Peasant economics
farm households and agrarian development

WYE STUDIES IN AGRICULTURAL AND RURAL DEVELOPMENT

Solving the problems of agricultural and rural development in poorer countries requires, among other things, sufficient numbers of well-trained and skilled professionals. To help meet the need for topical and effective teaching materials in this area, the books in the series are designed for use by teachers, students and practitioners of the planning and management of agricultural and rural development. The series is being developed in association with the innovative postgraduate programme in Agricultural Development for external students of the University of London.

The series concentrates on the principles, techniques and applications of policy analysis, planning and implementation of agricultural and rural development. Texts review and synthesise existing knowledge and highlight current issues, combining academic rigour and topicality with a concern for practical applications. Most importantly, the series provides simultaneously a systematic basis for teaching and study, a means of updating the knowledge of workers in the field, and a source of ideas for those involved in planning development.

Editorial Board
Henry Bernstein, Director, Wye College External Programme
Allan Buckwell, Professor of Agricultural Economics, Wye College
Ian Carruthers, Professor of Agrarian Development, Wye College
Dr Jonathan Kydd, Lecturer in Agricultural Economics, Wye College
Professor Ian Lucas, Principal of Wye College

Peasant economics

FARM HOUSEHOLDS
AND AGRARIAN DEVELOPMENT

FRANK ELLIS

Lecturer, School of Development Studies, University of East Anglia

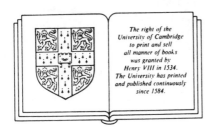

The right of the
University of Cambridge
to print and sell
all manner of books
was granted by
Henry VIII in 1534.
The University has printed
and published continuously
since 1584.

CAMBRIDGE UNIVERSITY PRESS

Cambridge

New York   New Rochelle   Melbourne   Sydney

Published by the Press Syndicate of the University of Cambridge
The Pitt Building, Trumpington Street, Cambridge CB2 1RP
32 East 57th Street, New York, NY 10022, USA
10 Stamford Road, Oakleigh, Melbourne 3166, Australia

First published 1988
Reprinted 1989

Printed and bound in Great Britain by Billings, Hylton Road, Worcester

British Library cataloguing in publication data

Ellis, Frank, *1947–*
Peasant economics : farm households and
agrarian development. – (Wye studies
in agricultural and rural development).
1. Peasantry – Economic aspects –
Developing countries   2. Households –
Economic aspects – Developing countries
I. Title
305.5'63   HD1521

Library of Congress cataloguing in publication data

Ellis, Frank.
Peasant economics.
(Wye studies in agricultural and rural development)
Bibliography
Includes index.
1. Peasantry – Developing countries – Economic
conditions.   2. Peasantry – Developing countries – Social
conditions.   3. Quality of life – Developing countries.
4. Developing countries – Rural conditions.   I. Title.
II. Series.
HD1542.E43   1988   338.1'09172'4   87–14815

ISBN 0 521 32446 7 hard covers
ISBN 0 521 31008 3 paperback

To Jane, Clare and Josie

Contents

Preface

This is a book on the economic analysis of peasant household agricultural production. It is about the ways people in peasant families make use of the resources at their disposal for production, for family survival, and, where possible, for improving the quality of their lives. It is also about the impact of social and economic change on peasant farming.

Some preliminary words are required regarding the level of the book, its aims, its approach, and its structure. The book is designed as a textbook for students of agricultural economics or related disciplines interested in the economics of peasant agriculture, either as part of an undergraduate degree or early in a postgraduate degree. The technical economic content of the book is pitched at a relatively elementary level. This is in part to take account of the often diverse educational backgrounds of students entering postgraduate courses in subjects like rural development, and in part to make the book accessible to the non-specialist reader or to the practitioner wishing to catch up on the topics which it covers.

The economic study of farm families in developing countries has undergone formidable increases in its scope and complexity in recent decades. A bewildering array of theories now exist on household decision making, the working of rural factor markets, paths of technical change, the internal relations of the farm household, and the prospects for peasants in a capitalist world economy. The purpose of this book is to disentangle some of these diverse theories, and to make the connections between them.

The book contains certain underlying ideas which serve to locate and unify the content of its individual chapters. These are summarised briefly here and are amplified at various points throughout the book:

1. *Definition of peasants for economic analysis.* A more specific economic conception of peasants is required than that they are either (i) the same as all

other farmers, or (ii) the same as the neoclassical profit maximising firm, or (iii) just small farmers. An economic concept of peasants advanced in the first chapter of this book is that they are family farmers only partially integrated into incomplete or imperfect markets. The threefold emphasis here is on family, on partial engagement in markets, and on the imperfection of those markets.

2. *The household as a unit of analysis.* The household as the primary unit of economic analysis always requires placing in context. The household is part of a continuum of dimensions of analysis which runs from relations between people within the household, through the household itself, and out into the larger economic system. Household economic behaviour involves interactions between individuals within the household, *and* interactions between the household and the wider society. Depending on the scope and intent of analysis this wider society may be the village, the region, the country, or the world economy.

3. *Women in peasant farm production.* The role and contribution of women to the economic welfare of the peasant farm family remains a neglected topic in peasant economics. The household as a unit of analysis tends to obscure the division of tasks between women and men, its impact on production decisions, and its significance for income distribution within the home. This book makes some effort to integrate women more fully into the economic analysis of peasants. This is done in part by emphasising in relevant places the defects of household theories in this respect, and in part by an extended chapter focused on the analysis of women in peasant farm households.

4. *Peasant political economy.* Important contributions to the understanding of peasants and their problems have been made by social scientists using Marxian theoretical perspectives. These contributions emphasise the larger social, political, and economic forces acting on farm household production in a capitalist world economy. They lend to the study of peasants dimensions of social change which are neglected in pure neoclassical economic analysis. This book deploys the themes and insights of Marxian analysis to interpret the wider relevance and limitations of economic theories of peasant production.

The book is structured in four parts. The first part is designed to provide the analytical basis for subsequent chapters, and it deals in turn with the definition of peasants (Chapter 1), the basic neoclassical economics of farm production (Chapter 2), and an introduction to the Marxian approach to peasant political economy (Chapter 3).

The content of Chapter 2 is essential for understanding the pure economic arguments and graphs of later chapters. However, its coverage is introductory and it may be regarded as optional by those readers already familiar with neoclassical production economics. Many agricultural economics students will not be so familiar with the approach set out in Chapter 3, which is relevant for understanding the connections made in later chapters between economic theories of peasant behaviour and the political economy of peasant societies.

The second part of the book sets out and explores five alternative microeconomic theories of peasant household behaviour. These are the profit maximising or efficient peasant theory (Chapter 4), the risk-averse peasant theory (Chapter 5), the drudgery-averse, or Chayanov, peasant theory (Chapter 6), farm household theories based on working factor and output markets (Chapter 7), and sharecropping theories (Chapter 8).

These chapters follow, as far as possible, a common format. This includes revision, where relevant, of underlying economic concepts; a statement of the theory; variants and extensions; empirical validation; policy aspects; and wider perspectives. The balance between these components varies according to their perceived importance for the theories under discussion. This part of the book concludes with a comparative summary of the assumptions, logic, and predictions of the various theories.

The third part of the book is concerned with intra-household economic analysis, and specifically with the analysis of women in the peasant household (Chapter 9). The household level theories of earlier chapters prohibit consideration of economic relations internal to the household, since they assume that the household as a unit maximises a single set of objectives over all its members. Chapter 9 subjects that assumption to critical examination, and introduces several additional concepts required to examine the subordination of women in peasant farm households.

The fourth part of the book extends the household economic analysis in a different direction, namely, farm size and technical change in peasant agriculture. The proposition that there exists an inverse relationship between the area size of farms and economic efficiency is considered (Chapter 10). The next chapter deals with the economic analysis of technical change in agriculture, and its application to farm mechanisation and new crop varieties (Chapter 11). A final chapter provides a summary of some of the main themes and strands of the book (Chapter 12).

This book is called *Peasant Economics* because it is at heart more of an economics textbook than one of social or political analysis. Nevertheless in the themes which underlie it, in the connections which it makes between different types of analysis, and in its references and asides to larger issues, it attempts to avoid too economistic an interpretation of peasant farm production. The agricultural economist concerned with the welfare and future prospects of people in farm communities in developing countries needs to be aware of the social and political forces which surround and constrain the application of economic analysis. It is only from such awareness that the limitations of the purely economic can be understood, naive mistakes of economic policy can be avoided, and fully informed debate about the goals and implementation of peasant farm policies can take place.

Acknowledgements

In writing this book I received encouragement and assistance from many people. Special thanks are due to Henry Bernstein for his advice, support, and enthusiasm. The early stages of formulation were helped by some penetrating comments by Michael Lipton, as well as comments on early draft chapters by Tony Barnett, Steve Biggs, John Cameron, Chris Edwards, Martin Greeley, John Harriss, and Adam Pain. The complete draft was commented on by Henry Bernstein, John Lingard, and Colin Thirtle, and I am indebted to them for the amount of work they put into this task, as well as for putting me straight on errors of theory and aspects requiring clarification. My chapter on women in the peasant household benefited from comments by Kate Young, Annie Whitehead, Sue Walters, Ruth Pearson, and Alison Evans to all of whom I extend my thanks for the trouble they took in reading that chapter. Any errors of analysis or interpretation which, no doubt, different readers will find in the book, remain entirely my responsibility.

The book was completed for publication while I was a Visiting Fellow at the Institute of Development Studies, Sussex University, and I am grateful for the time and facilities which this provided. I wish to express my thanks also to Olivia Graham and Venetia Biggs who provided research assistance at critical stages in the preparation of the draft, and to Barbara Dewing for drawing the graphs. The students in the various courses which I teach on these topics were both the inspiration to write the book in the first place and acted as a testing ground for much of its material. Finally I dedicate this book to my family who have accompanied me in many of my travels to countries with peasant societies, and without whose presence to provide support and relief to the writing I doubt if I ever could have embarked on such an enterprise.

Norwich   FE
February 1987

Part I

Peasants, economics, political economy

1

Peasants

Introduction

This book concerns the economic analysis of a kind of agricultural production which we refer to as peasant production. It is probable that at least a quarter of the world's population, over one billion people, belong to peasant farm households in the sense in which these are defined later in this chapter. Most of this large proportion of humankind live in the developing countries where they sometimes comprise as much as seventy per cent of the population. In some regions peasant farm households are disappearing under pressures of landlessness and concentration of farm holdings; in others they are a relatively stable feature of the rural social structure; and in still others they are created anew by the economic and social forces which bear on agricultural production.

Peasant populations occupy the margins of the modern world economy. With one foot in the market and the other in subsistence they are neither fully integrated into that economy nor wholly insulated from its pressures. Peasant populations are rarely prosperous, often precarious, and contain among them some of the poorest people in the world. In order to set about improving their prospects it is necessary to possess analytical methods which yield an accurate perception of the nature of their problems. That is what this book is all about.

The purpose of this chapter is to construct an economic definition of peasants consistent with the approach and concerns of the rest of the book. This is an important preliminary exercise. The choice of 'peasant', rather than some other term, to describe the farm households which are the subject of the book is not just a matter of vague inclination. Indeed the term possesses a disadvantage – its derogatory connotations in ordinary usage – which would lead to its avoidance if there existed an alternative with the same theoretical and descriptive meaning. In the absence of such an alternative we adopt the term peasant, and we seek a definition designed to fulfil the following criteria:

(a) It should serve to distinguish peasants not just from non-farm social groups, but also from other kinds of farm production be this plantation, estate, capitalist farm or commercial family farm;

(b) It should contain a sense of time as well as of change, in order to avoid mistakenly identifying peasants with stagnation and tradition;

(c) It should encompass the household as a unit of analysis, the larger economy, and the interaction between them;

(d) It should possess relevance for economic analysis, in the sense of delineating economic conditions of peasant life which differ analytically from those of other social groups or farm enterprises.

To anticipate the results of subsequent discussion, we find that such a definition centres on the idea that peasants are only partially integrated into incomplete markets. This idea has two aspects. The first is their partial integration into markets. The second is the degree of imperfection of the markets which peasants confront. This idea serves to distinguish peasants from their nearest relation, the commercial family farm which is wholly integrated into fully working markets. It also uncovers the implicit purpose of a large proportion of rural development policy, which seems to be to hasten the transformation of peasants into commercial family farms. It thus has the merit of making plain what is rarely stated explicitly, and it sharpens the economic perception of the peasant problem which is sometimes muddled in rural development books.

The rest of this chapter is concerned with filling in the detail of this idea. It begins by identifying components of the peasant definition which reside in distinctive features of peasant society compared to other societies. Second, it identifies components of the peasant definition which reside in the peasant farm household as an economic unit of production and consumption. Third, it ties these various components together and proposes a working definition of peasants for this book. Fourth, the chapter ends with some general points on the family and the household as units of economic analysis.

Peasant societies

The quest for a definition of peasants based on social characteristics which differ from other social groups is associated mainly with the field of social anthropology. The word 'social' here does not signify lack of economic content, it merely focuses on peasants as communities rather than as single individuals or households. A characteristic which is often stressed is that peasant societies in some sense represent a transition; they 'stand midway between the primitive tribe and industrial society' (Wolf, 1966: vii). One strand in social anthropology emphasises cultural aspects of this transition. Hence one of the best known earlier definitions of peasants describes them as 'part societies with part cultures' (Kroeber, 1948: 284), meaning that peasants are part of larger societies but retain cultural identities which set them apart. Another strand places more emphasis on the inferior status of peasants within the larger social systems of which they are a part. Thus 'it is only when ... the cultivator becomes subject to the demands and sanctions of power-holders outside his social stratum – that we can appropriately speak of peasantry' (Wolf, 1966: 11).

These earlier writings in anthropology on peasants contain several ideas which are pertinent for the concept of peasants to be derived here. These are set out in the following paragraphs, and between them they go some way to delineating the wider aspects of our peasant definition.

Transition

The idea of transition is a useful one because it injects a sense of history and change into the definition of peasants. Peasants are seen as representing a transition from relatively dispersed, isolated, and self-sufficient communities towards fully integrated market economies.

Transition implies change and adaptation but it must be stressed that the speed of change and its outcome are neither known nor determined in advance. Transition does not mean that peasants are here today and gone tomorrow, that they are inevitably and soon to be replaced by other, more 'modern', farm enterprises. What it does mean is that peasants are never just 'subsistence' or 'traditional' cultivators (terms often used by agricultural economists to describe them) caught in a timeless vacuum. Peasants come from somewhere, indeed they were often thrust out of where they were by powerful world forces outside their previous experience (e.g. colonialism) and they are undergoing a continuous process of adaptation to the changing world around them.

Markets and exchange

The idea of transition gives rise to several other relevant features of peasant societies. One of these is that peasants as a social group are always part of a larger economic system (Wolf, 1966: 8). A peasant society is never the isolated community that it may have been in the distant past. This means that peasant societies participate in exchange with the larger system, and that peasant production is exposed in some degree to market forces. The inputs and outputs of peasant farms are subject to valuation by the wider market, at prevailing prices, even if households participate in markets for only a small proportion of their requirements.

Markets provide both opportunities and pressures for peasants. Engagement in them may lead to higher living standards or more diverse consumption, but at the same time it exposes them to the possibility of ruin either from adverse price trends or from the exercise of unequal market power. Thus the relationship of peasants to the market contains a continuous tension between the risky advantages of market participation and the preservation of a non-market basis for survival.

Subordination

Many writers have stressed the inferior social and economic status of peasants as a central component of their definition. This aspect is referred to as their subordination. Hence 'It is correct to define the peasantry primarily in terms of its subordinate relationships to a group of controlling outsiders' (Wolf, 1966: 13); 'the structural subordination of the peasantry to external forces is an essential aspect of its definition' (Mintz, 1974: 94); or 'The underdog position – the domination of peasantry by outsiders' (Shanin, 1971a: 15).

The idea of subordination implies unequal social or cultural status, coercion of one social group by another, and unequal access to political power. However, most relevant for us is that it also implies the economic exploitation of peasants by other social groups. Peasants are 'rural cultivators whose surpluses are transferred to a dominant group of rulers' (Wolf, 1966: 3–4). These concepts of economic exploitation and surplus transfers are explained more fully in Chapter 3 of this book. The meaning attached to them requires some care in the context of economic analysis. In particular it is useful to distinguish between non-market coercion (e.g. the relations between overlords and serfs under feudalism), the exercise of unequal economic power in imperfect markets, and the adverse results for peasants of price trends originating in competitive wider markets.

Internal differences

By identifying peasants as a distinctive social or economic group, and by stressing their subordination to other social groups, there is a risk of overlooking differences of social and economic status within peasant society itself. Peasants are not a uniform, homogeneous, set of farm families all with the same status and prospects within their communities. On the contrary, peasant societies are 'always and everywhere typified ... by internal differentiation along many lines' (Mintz, 1974: 93). The word 'differentiation' here signifies that differences of social status, like many other aspects of peasants, are not a static, timeless, feature. Social structure changes over time according to the nature of forces acting on peasant society and to the adaptation of individual families to those forces.

It follows from this that subordination may not be a feature confined only to the relations between peasants and others; exploitation may occur between households of different status within a village or community. Thus 'it may appear that [peasants] consist entirely of the prey; in fact, some are commonly among the predators' (Mintz, 1974: 94). The importance of this aspect varies considerably across different peasant societies worldwide, and for practical purposes of economic policy it is not always relevant. On the other hand the existence of non-market and unequal forms of economic interaction between households within peasant society is, conceptually, an important element of the picture of peasants we are in the process of constructing.

The peasant farm household

The second point of entry to the definition of peasant is via its distinctive features as a farm enterprise. Here it is the dual economic nature of peasant production which is its central peculiarity. The peasant unit of production is both a family and an enterprise; it simultaneously engages in both consumption and production. This dual economic character of the peasant household has implications for its economic analysis which preoccupy a large proportion of the rest of this book. Here we direct attention to those features of this economic unit which distinguish peasant farm households from other economic actors in the market economy.

Dominant economic activity

In this book peasants are farmers; they obtain their livelihood from the land, mainly by the cultivation of crops, although livestock may have varying degrees of importance within their farm systems. When referring to the peasant household, other categories of rural dweller such as landless labourers, plantation workers, pastoralists, or nomads are excluded from the definition. Landless labourers and plantation workers may have previously been peasants, pastoralists and nomads may be on the verge of becoming peasants. In a wider concept of 'peasant society' all these and numerous other crafts and trades may be present, and for certain purposes of analysis they may be important for describing the economic activities and livelihood of peasant farm families. But for our main economic definition, peasant equals farmer.

Land

By defining peasants as farmers it is implied that they have access to the resource of land as the basis of their livelihood. This feature distinguishes peasants from landless labourers or urban workers. An important attribute of peasants worldwide is the significance of non-market criteria in the allocation of land. In many peasant societies families have complex traditional rights of access to land which prevail over and constrain the operation of freehold land markets. In some countries these traditional land rights are inalienable, and in others transfers of land outside ties of family are rare even though freehold markets do exist. In peasant society land is more than just another factor of production which has its price: it is the long term security of the family against the hazards of life, and it is part of the social status of the family within village or community.

Labour

It is widely agreed that reliance on family labour is a defining economic characteristic of peasants. Given that capitalist production is defined in part by the employment of wage labour and the separation of the ownership of the means of production from labour, the 'family labour' basis of peasant farms is what distinguishes them from capitalist enterprises. This feature does not rule out the use of hired labour in say, peak periods of harvesting; nor the sale by members of the farm household of their own labour outside the farm on an *ad hoc* basis; indeed for some peasant families this may be essential for survival. The predominance of family labour in production also has an effect on the working of labour markets in peasant communities, since various subjective criteria peculiar to individual households are likely to influence both the supply and demand for wage labour in the wider market.

Capital

Command over capital and its accumulation is a central attribute of capitalist production, as also is the notion of a rate of return on capital in the form of profit. Several writers have stressed the difficulty of defining a category of profit for household production. 'The peasant ... runs a household, not a business concern' (Wolf, 1966: 2). One problem resides in distinguishing profit from returns to family labour given the dual production and consumption nature of the peasant household. Another is that the purchase of capital inputs by the household may have both production and consumption aspects. An example would be the purchase of a tractor used both for production purposes (ploughing, driving a water pump or grain mill etc.) and for consumption purposes (family transport, firewood carrying etc.). The absence of a systematic category of rate of return to capital in such cases further distinguishes peasant households from capitalist enterprises.

Consumption

Perhaps the most popular defining feature of peasants amongst economists is the subsistence basis of their livelihood. Subsistence refers to the proportion of farm output which is directly consumed by the household rather than sold in the market, and peasants are often referred to as 'subsistence farmers' in this context. The degree of this subsistence is one reason why the integration of peasants into the market economy is only partial, but its significance should not be overstressed in the context of the many other factors which enter the definition of peasants. Many farm households worldwide are highly specialised commodity producers of cotton, sugarcane, bananas, coffee, tea, and so on, but they may still qualify as peasants according to other criteria we have discussed.

The economic definition of peasants

So far we have defined peasants with respect to notions of transition, exposure to market forces, subordination, internal differences, farming, access to land, family labour, ambiguity of profit, and, typically, a significant element of subsistence production. These give peasants a definite identity with dimensions of history, change, society, economic activity, and use of resources. They also distinguish peasants from other kinds of rural producer, from rural and urban workers, and from capitalist enterprises. They do not so far distinguish peasants from any other kind of family farmer, whether a 3000 hectare US grain farmer relying only on family labour, or an intensive small dairy farmer in the EEC.

What is lacking so far is an integrating concept, something which is common to all or many of the individual components, a concept which has theoretical import for economic analysis as well as descriptive content for evoking the image of a typical peasant. This integrating concept is the 'partial integration into markets' of peasants, and 'limitations in the operation of market principles' in the peasant economy (Friedmann, 1980:

164). In other words peasants are defined in part by their varying rather than total commitment to the market (implying also a variable capacity to withdraw from the market and still survive), and in part by the incomplete character of the markets in which they participate. It is this which ties together such distinct components as transition, subordination, subsistence, and the peculiarities of the access of peasants to factors of production. It is also this which distinguishes peasants from family farmers operating within fully developed product and factor markets. Since this view of peasants is central to their economic analysis throughout this book it requires more elaboration.

In economics market imperfection is a relative concept which is defined by comparison to a hypothetical ideal, perfect competition. Perfect competition emphasises the neutrality of the price mechanism and its role as the arbiter of all economic decisions. There are many buyers and sellers in the markets for both inputs and outputs. No producer or consumer is able to influence price levels by individual action. There is freely available and accurate information on market prices. There is freedom of entry and exit in any branch of activity, and, indeed, competition ensures that inefficient producers are forced out of production while only the most efficient survive. In the perfect competition model no coercion, domination, or exercise of economic power, by some economic agents over others, can exist.

To varying degrees peasant society sometimes features non-market, or *reciprocal*, transactions between farm households. Reciprocity refers to exchanges which are culturally defined, non-replicable between one event and the next, and involve unlike goods and services. For example you help me build my house, I agree to contribute a sack of cassava to the village school; you and your relatives help me with my harvest, my household throws a beer party for your extended family. There is an economic content in such exchanges – there are resource costs in the provision of goods and services – but the meaning of reciprocity is that such transactions are not valued by market prices. Reciprocity may also involve social norms of sharing and redistribution which are designed to ensure that all members of the community survive, irrespective of the year to year productive performance of individual households.

For some writers the reciprocal and sharing aspects of peasant societies are amongst their most distinctive features. The view that these often predominate over individual gain in the market has led to the peasant economy being described as a 'moral economy' (Scott, 1976). They have also been described as 'the economy of affection' in the context of African peasant societies (Hyden, 1980). It is, however, unnecessary to invoke an entirely distinct peasant economic logic in order to perceive the role of reciprocity in modifying market principles or evading their impact. What is implied is that 'competition does not exclusively or even principally define the relation of peasants to each other or to outsiders' (Friedmann, 1980: 165), and this is strengthened when there is no effective market in land since this inhibits the free entry and exit of producers from production.

In addition to partial engagement and reciprocal exchanges, the markets confronting peasants may be imperfect for reasons of low and uneven development of the economic infrastructure. Markets are not fully formed when they are spatially fragmented due to poor transport and communications. An important operative factor here is poor information. This favours those people in the social structure who do have information (merchants and officials) over those that do not (peasants).

It might be objected that since perfect competition is a Utopian construct, and family farm enterprises also operate in economies riddled with monopolies and other economic imperfections, then the distinction being made is not precise enough to be useful for analytical purposes. The answer to this is that although these considerations are matters of relativity and degree, in this case the degree of difference is quite large.

Consider, for example, the economic situation of a typical farm family in an industrial market economy. Such a farm family normally faces the following conditions external to the production process:

- credit is abundantly available from developed financial markets (banks, credit agencies etc.) at competitive market rates of interest;
- variable production inputs (fertilizer, seed, fuel, chemicals) are available up to any quantity that an individual farmer might wish to purchase from reasonably competitive suppliers;
- knowledge of the latest available technologies is widespread and discussed at length in all the farming magazines;
- there is a freehold market in land, so that the potential exists for new entrants to begin farming and unsuccessful farmers to exit from agriculture;
- information on prices of both inputs and outputs is available typically on a nationwide basis, reflecting the high degree of integration of markets and communications.

For the peasant farm family only a few, and possibly none, of these conditions is likely to prevail:

- capital markets are fragmentary or non-existent, credit is obtained from local landlords, merchants, or moneylenders at rates of interest which reflect the individual circumstances of each transaction, not a market clearing condition;

- credit and rates of interest may be tied to other factor prices like land and labour within a dependent economic relationship, thus factor markets may be locked together contractually rather than being independent;
- variable production inputs may be erratically available or unavailable, their quality may vary, access to them may involve formal or informal systems of rationing;
- market information is poor, erratic, fragmentary and incomplete, and there is a high cost for the farm household in acquiring information beyond the immediate confines of village or community;
- a freehold market for land does not always exist, and where it does non-market rights of access or non-price forms of tenancy are likely to predominate over open market transactions in land;
- markets and communications in general are not well integrated, and depending on place and infrastructure there are varying degrees of isolation between local communities, regions, and the more developed segments of the national economy.

We are now in a position to summarise the various components which make up the economic definition of peasants employed in this book. This definition is as follows:

> *Peasants are farm households, with access to their means of livelihood in land, utilising mainly family labour in farm production, always located in a larger economic system, but fundamentally characterised by partial engagement in markets which tend to function with a high degree of imperfection.*

There are three further points to be noted with respect to this definition. First, at no stage in the preceding discussion have we ascribed any notion of economic irrationality to peasants, and, indeed, nowhere do we do so in the rest of this book. For economic analysis peasants are engaged in the purposive pursuit of personal or household goals like any other economic agents. The only caveat to this, which applies to the economic method in general and not just to peasants, is that individual action always takes place in, and is modified by, larger social forces (Chapter 3 elaborates this point).

Second, our definition indicates the inadequacy of terms like 'traditional', 'subsistence', and 'small' often used by agricultural economists to describe the peasant farm household. The term 'traditional' seems to refer partly to production technique and partly to psychological factors, neither of which have entered our discussion. Like an earlier term, 'backward', its meaning only exists in contrast to the value-laden opposites of 'advanced' or 'modern' agriculture. Since many peasant farming practices are found to be ingenious adaptations to survival in difficult environments, these opposites have no objective content for economic analysis. The term 'subsistence' describes only one partial aspect of the peasant farm household, and not the most significant feature for economic analysis. Finally there is 'small farmer'. This is attractive because it lacks emotive connotations, but it has little theoretical content. It is not possible to set a farm size limit in the domain of peasant economics.

Third, according to our definition peasants cease to be peasants when they become wholly committed to production in fully formed markets; they become instead family farm enterprises. There is no rigid criterion by which such a transition could be marked, but one element of it would be a degree of specialisation and commitment to market transactions which would make it infeasible to continue farming in the face of a prolonged collapse of market prices.

Family, household, and women

The social unit which forms the basis of economic analysis through most of this book is the peasant farm household. The major exception to this occurs in Chapter 9 which is concerned with the economic analysis of women in the farm household. The term 'family' is often used interchangeably with household. For the central purpose of this book, which is the analysis of a type of farm enterprise, this mixing of terms is not that important. However, the reader should be aware of the difference for social science analysis of the terms family and household. A few points also need to be made about the scope and limitations of the household as a unit of analysis, especially for the integration of women into peasant economics.

The family is a social unit defined by the kinship relations between people. Since in different societies the major lines of kinship which constitute a family differ markedly, it is not possible to state a general rule concerning the boundaries of the term 'family'. One thing for certain, however, is that in most peasant societies the concept of family is not limited to two adults living with their children, as in the Western concept of a nuclear family. This is nearer in meaning to the term 'household' than to the kinship definition of family.

The household is a social unit defined by the sharing of the same abode or hearth. As such it is evidently a sub-set of the family, though the extent to which families may be split up among separate households again varies across different societies. Economics finds the household a useful unit of analysis on the implicit assumption that within the household resources are pooled, income is shared, and decisions are made jointly by adult household members. It is also convenient, and not that far off the mark in most cases, to associate the household, rather than the larger family, with the farm as a production enterprise.

An explicit purpose of this book is to integrate women into the economic analysis of peasants. Taking the household as a single unit of economic analysis poses problems for this aim, since it subsumes the distinct economic position of women and men to the joint economic behaviour of the household. The best we can do to overcome this is to make cautionary remarks at relevant points about what is hidden in the results and predictions of household theories. However, in Chapter 9 we open up the closed box of the household to critical scrutiny, and this permits a number of important economic issues concerning women in peasant agriculture to be brought to light.

Summary

1 This chapter concerns the construction of an economic definition of peasants appropriate to the content of the rest of the book.

2 This definition is approached by examining (a) some distinctive characteristics of peasant societies which set them apart from other social groups, and (b) features of the peasant farm household which differ from other kinds of farm enterprise.

3 Bringing together the various components, a definition of peasants is found in their partial integration into incomplete markets.

4 The first part of this definition emphasises that peasants are not, like other farm enterprises, wholly and inextricably linked to the market economy. Their main factors of production – land and family labour – are not purchased in the market, and, often, only a proportion of their output is sold in the market.

5 The second part of the definition emphasises the incompleteness and imperfection of the markets confronting peasants. Markets for some factors of production may not exist, for others may be fragmented or distorted, and market information may be highly imperfect. This contrasts with family farm enterprises operating in markets which are at least fully formed, even though not perfect in the strict economic sense.

6 The chapter concludes with some observations regarding the family and the household as units of economic analysis. Although the household is taken as the basic unit of economic analysis

through most of the book, the reader is cautioned that this obscures a number of important matters concerning the economic relationships between people within the household, and this applies especially to the role and status of women in peasant societies.

Further reading

By far the best introduction for readers of any discipline to the study of peasants is the excellent book by Wolf (1966). This is concise, readable, and contains matters of emphasis and insight which remain just as pertinent today as when the book was written. Other useful and accessible sources on the definition of peasants are Wolf (1955), Shanin (1971a; 1971b), Mintz (1974), and Williams (1976). The main inspiration of the unifying theme of this chapter is a paper by Harriet Friedmann (1980). This is a difficult paper for the reader not conversant with Marxian terminology (see Chapter 3), but it contains a wealth of interesting ideas for the location of peasants in economic analysis.

Reading list

Friedmann, H. (1980). Household production and the national economy: concepts for the analysis of agrarian formations. *Journal of Peasant Studies*, Vol. 7, No. 2.

Mintz, S.W. (1974). A note on the definition of peasantries. *Journal of Peasant Studies*, Vol. 1, No. 3.

Shanin, T. (1971a). Introduction. In his (ed.), *Peasants and Peasant Societies*. Harmondsworth: Penguin.

Shanin, T. (1971b). Peasantry: delineation of a sociological concept and a field of study. *European Journal of Sociology*, Vol. 12.

Williams, G. (1976). Taking the part of peasants. in Gutkind P. & Wallerstein I. (eds.), *The Political Economy of Contemporary Africa*. London: Sage Publications.

Wolf, E.R. (1955). Types of Latin American peasantry: a preliminary discussion. *American Anthropologist*, Vol. 57, No. 3.

Wolf, E.R. (1966). *Peasants*. Englewood Cliffs, New Jersey: Prentice-Hall.

2

The neoclassical theory of farm production

Farm decision making

This chapter sets out the basic tools of analysis of the neoclassical economic theory of farm production. A grasp of these analytical tools is indispensable for understanding a wide range of topics and debates in the economics of peasant agriculture. They are applied and extended in many different ways in later chapters of the book.

The theory begins with the farmer as an individual decision maker concerned with questions such as how much labour to devote to the cultivation of each crop, whether or not to use purchased inputs, which crops to grow in which fields, and so on. It thus centres on the idea that farmers can *vary* the level and kind of farm inputs and outputs.

Three kinds of relationship between farm inputs and outputs are typically recognised as encompassing the economic decision making capacity of the farmer. These three relationships also correspond to three main steps in the construction of the theory of the farm firm. They are as follows:

(a) The varying level of output corresponding to different levels of variable inputs (e.g. variations in maize output resulting from different levels of nitrogen fertilizer). This is called the factor–product or input–output relationship. It is also the *production function* i.e. the physical relationship between inputs and output to which all other aspects of the production process are ultimately related.

(b) The varying combination of two or more inputs required to produce a specified output (e.g. the different amounts of land and labour which could result in the same quantity of paddy production). This is called the factor–factor relationship. It is also sometimes referred to as the *method* or *technique* of production.

(c) The varying outputs which could be obtained from a given set of farm resources (e.g. the different quantities of cassava or beans which could be obtained from the same area of land). This is called the product–product relationship. It is also termed *enterprise choice*.

This threefold capacity for varying the way in which farm production is organised only attains analytical relevance when placed in the context of the *goals* of the farm family and the resource *constraints* of the individual farm. In practice farm families may have many different goals: long term income stability, family food security, achievement of certain preferences in consumption, fulfilment of community obligations and so on. The farm may also face constraints of varying severity which limit the capacity to vary the organisation of production. An evident constraint is the land area of the farm which in many cases is fixed over considerable periods of time. However, for peasant farmers in the tropics this may be the least of problems: working capital may be scarce and expensive; purchased inputs variable in availability, quality, and price; security of tenure on the land low; and capability to market alternative crops variable and sometimes non-existent.

The basic theory of farm production involves some important simplifications with respect to this myriad of possible goals and constraints. The consumption side of the farm household is ignored. Only a single goal, that of short term profit maximisation, is explored. Only a single decision maker, the farmer, is permitted. Dissension amongst members of the farm household is certainly not allowed at this stage. Other assumptions include competition in the markets for farm outputs and inputs, and unlimited working capital for the purchase of variable inputs. This chapter proceeds to examine in turn the three components of decision making under these conditions.

The production function
The physical relationship between output and inputs

Many students seem to have difficulty in grasping the concept of a production function, even when in other respects they have attained a competent working knowledge of economic theory. Perhaps this is because the production function tends to be presented in a rather abstract and mathematical way in microeconomic textbooks, making it difficult to envisage a practical example which would make the concept clear.

While it is true that for some purposes the production function is an abstract concept and does not refer directly to real world situations, in the context of farm production it has several realistic applications. Consider, for example, the response of rice (paddy) output to changes in the application of nitrogen fertilizer. Commonsense would suggest that output rises with increasing quantities of fertilizer, but only up to a certain point. Beyond that point an imbalance occurs between the fertilizer and other plant nutrients in the soil so that output levels off, and eventually declines if even more fertilizer is applied.

The relationship between paddy output and fertilizer input *is* a production function. This relationship may be illustrated by a graph as in the top half of Figure 2.1. The graph shows that, holding other inputs at a constant level, paddy output is 2200 kg with no fertilizer, it rises to a peak of 3762 kg as fertilizer is increased by up to 125 kg, and it falls thereafter. The

Figure 2.1. The production function.

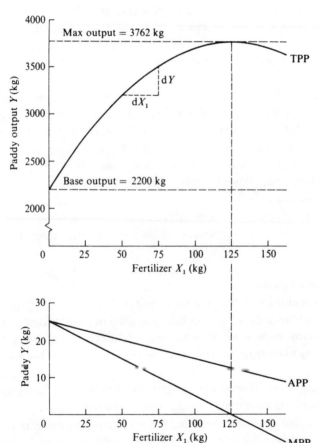

graph shows the *production function* of paddy output for varying levels of fertilizer use. This production function is described as the total physical product (TPP) curve.

The same relationship can also of course be described mathematically, either in a general form which says that paddy output (Y) is some function of different levels of a variable input (X_1), or $Y = f(X_1)$; or in a specific form which tries to give the exact relationship between output and input. The exact mathematical relationship which describes the graph shown in Figure 2.1 is a quadratic equation which is written as follows:

$$Y = 2200 + 25X_1 - 0.10X_1{}^2$$

An equation of this kind is fairly common for describing the response of a crop output to fertilizer use, and the numbers in it are obtained by sample measurements. However, this is not the only mathematical form a farm production function can take, and it is sufficient at this stage to be aware that the production relationship can be specified in this way. In this example the land input is held constant at one hectare, so that what is described in Figure 2.1 is the per hectare yield response to successively greater applications of fertilizer. Although the example is hypothetical it is not wildly removed from the farm level response of high yielding varieties of rice to nitrogen fertilizer which has been estimated in Asian countries (IRRI, 1978: 181).

In general, the production function in economics describes the technical or physical relationship between output and one or more variable inputs. This is so no matter how many variable inputs are included in the function. Inputs are rates of resource use and output is rate of production over a specified time period, usually the crop season. A function describing the response of output to a single input, as in our example, is often referred to as a single input response curve. In this example, as in cases of two or more variable inputs, those resources not included in the production function are assumed to be held constant, as also is the overall state of farm technology.

Returning now to the example of Figure 2.1, the production function summarises a considerable amount of information concerning the nature of the output response of paddy to fertilizer. What is true of this example is also more generally true of the production function as a theoretical device, and is described in the following paragraphs.

First, there is the output which would occur without any application of fertilizer. This is described in the figure as the base output and it is given as 2200 kg. For some kinds of farm inputs, for example fertilizers, irrigation water, weedicides, pesticides, etc., one would often expect some level of output to occur even in the complete absence of the input. For others, for example seed, labour hours, or land, a zero level of input would cause zero output and the production function would in this case begin at the origin of the graph.

Second, there is the highest output which can be achieved by successive increases in the application of fertilizer, holding all other production inputs constant, and this is given as 3762 kg. This peak output is sometimes referred to as the *technical maximum* level of output.[1] As is shown shortly this differs from the economic optimum level of output.

Third, the shape of the curve is crucial. It describes a situation in which although output grows with successive equal increases in fertilizer application, the amount by which it grows gets less and less. This can be confirmed simply by comparing the rise of output for an equal 25 kg increase in fertilizer use at two places on the graph, one at a low level and the second at a higher level. The quantity of additional output which is obtained for each successive additional unit of input is called the marginal physical product (MPP). The tendency for this additional output to get smaller as the amount of an input increases is the famous *Law of Diminishing Marginal Returns*.

The marginal physical product of an input can be expressed in a number of different ways, and this brings us to the bottom half of Figure 2.1. Mathematically, the MPP is the *slope* of the total product curve at any particular point. This is expressed by what is called the first derivative of the curve, dY/dX_1, which means the amount of output (vertical distance on the graph, dY) obtained for a very small increase in the amount of input (horizontal distance on the graph, dX_1).[2] The lower part of Figure 2.1 graphs the MPP as fertilizer use increases. In correspondence with what we already know from the total product curve, the MPP curve slopes continuously downward reflecting lower and lower additional output for each successive unit of input. The MPP curve crosses from positive to negative at exactly the point of maximum output, after which it is increasingly negative and total output declines accordingly.

Fourth, there is the productivity measure given by the average physical product of the input. The average physical product (APP) is defined as the total physical product divided by the total amount of the input used in production. It is expressed as Y/X_1. This definition is the general case and it applies without difficulty to inputs like land and labour for which the level of output is zero when input use is zero. However, for an input like fertilizer, where a certain volume of output occurs even with zero input, it is sometimes more useful to consider the average physical product as the total output above the base level divided by the total amount of the input applied.

Thus with reference to our example in Figure 2.1, when total output is 3200 kg and fertilizer is 50 kg, the APP of fertilizer is 20 kg paddy (3200 kg minus 2200 kg = 1000 kg, divided by 50 kg fertilizer = 20 kg paddy for one kg fertilizer). Likewise when output is 3700 kg and fertilizer is 100 kg, the APP is 15 kg paddy.

The curve for average physical product in the lower graph has the same point of departure as that for the marginal physical product, but it declines less steeply. Precisely because the top graph displays declining MPP from the outset, the APP is at a maximum for the first unit of fertilizer applied and this is the same quantity as the MPP: in this example the first unit of fertilizer increases output by 25 kg. Thereafter MPP is declining and thus pulling down APP in its wake, but not as fast as the decline of MPP itself since APP is measuring the productivity of *all* the units of fertilizer applied up to that point, not just the last one.

The precise shape of the MPP and APP curves is not important to these results. In Figure 2.1 they are straight lines, i.e. linear, because this happens to be a characteristic of the quadratic equation for the production function from which they are derived. Other mathematical specifications of the production function would give curves rather than straight lines for APP and MPP, but these curves are nonetheless generally negatively sloped downwards from left to right as a consequence of diminishing marginal product.

A *fifth* measure of the physical relationship between output and a single variable input is the *input elasticity*, also known as the partial elasticity of production. This is defined as the percentage change of output resulting from a given percentage change in the variable input:

$$E = \frac{\% \text{ change in output}}{\% \text{ change in input}} = \frac{dY/Y}{dX_1/X_1} = \frac{dY}{dX_1} \cdot \frac{X_1}{Y}$$

$$= MPP \cdot \frac{1}{APP} = \frac{MPP}{APP}$$

The point about an elasticity is that by taking the ratio of two proportional changes it obtains a measure of the impact of one variable on another which is independent of the physical units in which the variables are denominated. The relationship between the input elasticity, the MPP, and the APP should be noted. The area of diminishing marginal returns on the production function occurs when MPP < APP, but is not negative, i.e. when E is between 1 and zero:

$$0 < E < 1$$

$E > 1$ and $E < 0$ define areas of the production function in which it would not be economically logical for the farmer to operate: the first because output grows more than proportionately with any increase in input which means the farmer could always gain by using more of the input (this possibility is not shown on our graph), and the second because output decreases as a consequence of using more of the input and the farmer clearly does better by reducing input use.

In summary, then, the production function defines the *physical* relationship between output (Y) and any number of production inputs ($X_1, X_2, \ldots, X_n$):

$$Y = f(X_1, X_2, \ldots, X_n)$$

Typically the concern is only with one or more variable inputs, other inputs and the state of technology being held constant. This is written:

$$Y = f(X_1, X_2, \ldots, X_m / X_{n-m})$$

where $X_1, \ldots, X_m$ are variable inputs, and the bar indicates that all other inputs are held constant. The precise equation of the production function depends on the kind of input response under study and the degree of abstraction from actual production processes. However, all production functions must satisfy two conditions to make economic sense: the marginal physical product should be positive, and it should be declining. For these conditions to be met the equation should have a positive first derivative ($dY/dX > 0$), and a negative second derivative ($d^2Y/dX^2 < 0$) i.e. the response of output to increasing levels of input(s) must be rising, but at a decreasing rate.

Economic optimum level of resource use

The most efficient level of a variable input depends on the relationship between the price of the input and the price of output. In Figure 2.2 the information of our previous example has been converted to value terms assuming an output price of paddy of $0.10 per kg at the farm gate, and an input price of $1.00 per kg of fertilizer. The shape of the product curves remains the same: they are simply the physical curves multiplied by the paddy price of $0.10 and the vertical axes of the graphs are relabelled in value terms accordingly. They thus become total value product (TVP), average value product (AVP), and marginal value product (MVP).

Note that MVP is the general term for describing the rate of change of TVP, and it includes the possibility, not relevant here, that the output price might vary as the level of output changes. Some textbooks prefer to use the term 'value of the marginal product' (VMP) when the farm enterprise is a price taker in competitive markets. In other words VMP describes the pure case when MVP equals p.MPP i.e. when a single price, p, applies across all levels of output.

The additional information contained in Figure 2.2 is the total factor cost (TFC) line in the upper graph, and the marginal factor cost (MFC) line in the lower graph. Total factor cost simply traces out the cumulative cost incurred as fertilizer use increases. Each 25 kg of fertilizer increases total cost by $25, and this is a linear relationship. The marginal factor cost is just another way of describing the price of the variable input. This is a straight line at the level of $1 on the lower graph: each successive unit of fertilizer costs the same.

Figure 2.2. Optimum use of a single input.

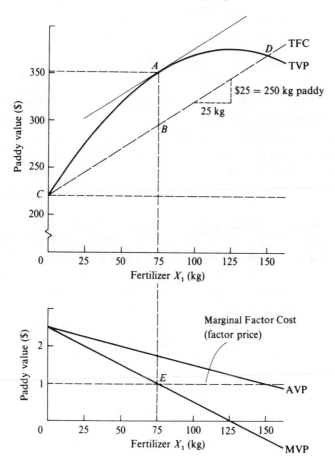

The *economic optimum* level of input occurs when the marginal value product of the input is equal to the price of the input (point E on the lower graph). This is commonsense. In the area to the left of point E the additional return generated by an extra unit of input is greater than the unit cost of the input, $MVP > MFC$, and it pays to increase the level of the input. In the area to the right of point E the additional return obtained from an extra unit of the input is less than the unit cost of the input, $MVP < MFC$, and profits are being reduced. $MVP = MFC$ in the lower graph corresponds in the upper graph to the point where a line parallel to the total factor cost curve is tangent to the production function i.e. where the slope of the two curves is equal. This makes sense given that MVP *is* the slope of the production function, and MFC *is* the slope of the total factor cost curve. At this point the surplus between total cost and total revenue, the gap AB, is at its maximum: profit is being maximised.

With the aid of some simple mathematics this optimum level of a single input can be usefully expressed in several different ways. Defining:

P_X = price per unit of input X (i.e. MFC)
P_Y = price per unit of output Y

Then, $MVP_X = MPP_X \cdot P_Y$, i.e. the marginal value product of input X equals its marginal physical product multiplied by the output price. There are then three ways of looking at the optimal point:

(a) At the economic optimum extra return equals extra cost, $MVP_X = P_X$. If $MVP_X > P_X$ then the farmer is applying too little of the variable input; if $MVP_X < P_X$ then the farmer is using too much.

(b) By rearranging this expression, the optimum condition can also be stated as $MVP_X/P_X = 1$. The ratio of the marginal value product to the price of the input should equal one. This way of expressing the economic optimum is often found in journal papers concerned with research into the economic efficiency of peasant farmers, where the question is asked whether or not this ratio is statistically different from one for each variable input, and if so, in what direction. Again if $MVP_X/P_X > 1$ the farmer is applying too little of an input; if $MVP_X/P_X < 1$, the farmer is applying too much.

(c) Since $MVP_X = MPP_X \cdot P_Y$ the optimum condition can also be stated as $MPP_X = P_X/P_Y$. The marginal physical product should equal the inverse (factor–product) price ratio. This is referred to as the 'inverse' price ratio because it reverses the ordering of the variables with respect to the graph. In our example the price of fertilizer is $1 per unit, and the price of paddy is $0.10 per unit. Thus the inverse price ratio is $1/$0.10 = 10, and profit is maximised at the point on the production function where the MPP is 10 kg.

In order to relate this to the graph, note that the inverse price ratio P_X/P_Y is the same as the quantity of output, Y, which could be purchased for the same price as one unit of fertilizer, X_1. As shown in Figure 2.2 on the total factor cost curve, 250 kg of paddy (vertical distance on the graph) could be purchased for the same price as 25 kg of fertilizer (horizontal distance on the graph), and thus the slope of the total cost curve (also the slope of the tangent at A) expressed in physical terms is 250 kg/25 kg = 10.

The impact of price changes and the supply curve

This brings us to the impact of *price changes* on the optimum levels of input and output in this model. The foregoing discussion should have made it clear that what is important is not the absolute levels of input or output prices but the ratio between them. In the preceding example it was not the prices of $1 and $0.10 for fertilizer and paddy respectively which determined the optimum position, but the ratio between them, i.e. 10:1. The economic optimum was found where the MPP at 10 kg equalled the amount of output which could be purchased for the price of one unit of fertilizer, also at 10 kg.

It follows that changing the price ratio between input and output alters the position of the economic optimum. If P_Y falls, then P_X/P_Y (the slope of the line that was tangent at A) rises. The line is steeper and gives a new tangency at a lower input level. For example, if the paddy price falls to $0.05 per kg the inverse price ratio rises to 20:1 and the economic optimum occurs at an MPP of 20 kg, i.e. lower down the production function. Similarly if the paddy price increased to $0.20 per kg the inverse price ratio would fall to 5:1 and the economic optimum would occur at an MPP of 5 kg, i.e. much nearer the top of the production function.

The outcome of this for supply at different output prices is shown in Figure 2.3. This graph may appear rather complicated at first sight, but is not that difficult. The upper half shows our old friend the fertilizer production function, with two points of tangency on it, one at A being the same optimum position as in Figure 2.2, and the second one at B being the point of tangency appropriate to an input:output price ratio of 20 (fertilizer price held constant at $1, paddy price fallen to $0.05). The upper graph also contains a 45° line. This is simply a graphical device used to reproduce the vertical axis for output in the top graph as a horizontal axis for output in the bottom graph, keeping the same scale in both cases. The bottom graph shows the optimum output levels for different levels of the paddy price, holding the fertilizer price constant at $1: it is a *supply curve*. The way to read Figure 2.3 is to start from the points of tangency on the production function, which represent the optimum levels of output corresponding to different fertilizer:paddy price ratios, thence via the 45° line to the supply curve which graphs the same optimum output levels against the paddy prices which generated them.

Note that the supply curve is sloped upwards. Each equal increase in the paddy price achieves ever smaller increases in output. This is an evident corollary of the law of diminishing marginal returns. It occurs because ever

Figure 2.3. Derivation of a supply curve.

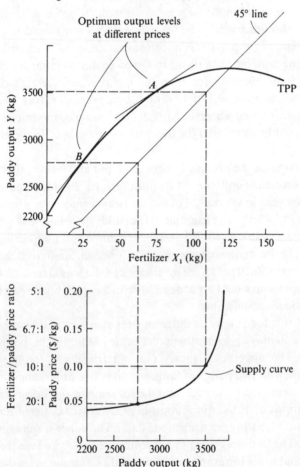

larger quantities of fertilizer (at a given cost per unit) are required in order to obtain each extra unit of output. If we define the price for each unit of output as the Marginal Revenue (MR), and the increasing outlay on fertilizer required to obtain each extra unit of output as Marginal Cost (MC), then our previous profit maximising condition can be restated as MR = MC. In terms of the lower graph in Figure 2.3, this means that the supply curve is synonymous with the marginal cost curve for fertilizer.

The translation from MVP = MFC to MR = MC involves two different ways of expressing the same profit maximising condition. The former expression focuses on the value of the additional output (MVP) obtained from each extra unit of fertilizer. The latter expression focuses on the cost of the additional fertilizer (MC) required for each extra unit of output. The derivation of the supply curve in Figure 2.3 is a graphical representation of this shift between two alternative ways of looking at profit maximisation. The top diagram gives us different points on the production function where MVP = MFC for different output prices. The bottom diagram restates these points by equating the different output prices (MR) to the rising marginal cost (MC) of fertilizer incurred for each unit increase in output.

A final point on this analysis is to emphasise that it is the changing price ratio between input and output, not the absolute level of their prices, which is relevant. The same supply response would occur by lowering the fertilizer price while keeping the paddy price constant, as by increasing the paddy price while holding the fertilizer price constant.

Substitution between inputs

The physical interaction between inputs

Even though the idea of output response to varying levels of inputs yields some powerful conclusions about resource use in farm production, it does not adequately describe the interaction between inputs for the case of more than one input. Any production function relating output to two or more inputs contains the possibility that a given level of output could be produced with more than one combination of inputs. For example 3 metric tons of maize might be produced using 1 hectare of land and 4 workers, or 2 hectares of land and 2 workers.

This idea that two or more variable inputs may be combined in different quantities to produce the same output is called the *principle of substitution*. It is also sometimes referred to as the *law of variable factor proportions*. It is the second major component of the neoclassical approach to farm production, and it has wide application with respect to choice of technique in agricultural production. The treatment which follows restricts attention to the relationship of two variable inputs to a single output, and it assumes that input combinations may be varied continuously over the range of economic interest.

Consider the possibility that specified quantities of paddy could be produced with varying amounts of labour and land. For example 1 metric ton of paddy might be produced either with 100 days of labour and 0.5 hectare of land, or with 75 days of labour and 0.75 hectare of land, or with 50 days of labour and 1 hectare of land. The graphical device which permits us to describe the entire range of such combinations, within plausible limits, is an iso-product curve or *isoquant* ('iso' being Greek for 'the same'). Figure 2.4 shows several such isoquants. Each curve represents a given quantity of paddy output (Y) in metric tons. The varying quantities of labour (X_1) and land (X_2) used to produce these given outputs are shown on the horizontal and vertical axis of the graph. Isoquants are expected to have certain general characteristics deriving in the main from a commonsense view of how inputs relate to each other in farm production.

First, it should be appreciated that isoquants are just a (graphical) restatement of the production function. For example in the two variable input case, $Y=f(X_1, X_2)$, they are obtained by holding Y constant and discovering the different levels of X_1 and X_2 required to achieve the given level of output. In fact what is described in Figure 2.4 is a continuous production surface for all feasible levels of Y, out of which certain specific levels of Y have been selected and drawn as isoquants.

Figure 2.4. Variable factor proportions – isoquants.

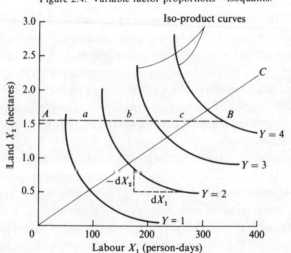

Second, the slope of the isoquant curve describes the quantity of input X_2 (vertical axis) replaced by one extra unit of input X_1 (moving outwards along the horizontal axis). This slope has a negative value, since each extra unit of input X_1 implies a reduction in the use of input X_2. As shown in Figure 2.4 on the isoquant for $Y=2$ metric tons, the slope of the isoquant equals $-dX_2/dX_1$. This slope is called the marginal rate of substitution (MRS) between X_1 and X_2.[3]

Third, isoquants have a shape which is convex to the origin. This means that the marginal rate of substitution, i.e. the slope of the curve, tends to diminish as more of one factor is used to replace the other. The curve gets flatter. This *diminishing marginal rate of substitution* results from the principle of diminishing marginal returns: as substitution proceeds it requires more and more of input X_1 to replace a single unit of input X_2 in order to maintain the same level of output. This is because input X_1 is subject to diminishing marginal returns and it eventually tends towards a technical maximum productivity as a single input.

The presence of diminishing marginal returns to a single input in an isoquant diagram can also be shown in a slightly different way. Consider the dotted line AB which shows the amount of labour which would be required to achieve successive equal increases in output (from $Y=1$, to $Y=2$, to $Y=3$, etc.) while holding the amount of land constant at 1.5 hectares. The gaps a, b, c along this line are successively wider, meaning that an increasing amount of labour is required to achieve equal increases in output for a given amount of land.

One further aspect of the physical relationships shown in Figure 2.4 should be noted, and this is *returns to scale*. Returns to scale are defined as what happens to output when both (or all) inputs are increased in the same proportion. A straight line drawn from the origin of an isoquant diagram, such as the ray OC in Figure 2.4, represents all those points for which the ratio of the two inputs stays the same as output increases. If, as in Figure 2.4, isoquants representing equal successive increases in output are spaced equally apart along a ray like OC, this demonstrates *constant returns to scale*, i.e. an equal percentage increase in both results in the same percentage increase in output. When successive isoquants representing equal increases in output move closer together going out from the origin, this is increasing returns to scale; and when they move further apart it is decreasing returns to scale. Issues of returns to scale in farming are examined more fully in Chapter 10 of this book.

The optimum combination of inputs

The optimum combination of inputs in economic terms is determined by the ratio of their prices. The price levels of different variable inputs determine how much of each input could be purchased for a given total cost of production. The way in which the most efficient combination of inputs is approached is to discover, for a given output, the least cost quantities of inputs given their different price levels. In other words the optimisation problem is seen here as one of cost minimisation, rather than the profit maximisation of the preceding section.

Cost information is represented on an isoquant diagram by a series of straight lines, each showing a given total cost corresponding to different combinations of two inputs. These are called *iso-cost* lines. In Figure 2.5 the iso-cost lines represent levels of total cost when the price of labour in paddy production is $2 per day and the price of land is $300 per hectare. The meaning of these lines can be clarified by way of an example. Take the iso-cost line for $600 shown in Figure 2.5. This represents the total amount of money which is available to spend either on land, or on labour, or on some combination of both inputs. If all the money is spent on land at $300 per hectare it will obtain 2 hectares; if all the money is spent on labour at $2 per day it will purchase 300 days of labour. The straight line connecting 2 hectares on the vertical axis and 300 days of labour on the horizontal axis

Figure 2.5. Optimum factor proportions.

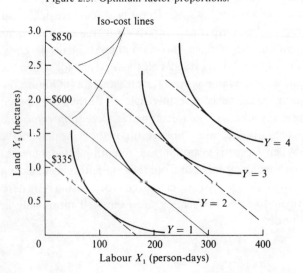

gives all the different combinations of land and labour which could be purchased for $600.

The slope of an iso-cost line is equal to the *inverse ratio of input prices* and it is negative. It is the number of units of X_2 (vertical axis) which can be purchased for the price of one unit of X_1 (horizontal axis). Since in this example $P_2 = \$300$ and $P_1 = \$2$, the slope of the curve is $P_1/P_2 = 2/300 = 0.0067$.[4] This is the amount of land which could be purchased for the price of one unit of labour. The slope is negative since each extra unit of input X_1 results in a reduction in the units of X_2 which can be purchased for a given total cost.

The least cost combination of inputs, for a given level of output, occurs at the point of tangency between the isoquant and the iso-cost line which makes the tangent. Any other points to the left or right of this point on the isoquant would clearly lie on a higher iso-cost line than the one which makes the tangent, and would therefore incur a higher total cost for the same output. At the point of tangency the slopes of the two curves are equal. The marginal rate of substitution equals the inverse ratio of input prices.

As in the case of the optimum point on the production function, some simple mathematics helps to explore the implications of this conclusion. First we are dealing here with a production function which has two variable inputs, and which is of the general form:

$$Y = f(X_1 \ X_2)$$

Each of the inputs in this production function is associated with its own marginal physical product, so that we have:

$$\text{MPP}_1 = \mathrm{d}Y/\mathrm{d}X_1, \text{ and } \text{MPP}_2 = \mathrm{d}Y/\mathrm{d}X_2$$

It works out that the inverse ratio of marginal physical products equals the marginal rate of substitution:[5]

$$\text{MPP}_1/\text{MPP}_2 = (\mathrm{d}Y/\mathrm{d}X_1)\cdot(\mathrm{d}X_2/\mathrm{d}Y) = \mathrm{d}X_2/\mathrm{d}X_1 = \text{MRS}_{12}$$

But as we have already seen in the context of Figure 2.5, at the optimum point the marginal rate of substitution equals the inverse ratio of input prices, P_1/P_2. Therefore the inverse ratio of the marginal physical products of each input equals the inverse ratio of their prices:

$$\text{MMP}_1/\text{MPP}_2 = P_1/P_2$$

or by cross-multiplying:

$$\text{MMP}_1/P_1 = \text{MPP}_2/P_2$$

In other words the optimum, least cost, combination of inputs occurs when the ratios of marginal physical products to unit costs are the same for all inputs. And this is the same as saying that the MPP per \$1 outlay should be equal across all inputs.

The least cost combination of inputs changes either if there is a change in the technology of production (altering the location or shape of the isoquants), or if there is a change in the ratio of factor prices. The economic analysis of such changes is deferred to Chapter 11 of this book on technical change in peasant agriculture.

Enterprise choice
The physical interaction between outputs

The third dimension of the farm production process which the farmer can vary is the pattern of farm output between different crop or livestock enterprises. The way in which this dimension is approached is to consider the combinations of alternative outputs which can be produced for a given set of resources. It thus reverses the logic of the factor proportions problem, and in many respects appears as its mirror image. This component is usually referred to as the product–product relationship.

The main consideration here is that alternative farm enterprises are likely to compete with each other for a given availability of inputs. For example, different annual or perennial crops grown in pure stands compete with each other for a fixed resource of a given quality of land. Two crops which ripen in the same month of the year would compete at harvest time for a fixed labour resource, and so on.

It should be noted, however, that not all outputs necessarily compete for all resources, and there are many examples from tropical agriculture of farming systems which minimise output conflicts with respect to specific resource constraints. One example is growing two different successive crops with short growing seasons on the same land; another is utilising different kinds of land for the crops most suitable to the different soils; another is the practice, highly prevalent in peasant agriculture, of mixed cropping which permits a fixed labour resource to cultivate simultaneously several different crops.

Consider, first, the simplest possible case of two outputs competing for one fixed resource as shown in Figure 2.6. The two crops are paddy and sugarcane, the variable resource in limited supply is labour – 2 people with 300 days of labour available for farm work between them. In a manner analogous to the presentation of isoquants, a curve may be drawn which describes all the different combinations of paddy and sugarcane which can be grown with 300 person-days of labour. This curve is called the production possibility frontier (PPF), and it is the third component in our threefold toolkit of farm production economics. The PPF represents the *maximum* product combinations for a given input level, which is why it is called a frontier. Notes on this construction are as follows:

First, the points at which the PPF hits each axis are the maximum quantity of each output which can be produced with the given amount of labour. Assuming at the extremes an average productivity of labour of 100 person-days for a metric ton of paddy and 2 person-days for a ton of sugarcane, then the maximum outputs are 3 metric tons of paddy or 150 metric tons of sugarcane.

Second, the slope of the PPF measures the rate at which one output can be substituted for the other given the fixed level of the resource. It is the amount of paddy on the vertical axis (dY_1) which can be obtained by giving up one unit of sugarcane on the horizontal axis (dY_2). The slope, $dY_1/-dY_2$, is negative since more of Y_1 can only be produced at the expense of less Y_2. The slope is called the marginal rate of transformation (MRT). It measures the increase in Y_1 which results from a small decrease in Y_2.

In contrast to isoquants the shape of the PPF is concave to the origin. The marginal rate of transformation is expected to increase (i.e. become less negative) as more of the input is transferred from one output to the other. This again is commonsense. As successive units of a single variable input are removed from Y_2 to Y_1, the sacrifice of Y_2 for each additional unit of Y_1 gets larger and larger. Thinking back to the production function, the output

Figure 2.6. Production possibility frontier.

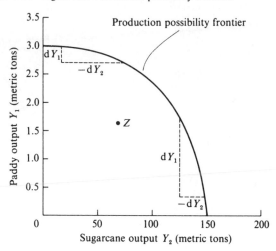

from which the input is being taken will experience rising MPP as we move down the production function, while that to which the input is being transferred will experience declining MPP as we move up the production function, even possibly to the point where very large sacrifices indeed of the first output would be required for minuscule gains in the second output. This is the situation depicted towards the top of the curve in Figure 2.6, where a large decline in sugarcane output is required for a minor rise in paddy output.

Third, technical efficiency in production requires operation at some point *on* the PPF. Any point (e.g. Z) inside the frontier is inefficient in technical terms, either because it represents less than full employment of the available resource or because it implies a lower efficiency of resource use than could be obtained given the production technology confronting the farmer.

The economic choice of enterprise

The economically optimum choice of enterprises is determined by the ratio of output prices. By now the logic of this should not be surprising or difficult. In addition to the PPF, Figure 2.7 contains a number of parallel straight lines, which describe the different combinations of paddy and sugarcane which yield given levels of total revenue. These lines are called *iso-revenue lines*. For example the iso-revenue line for $500 represents the different combinations of paddy, at $250 per metric ton, and sugarcane, at $10 per metric ton, which would yield a gross income of $500. This money could be obtained by selling 2 metric tons of paddy, 50 metric tons of sugarcane, or various alternative combinations between those two.

Figure 2.7. Optimum choice of enterprise.

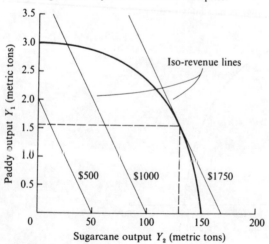

The slope of the iso-revenue lines equals the inverse ratio of output prices. It is the number of units of Y_1 which must be sold to earn the same revenue as one unit of Y_2, which in this case is \$10/\$250 equals 0.04. The slope is negative because for total revenue to remain constant, increased income from one output is associated with decreased income from the other.

The optimum combination of enterprises must lie on the PPF, as already discussed, and should also represent the maximum total revenue consistent with location on the PPF. This obviously occurs at the point of tangency of an iso-revenue line with the PPF, since any iso-revenue lines to the left of this point would represent lower total returns, and any iso-revenue lines to the right lie outside the boundary of production possibilities. In Figure 2.7, the optimum combination of paddy and sugarcane occurs at 1.6 metric tons of the former and 135 metric tons of the latter, yielding a total revenue of \$1750. The same point is defined where the marginal rate of transformation dY_1/dY_2 equals the inverse price ratio of the two outputs $P(Y_2)/P(Y_1)$.

In the case of the production possibility curve we have two production functions relating two separate outputs to a single resource:

$$Y_1 = f(X_1) \text{ and } Y_2 = f(X_1)$$

The single variable input, X_1, has two marginal physical products, one for each output:

$$MMP(Y_1) = dY_1/dX_1 \text{ and } MMP(Y_2) = dY_2/dX_1$$

The marginal rate of transformation of output Y_1 into output Y_2 has already been defined as:[6]

$$MRT_{12} = dY_1/dY_2$$
$$= MPP(Y_1)/MPP(Y_2)$$

This is by substitution from the MPP definitions. Thus the marginal rate of transformation equals the ratio of marginal physical products for a given resource between the two enterprises. Profit is maximised when:

$$MRT_{12} = P(Y_2)/P(Y_1)$$

Therefore at the optimum point:

$$MPP(Y_1)/MPP(Y_2) = P(Y_2)/P(Y_1)$$
$$MPP(Y_1) \cdot P(Y_1) = MPP(Y_2) \cdot P(Y_2)$$

by cross-multiplying.

Therefore:

$$MVP(Y_1) = MVP(Y_2)$$

This is an important result. It says that the optimum choice of enterprise occurs when the marginal value product per unit of a variable resource is equal in both enterprises. This is called *the principle of equi-marginal returns*. It says that a variable input should be transferred from one enterprise to another up to the point where the MVP of each unit of the input is equal for both enterprises. In terms of our example, this means that labour is transferred from paddy to sugarcane production up to the point where the additional revenue derived from one person-day of labour is equal in both crops.

Opportunity cost and comparative advantage

A concept closely related to the economic choice of enterprise is that of *opportunity cost*. The preceding analysis shows that with a given technology of production and fixed resources at the farmer's disposal, the output of one enterprise can only be increased by withdrawing resources from some other activity. The consequent reduction in output in other activities represents a 'cost' measured by the income foregone.

More generally, the opportunity cost of any resource may be defined as the maximum income that the resource could have obtained in an alternative use. For example if farm land could earn more by turning it into a holiday resort, then the opportunity cost of continuing to use it in farming is the income which could have been obtained by leasing it to a hotel operator. Another application of the opportunity cost principle is the subsistence consumption of farm output. The opportunity cost of on-farm consumption is the income which could have been obtained by selling the same amount of output in the market.

One further economic principle which relates to choice of enterprise is that of *comparative advantage*. Comparative advantage refers to the physical resources best suited to the production of different crops of livestock which exist *in different locations*. For example, at the level of a single farm which has land of different qualities, it makes sense to grow alternative crops on the land economically best suited to each individual crop. A farmer would not grow beans on swampy land and rice on a stony hillside.

For the farm sector as a whole the principle of comparative advantage refers to production alternatives in different locations. Crops should be distributed spatially so that they make the best use of the physical resources (climate, soils, topography, labour, transport infrastructure etc.) present in different locations. This means, first, that the resource needs of different enterprises are matched with resource availabilities in different locations and, second, that enterprises requiring greater amounts of certain resources are located in places where those resources are in most abundant supply.

Both on-farm and farm sector comparative advantage may change over time due to (a) changes in technology (e.g. new varieties or different equipment) which alter the input requirements of alternative enterprises, (b) land improvements (e.g. by drainage, irrigation, terracing etc), (c) changes in relative input costs or output prices in different locations, (d) changes in transport costs (e.g. new roads), and (e) development of substitute outputs (e.g. synthetic fibres which take away the comparative advantage of natural fibres).

Constrained production: the linear programming approach

An approach to resource use which can usefully be introduced in connection with the preceding concept of a production possibility frontier is linear programming. Linear programming (LP) is an operational method for studying the allocation of resources between enterprises when inputs are limited in their total amounts or are otherwise constrained, for example, a particular area of land may be suitable for one type of crop but not others.

The mathematical method underlying linear programming means that production functions are linear. More than that they are *fixed proportion* production functions of the special form:

$$Y = \min (a_1 X_1, a_2 X_2)$$

The meaning of this is shown by a simple example. Say paddy (Y) is produced on the basis of 2 metric tons per unit of land ($2X_1$) and 0.5 metric tons per unit of labour ($0.5X_2$) in a situation where the amount of land is fixed at 2 ha and the amount of labour is fixed at 6 persons. Then there is enough land to produce 4 metric tons paddy, but only enough labour to produce 3 metric tons paddy. The limiting input is labour and the feasible output is the minimum of the latter two figures i.e. it is 3 metric tons paddy. This in turn means that only 1.5 ha out of the available 2 ha of land is utilised, the remaining 0.5 ha is surplus.

This example conveys the general principle of LP: the level of output is determined by the *most limiting input*, and this level of output in turn determines the level of use of other inputs. This principle may be further illustrated by an extension of the above example, cast within the PPF framework.

Suppose we have two outputs, paddy (Y_1) and sugarcane (Y_2). We also have three variable inputs in limited amounts, which are labour (X_1), type 'A' land (X_2) which is more suitable for paddy than for sugarcane, and type

'B' land (X_3) which is more suitable for sugarcane than for paddy. The amount of each output which can be obtained per unit of the inputs, and the maximum level of each input, are set out in Table 2.1.

When placed on a PPF-type graph, these production conditions yield the situation shown in Figure 2.8. A total of 1.5 person-years of labour permits *either* 3 metric tons of paddy to be produced, *or* 150 metric tons of sugarcane, *or* some combination between these limits. This is the labour constraint. Similarly 2 hectares of 'A' land permit a maximum of either 6 metric tons of paddy, or 100 metric tons of sugarcane; 5 hectares of 'B' land permit a maximum of either 2.5 metric tons of paddy, or 400 metric tons of sugarcane. These are the 'A' land and 'B' land constraints respectively. The

Table 2.1

Input	Units of output per unit of input		Total input available
	Y_1	Y_2	
Labour X_1	2	100	1.5 person-years
'A' Land X_2	3	50	2 ha
'B' Land X_3	0.5	80	5 ha

Figure 2.8. Linear programming: graphical solution.

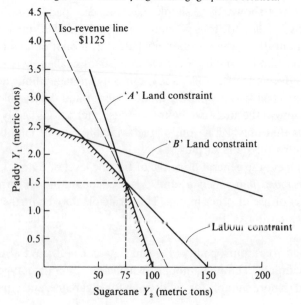

constraints are straight lines due to the linear nature of the model: the average products (APPs) of labour and land are constant over all positive levels of output. The production possibility frontier is indicated by the shaded area of Figure 2.8. It is the frontier describing the maximum combinations of paddy and sugarcane permitted by the limited quantity of each resource.

The comparability of Figure 2.8 to the previous analysis of enterprise choice is evident. Also the same is the graphical determination of the optimum choice of enterprise, which occurs at a point of contact between the PPF and the highest possible iso-revenue line. For the same output prices as Figure 2.7, $250 per metric ton paddy and $10 per metric ton sugarcane, the optimum 'solution' to this linear programming problem is 1.5 metric tons rice and 75 metric tons sugarcane for a gross revenue of $1125. LP problems are not typically so simple as to be susceptible to graphical solution, but they lend themselves readily to computer solution methods.

This treatment of linear programming is inevitably rather brief. The main intention is to demonstrate how LP relates, as a methodological approach to resource allocation, to the idea of constrained production possibilities due to restrictions on resource availability. Such constraints are a crucial feature of the economic situation of most peasant farmers, and the idea of identifying the most limiting resource has widespread application in the design of small farm economic policies.

One further feature of the LP approach requires mention. The solution of the maximisation problem, such as that depicted in Figure 2.8, also implies an implicit value per unit of each resource to the farmer in the region of the profit maximising position. This implicit value, which is termed the *shadow price* of the resource, measures the addition to total farm revenue which would result if one more unit of a limiting input were made available.

In our example these shadow prices are $250 per year for labour, $380 per hectare for type 'A' land, and zero for type 'B' land. Type 'B' land has a zero shadow price because it is in surplus in the optimal farm plan. Since this surplus cannot be used productively due to other binding constraints it has no implicit value to the farmer. The shadow prices are equivalent to the MVPs of the conventional theory. They are obtained by the solution of what is called the 'dual' of the maximisation problem, a feature of LP which would take us beyond the ambitions of this chapter but good introductions to which can fortunately be found elsewhere.[7]

Summary

We are now in a position to summarise the main propositions of the neoclassical economic model of farm production. This section gives in turn, first, a summary of the results concerning optimum resource use in farm production; and, second, a restatement of the theoretical principles which underpin a great proportion of the economic analysis of farm production.

Optimum resource use in farm production

The three components of the farm production model yield three conditions of economic efficiency:

1 For any variable input in farm production, the optimum level of its use occurs when the extra return just equals the extra cost per unit:

$$MVP_X = P_X$$

This means that the *rate of technical transformation* of factor into product (dY/dX or MPP_X) should equal the inverse (factor/product) price ratio (P_X/P_Y)

2 For any single enterprise, and several variable inputs, the least cost method of production occurs when the marginal product per \$1 spent is the same for each resource:

$$MPP_1/P_1 = MPP_2/P_2 = MPP_3/P_3 \ldots$$

This also coincides with the point where the *rate of technical substitution* between inputs (dX_2/dX_1 or MPP_1/MPP_2) equals the inverse ratio of input prices (P_1/P_2).

3 For a single variable input used in several enterprises, the maximum profit combination of enterprises occurs when the marginal value product is the same in each enterprise:

$$MVP(Y_1) = MVP(Y_2) = MVP(Y_3) \ldots$$

This is called the principle of equi-marginal returns. It also coincides with the point where the *rate of technical transformation* between outputs (dY_1/dY_2) equals the inverse ratio of output prices ($P(Y_2)/P(Y_1)$).

Combining these results, efficient farm production means that the marginal value product per unit of outlay on inputs should be equal for all resources in all enterprises.

Seven main principles

Using a slightly modified version of a scheme suggested by Dillon & Hardaker (1980, pp. 3–6) we can set out seven principles which together form the backbone of the neoclassical economic approach to farm production. These principles provide a convenient summary of the material covered in this chapter, as well as a reference point for later chapters.

1 *The principle of variable versus fixed resources.* The distinction of farm resources between *variable* and *fixed* inputs underlies much economic analysis of farm production. Variable inputs are those which change with the volume of output over a specified time period (e.g. fertilizer, seeds, pesticides, fuel, harvest labour etc.). Fixed inputs are those which remain the same regardless of the volume of output actually achieved (e.g. land rent, labour required for cultivation irrespective of final yield, bullocks, tools, machinery, and buildings). The same distinction lies between *variable costs* (which vary with output) and *fixed costs* (which are incurred irrespective of the level of output).

2 *The principle of diminishing marginal returns.* The principle of diminishing physical and economic returns is critical to agricultural production economics. Without it no production 'problem' could be identified since increases of output would be the same or greater than increases in variable input(s) (i.e. there would be no resource constraint). It is the existence of diminishing returns which determines the best level for any production practice or activity on the farm.

3 *The principle of substitution.* The principle of substitution, or variable factor proportions, applies whenever farm output can be produced by alternative combinations of inputs. Different input combinations for a given output can be referred to as different 'methods' or 'techniques' of production.

4 *The principle of enterprise choice.* This principle states that, in most cases, farmers are able to produce various different outputs from the resources at their disposal. Thus there exists an economic problem of selecting the optimum combination of enterprises in the light of farmers' goals.

5 *The principle of the most limiting resource.* This principle recognises that farmers often confront constraints on the quantity of farm inputs and on their use between alternative activities. The most limiting resource is the input constraint which determines the

maximum feasible level of output, notwithstanding surplus amounts of other resources. Linear programming provides an operational method for finding the optimum combination of enterprises where there are many constraints, and also for valuing resources according to their marginal contribution to farm income.

6 *The principle of opportunity cost.* This principle states that the transfer of resources from one activity to another has an implicit 'cost', which is the income lost from reducing the level of output in the activity from which resources are withdrawn. The strict definition of opportunity cost is the *maximum* income that the resource(s) could have yielded in an alternative use, and this may include off-farm as well as on-farm deployment of available resources.

7 *The principle of comparative advantage.* This principle refers to the geographical distribution of physical resources best suited to the production of different crops and livestock in different locations. It states that alternative farm activities should take place in those locations where the climate, soils, terrain, labour availability etc. favour their lowest cost production compared to other locations.

Notes

1 The technical maximum on a single production function should not be confused with the more general concept of 'technical efficiency' which refers to operation on the best production function available (see Chapter 4).

2 As shown on the graph these increases strictly should be labelled ΔY and ΔX_1 meaning discrete changes. Mathematically dY/dX_1 refers to a point on the curve, and this is approached as ΔX_1 tends to dX_1, a very small change. The same applies for other graphs of this chapter where slopes of curves have been illustrated by discrete changes.

3 The marginal rate of substitution is negative. An alternative expression, the rate of technical substitution (RTS) is often used to describe the same thing while avoiding the minus sign, i.e. $RTS = -MRS$.

4 Due to the scales used on the graph in Figure 2.5, the slope of the iso-cost lines does not of course look like -0.0067 (it looks more like -1). Nevertheless given the measurements, the figure cited is arithmetically correct. The same explanation also applies to the slope of iso-revenue lines which appear in Figure 2.7 further on in this chapter.

5 This and subsequent equations ignore minus signs which should be on both sides of the equation and which therefore cancel each other out.

6 Similarly to the analysis of isoquants, the marginal rate of transformation (MRT), which is negative, has an alternative definition, the rate of product transformation (RPT), which is positive. Again here we have chosen to ignore minus signs which occur on both sides of the equation, rather than confuse the reader with a multiplicity of definitions (see Notes 3 and 4 above).

7 See for example Upton (1973, Ch. 16), Doll & Orazem (1984, Ch. 9), or Beneke & Winterboer (1973).

Further reading

A great many agricultural economics textbooks describe the farm production model. The classic original was Heady (1952). Useful more recent introductions are Upton (1973) with similar coverage to this chapter, Upton (1976) which is a little more advanced, and Ritson (1977) which is a general agricultural economics textbook. An excellent textbook which illustrates the material with numerous examples, and which has the clearest introductory chapter on linear programming this author has seen, is Doll & Orazem (1984). For more advanced treatment of neoclassical production theory Beattie & Taylor (1985) is recommended.

Reading list

Beattie, B.R. & Taylor C.R. (1985). *The Economics of Production*. New York: Wiley.

Doll, J.P. & Orazem F. (1984). *Production Economics: Theory with Applications*, 2nd edn, New York: Wiley.

Heady, E.O. (1952). *Economics of Agricultural Production and Resource Use*. Englewood Cliffs, New Jersey: Prentice-Hall.

Ritson, C. (1977). *Agricultural Economics: Principles and Policy*. London: Crosby Lockwood Staples.

Upton, M. (1973). *Farm Management in Africa: The Principles of Production and Planning*. London: Oxford University Press.

Upton, M. (1976). *Agricultural Production Economics and Resource-Use*. Oxford University Press.

3

Elements of peasant political economy

Peasants and political economy

Although this is a textbook about the economic analysis of the peasant farm household it contains many underlying themes and perceptions about the nature of peasant economy which fall outside the scope of neoclassical economics. We have already encountered some of these themes in our definition of peasants in Chapter 1. Themes of history and change, of tension between subsistence and market participation, of peasant subordination to other social groups, and of social differences within peasant communities are all part of a larger picture of peasant economic life which we use to interpret, and sometimes to modify, the results of neoclassical economic analysis.

The approach which lends some theoretical coherence to this wider conception of peasants is that of Marxian political economy. The purpose of this chapter is to introduce the student to concepts in the Marxian theoretical method which are useful for the study of peasants, and to summarise certain large strategic issues about the future of peasants to which these concepts have been applied. Some cautionary observations are first required concerning comparisons and differences between the Marxian and neoclassical theoretical approaches, and these are set out as follows:

(a) Although both theories set out to analyse the same economic system – the market economy or capitalism – they do so from entirely different points of entry and methodology.

(b) The starting point of neoclassical economics is the individual economic unit – firm, consumer, or household – and the working of the larger economic system is deduced from predictions concerning individual action. The starting point of Marxian political economy is society as a

whole – the entire economic system – and individual action is governe
circumscribed by the way this larger system works.

(c) The neoclassical approach separates the economic from the social
and political and hives off the last two for treatment in different disciplines.
The Marxian approach emphasises the inseparability of economic, social
and political dimensions of human societies.

(d) The logical method of neoclassical economics is deduction from a set
of prior assumptions. The more precisely this deduction can be formulated
(e.g. by mathematical logic) the happier is the neoclassical economist since it
seems to lend the discipline a 'scientific' character.

(e) The method of Marxian political economy is dialectical, i.e. it focuses
on tension and contradiction between opposites both as the focus of
theoretical interest and as an explanation of the forces which drive society as
a whole in particular directions. Some relevant opposites are production for
use versus production for exchange, owners versus non-owners of productive resources, capital versus labour, profit versus wages, and so on.

(f) Neoclassical economics emphasises social harmony. Individual economic units only interact with each other through exchanges in the market
and, since each individual is assumed free to choose whether and when to
enter the market, no conflict between people can arise.

(g) Marxian political economy emphasises contradiction and potential
conflict in the relations between social classes as a central explanation of the
way societies change over time. This does not mean that Marxian analysis is
only preoccupied with social turmoil. Conflict and tension are creative as
well as destructive forces, and recognition of them often provides a sounder
basis for explaining the patterns and direction of social change than appeals
to an imaginary social harmony.

(h) The domain of interest of neoclassical economics is largely confined
to problem solving of a technical–economic character over a time horizon
which holds social, political, and technological factors constant. The
domain of interest of Marxian political economy is social change writ large.

Because both theoretical approaches were developed to understand
better the same economic system, they are not incompatible over many
aspects of pure economic analysis. A Marxian economist would not argue
with profit maximisation as the goal of capitalist enterprises, nor with the
short term predictions of the neoclassical theory of the firm about resource
use and the impact of relative price changes. However, few Marxian
economists would regard such matters as the most pertinent feature of
capitalist enterprise. They would be much more interested in what the
predictions meant for different groups of people, capitalists and wage

labour, who relate to the social activity of production in quite distinct ways. The incompatibility of the theories resides not so much in disagreement about the mechanics of the working of the market economy, but in the *meaning* attached to this working. And here the Marxian emphasis on the social nature of all productive activity, on contradiction, and on social change differs greatly from the neoclassical preoccupation with the nuts and bolts of individual economic decision making.

The chapter proceeds as follows. First, it gives a brief account of the meaning of concepts and terms in political economy which are used in the rest of this chapter and elsewhere in the book. Second, it examines the way these concepts have been applied to the study of the status and future of peasant farm production in the world economy. Third, it considers the meanings of 'surplus' and 'exploitation' in the context of peasant production. Fourth, it makes some brief observations on the state as a force for influencing the conditions and prospects of peasant farm production.

Concepts in Marxian political economy
Social relations of production

In any society the livelihood of different groups of people is crucially determined by (a) who possesses effective control over productive resources, and (b) what happens to the output created with those resources. Productive resources – such as land, variable inputs, instruments of production, and machines – are referred to in Marxian terms as the *means of production*. The output obtained by productive activity may be consumed directly by its producers, in which case it is production for use, or it may be sold in the market, in which case it is production for exchange.

Control over means of production and what happens to output are inextricably linked. The Marxian concept which describes this link and places it in a social context is that of *social relations of production*. Social relations of production refer to the access of different groups of people to productive resources, and hence to control over what they produce, in *society at large*, not in the individual production unit. The concept thus embodies the idea that in different societies, in different historical eras, there are dominant ways in which groups within society relate to each other for the purposes of production.

For example under feudal social relations of production, land as a productive resource was owned or controlled by one social class, the feudal lords, and its access by another social class, the serfs (a kind of peasant), was contingent on control by the feudal lords over the labour of the serfs and over a share of the output produced by the serfs. Likewise under capitalist relations of production, one social class, the workers, do not own productive resources, and they must thus work for another social class, capitalists, in order to obtain their livelihood. These two examples describe *class* societies: in both cases the dominant relations of production are such as to create a distinction between those who apply their labour to production, and those who own the means of production.

Mode of production

An extension of the concept of social relations of production is that of *mode of production*. We have already seen that social relations of production refer to the dominant way production is organised in societies over spans of their history. The concept of mode of production summarises such dominant systems of social and economic organisation as a whole. In addition to social relations of production it encompasses the characteristic technological development of the system (the 'forces of production'), and the various legal, institutional, and cultural norms (the 'superstructure') which regulate its operation.

It is generally accepted that capitalism is the dominant mode of production in the contemporary world economy, and this has important implications for the viability and prospects of peasant production within this dominant mode.

Labour, social reproduction, and surplus value

In political economy labour is not thought of as just another input into production like sacks of fertilizer or drums of diesel. Labour is performed by people, and it involves a *social* relationship between people who come together for the purpose of production. Nor is labour synonymous with work. Labour applies to situations of social production, while work could equally be performed by a Robinson Crusoe living in isolation on a desert island. Once Man Friday appears on the scene, a social relation is established, and *labour* comes into existence.

Social labour underlies the concept of *social reproduction*. It is the outcome of production relations between people which enables a society to renew itself in all its various dimensions over time. Social reproduction refers to this material capacity for social renewal, it does not mean the biological reproduction of human beings although the latter is evidently one aspect of social reproduction.

Social reproduction may be of two kinds. It can be *simple reproduction*, in which social labour produces just enough to ensure that the society keeps ticking over at the same material level year after year. This 'just enough' must be sufficient, of course, to enable production to continue at the recurrent level. For example in an agrarian community, enough of the previous season's crop must be kept aside for sowing in the next season, and a proportion of labour time must be set aside for repairing and maintaining the existing means of production of the community.

Social reproduction may, alternatively, take the form of *expanded reproduction*. Expanded reproduction requires *both* that society produces more than is strictly required to maintain it in the same conditions in successive time periods, *and* that this 'extra' production is utilised to raise output still further over time. In other words it requires the *investment* of this extra output in new means of production.

The difference between this extra production and the level needed for simple reproduction gives us a first indication of what is meant by the term 'surplus'. The production of a 'surplus' over and above recurrent needs is a prerequisite for society to experience rising output and standards of living. However, it does not on its own guarantee rising output, and this is where the class structure of society becomes important. In feudal societies, for example, serfs produced a surplus above their own needs of simple reproduction, but because the feudal lords appropriated this surplus mainly for consumption purposes the society at large did not undergo expanded reproduction. Similarly, it has been observed in some contemporary developing countries that the state bureaucracy consumes a large proportion of the surplus produced by peasant farmers (e.g. Ellis, 1983), and this again means that expanded reproduction in the society at large is inhibited.

There are many examples in history of societies, even great empires, based on the consumption by one social class (overlords, chiefs, rulers, slave owners) of surpluses produced by other social classes. These societies correspond to various pre-capitalist modes of production. A central feature of such societies was that they depended for their expansion not on cycles of investment leading to sustained increases in output, but on the coercion of ever greater surpluses from their subject peoples for direct consumption. These societies did not experience expanded reproduction, and they were prone to collapse if for one reason or another the volumes of surplus on which they depended could no longer be sustained.

The capitalist mode of production involves expanded reproduction because surpluses produced above recurrent output levels are continuously reinvested in new means of production which raise future output. Like earlier modes of production, capitalism is based on a social class structure to achieve these surpluses. One class, the workers, produces a level of output which is substantially above that required for their own reproduction as a social class. The other class, the capitalists, utilises the surplus produced by labour for investment in new means of production which raises output still further in successive periods. The capitalist class is in a position to do this because it owns, or has command over, the means of production necessary for social reproduction. Workers do not have command over resources by which they could secure their own reproduction, and they must therefore sell their labour power to the capitalist class, for a wage, in order to survive.

Marxian theory specifically makes labour the source of the capacity of capitalist society to renew itself over time in a continuously expanding cycle. For this reason the *value* to society at large of what is produced, manifested by the ability of capitalists to sell in the market, is attributed to labour, not to capitalists nor to consumers. Likewise, the proportion of this social value which constitutes a surplus above the wage costs of production is referred to as *surplus value* produced by labour.

In world history the capitalist mode of production is unique in its systematic and sustained achievement of expanded social reproduction on the basis of the uncoordinated actions of individual capitalists. The mechanism by which this occurs combines the appropriation and reinvestment of surplus produced by labour with (a) production for exchange in the market, not for direct use, and (b) competition between capitalists which continuously forces them to seek new ways of maintaining their individual capacity to generate surplus.

Competition and the market pervade all social relations under capitalism. The market sets the terms under which individual production units survive or perish; competition continuously redefines these terms and ensures a continuous process of adaptation to them. The Marxian approach emphasises the market and competition as social forces to which individual economic agents must conform in order to survive. This contrasts with neoclassical economics which stresses freedom of choice in the market economy.

Application to peasant production

According to our earlier definition of peasants (Chapter 1) they are always part of a larger economic system which in varying degrees establishes the conditions under which they survive as agricultural producers. Peasant household production is never a mode of production in itself, it is always located in a larger society where a particular dominant mode prevails. This means that social reproduction as a whole obeys the rules of the dominant mode of production, even if peasants possess a limited ability to reproduce themselves independently of that mode.

The position of peasants is clearer under the feudal mode of production than under capitalism. Under feudalism peasants are the social *class* which produces the surplus necessary for the renewal over time of feudal social relations. The subordinate social status of peasants in this case is unambiguous, as also is the non-market basis of surplus extraction. Under capitalism, peasant production no longer corresponds to the dominant mechanism of social reproduction. Moreover, peasants in varying degrees have the capability, via their access to land, for simple reproduction outside the dominant mode. Nevertheless, participation in market transactions means that they are never wholly independent of capitalist relations, and the more enmeshed they become in market exchanges the more they must conform to the dictates of productive efficiency set in the capitalist market place.

The central debate in Marxian theoretical work on peasants concerns the sustainability, or persistence, of peasant forms of production within the dominant capitalist mode of production. We have already seen in Chapter 1 that this question turns in part on the attributes of family or household forms of farm production which enable them to compete successfully within a prevailing system of capitalist production relations. For peasants it also turns on their partial ability to disengage from the market when the going gets tough. Two opposing lines of reasoning about the persistence of peasants are described in the following paragraphs.

The classic Marxist position, as set out by Lenin (1967), is that the pressures on peasants created by capitalist production relations must, inevitably, result in their disappearance as a distinct form of production. The process by which this occurs is called *social differentiation*, in which peasant communities are predicted to disintegrate into the two social classes of capitalist farmers and rural wage labour. The reasons this may happen are manifold, but they include such factors as the institution of private property in land, the differential adoption of improved cultivation practices by different individual farmers, the enforced abandonment of their holdings by peasants unable to compete in the market with their more advanced neighbours, the foreclosure by creditors on farmers who have run into debt, and the increasing employment of wage labour by those farmers who are successful.

Some writers have considered this not just an inevitable process under capitalism, but also a required process in order for the agricultural sector to make a proper contribution to economic growth. Hence it is sometimes expressed not as an objective process that works itself out in fullness of time, but as a strategic necessity so that a more efficient and market oriented agriculture can provide the non-farm sector with cheap food, raw materials, and labour.

An opposing line of reasoning is that family farm production, of which peasants comprise a major type, possesses an internal logic which permits it to resist the pressures of capitalist production relations and thus to reproduce itself indefinitely. Components of this position include:

(a) the capability of peasants to maintain their needs of simple reproduction due to their control over means of production, especially land;

(b) the social norms of peasant communities which are directed towards reciprocity rather than individual profit maximisation (the 'moral economy' argument advanced by Scott (1976));

(c) demographic factors in the life cycle of peasant families from one generation to another which oppose the concentration of land in the hands of a few farmers due to the subdivision of land on inheritance;

(d) the capacity of peasants to overcome market pressures by intensifying the amount of labour committed to production (sometimes referred to as the capacity of peasants for 'self-exploitation');

(e) natural or technical factors specific to farming which make agriculture unattractive to capital (e.g. the length of the production cycle, variability of climate, higher risk of output failure, difficulties of supervision);

(f) functional advantages for capitalism (e.g. cheaper food, less risk) from leaving agriculture in the hands of peasants (related to reasons (d) and (e));

(g) other flexibilities possessed by household production with respect to cropping patterns, labour use, and sources of income between farm and off-farm activities.

One of the theories of this position is a non-Marxian model of peasant household behaviour which stresses the simple reproduction motivation of peasants linked to demographic factors internal to the farm household. This is Chayanov's model of peasant economy, the logic of which is examined in Chapter 6 of this book. As an explanation of the stability of peasant society it relies heavily on the assumption that the goal of peasant households is simple reproduction rather than profit maximisation. This ensures that capital accumulation, which would be almost bound to occur unevenly between farmers over time, does not take place.

There are also several arguments which seek to locate some of the above reasons for the persistence of peasant household production *within* the logic of capitalism and the market. These arguments originate in the orthodox Marxian approach, but they concede a number of forces working against the inevitable dissolution of household production. Two of these arguments are summarised in the following paragraphs.

First, lack of accumulation in the peasant economy may occur not due to the limited material motivation of peasants but because capitalist production relations continuously push peasants back towards simple reproduction. Two main reasons are advanced:

(a) Surplus appropriation. The wider system captures any surplus which peasants produce, thus leaving them always at the level of simple reproduction. The forms such surplus appropriation can take are examined in the next section but may include rents of various kinds, price squeezes, and taxes.

(b) Lowering the social value of peasant labour time. This is called 'devalorisation' of peasant labour. It refers to the impact of lower cost production methods on the viability of peasant production. Innovations occurring outside the peasant economy which reduce the price of commodities produced by peasants either result in lower peasant income, or more work by peasants to sustain the same level of income (refer to point (d) in the previous list).

Both these factors may be described as a 'simple reproduction squeeze' imposed by the market on peasants (Bernstein, 1979). They may be offset by the adoption by peasants themselves of lower cost or higher output production methods. It has also been argued in the same context that the purported superior efficiency of peasants is a *result* of these external pressures imposed on them (causing them always to work harder for less) not an inherent *capability* they possess for long run survival.

Second, it has been argued that certain aspects of farm production are awkward for capitalist production relations and this discourages the advance of capitalism in agriculture. The principal factor is the length of the farm production cycle compared to the time in which labour is productively employed (Mann & Dickinson, 1978). This refers to the seasonal pattern of labour use, which in family production means that household labour is applied unevenly through the year. For capitalist production this poses the problem either of paying for permanent wage labour when it is not needed all the time or of depending on the uncertainties and social disruption of migrant labour.

It is observed from the foregoing that many of the reasons advanced for the survival of peasant production are, more generally, reasons for the persistence of family farm production under advanced capitalism. It follows that capitalist farming is not the only route which may be taken in paths of agrarian change; an alternative route is the transition from peasant farming to commercial family farming in a context of fully developed input and output markets (Friedmann, 1980).

In summary, then, there exist various opposing forces influencing the long run viability of peasant household production. In practice it is the interplay between these forces, rather than the complete dominance of one or another, which determines the fate of peasant societies. In certain conditions the forces of disintegration are observed to dominate; in others the forces of stability or persistence seem to prevail. In contemporary agrarian societies the relative strength of these opposing forces is influenced by two factors which merit further consideration. One is the intensity of the pressure imposed on peasants to yield a surplus which is captured by other social groups. The second is the role of the state in contributing to the stability or instability of peasant production. This chapter concludes with a brief summary of these two aspects.

Peasants and surplus

Many different definitions of surplus can be encountered in writings on peasant economy. Some writers refer to 'marketed surplus' meaning the proportion of the physical output of peasants which is sold in the market rather than retained for home consumption. Other writers refer to 'financial surplus' meaning the proportion of the sales value of peasant marketed output which is not passed back to producers in the farm-gate price they receive, less the necessary costs of crop marketing.

A broader view of surplus which follows from our discussion of Marxian concepts is the proportion of the social value produced by peasant labour above the simple reproduction needs of the peasant household. This is similar to, but should not be confused with, the 'surplus value' produced by labour under capitalist production relations. It differs from the latter because, for one thing, peasants may be able to retain for themselves some share of this surplus, and, for another, it is not necessarily capitalists who capture part of the surplus.

In keeping with this notion of surplus, we can consider 'surplus appropriation' as those components of the total product of peasant labour which are captured by other groups or classes in the wider society. Deere & de Janvry (1979) identify seven mechanisms which they interpret as ways in which part of the product of peasants is captured by other social groups. Three of these mechanisms operate via rents, three via markets, and one via the state. Some of these mechanisms are doubtful, since they could be considered as normal payments for the use of factors of production. Nevertheless we set them out in full here, and defer comment on them to the end of this section:

(a) *Rent in labour services*. This refers to the practice prevalent under feudal relations of production by which the access of peasants to land to meet their own subsistence is contingent on the fulfilment of labour obligations to their landlord. It survives to this day in some Latin American societies.

(b) *Rent in kind*. This refers to sharecropping whereby the tenancy contract between a peasant and landlord specifies the rent as a proportion of farm output. Again this was common under feudal relations of production, and it remains a major feature of peasant production in many developing countries. Sharecropping poses interesting problems about microeconomic efficiency and the working of factor markets which are examined in Chapter 8.

(c) *Rent in cash*. Cash payment for rights of access to land is the typical tenancy contract under capitalist production relations. The level of cash rents reflect the intensity of pressure for access to land and the productivity of peasant farming. Where competition for tenancies is intense it is to be expected, under the normal working of the market, that rents will tend to adjust upwards with increases in productivity so that the standard of living of tenants may remain at or near the subsistence level.

(d) *Appropriation of surplus value via the wage*. When part of the peasants' income is obtained by wage labour off the farm, then the peasant – this time as wage worker – creates surplus value in the orthodox Marxian sense as applied to capitalist production.

(e) *Appropriation via prices*. This refers to the potential for peasant incomes to be squeezed, either through falling prices for output sold in the market or through rising prices of market inputs, or a combination of both. The concept used to describe market price squeezes is that of the changing *terms of trade* confronting peasant producers which measures the ratio of output prices to input prices over time.

(f) *Appropriation via usury*. Usury refers to the advance of loans to peasant farmers at levels of interest rate which do not reflect competitive market rates in the wider national or international economy. This may occur for various reasons, but the most pernicious form is where peasants are caught in a cycle of permanent debt to an individual landlord, moneylender, or trader who can charge as high interest as they consider the peasant able to afford because the peasant's continued survival depends on meeting repayment obligations to the creditor.

(g) *Peasant taxation.* This is the form in which the state extracts part of the product of peasants. For reasons of administrative difficulty peasants are rarely taxed directly on their net income. Rather taxation of peasants is usually indirect and operates by taxes on the inputs or outputs of the farm. In some countries export taxes on commodities produced by peasants have constituted a major mechanism by which income is transferred from peasants to the state.

Note that the first two of these mechanisms are non-market in character and involve non-capitalist social relations between peasants and others. The sixth, usury, tends to be closely related to the second, and is associated with incomplete or non-working markets under capitalism. The third, rent in cash, and the fifth, price squeezes, are consistent with capitalist production relations but they may be intensified by unequal exercise of market power in imperfect markets. The seventh, state taxation, is common to all societies and whether its incidence falls especially heavily on peasants is a matter for investigation in particular cases. Only the fourth, wage labour off the farm, corresponds to direct 'exploitation' of labour by capital in its strict Marxian sense.

In short the 'exploitation' of peasants under capitalism, sometimes alluded to in books on peasants, is conceptually dubious. If peasants are exploited, it is more likely to be a function of non-capitalist social relations, or the unequal exercise of market power, than a function of capitalism *per se.* Much of the supposed exploitation of peasants, price squeezes in particular, corresponds to the normal working of the capitalist economy in which only the most efficient producers survive in the longer run. The major exception to this is when the state uses prices to squeeze surplus from peasants.

Peasants and the state

The role of the state is played down in much of the writing on the political economy of peasants. This originates in part from the orthodox Marxist view that the state is merely an apparatus for oiling the wheels of capitalism, namely for providing the legal and institutional apparatus to enforce private property rights and legal contract, and for providing public goods and services (utilities, roads, telecommunications etc.) which are too large and diffuse in their spread for private capital itself to handle. Likewise free market economists often advocate a minimum role for the state in the economic life of society.

This view of the state is misplaced in the context of societies with large agrarian populations obtaining their livelihood from peasant production.

A common situation is one of a powerful central state drawing its support and legitimacy from a small minority of the population with a foothold in the more advanced sectors of the economy (or in the military), and with little or no effective representation of its peasant population. In extreme cases where the development of capitalist production relations is weak and uneven, the state itself (as a social group of bureaucrats and politicians) may not have the material basis to survive unless it extracts large surpluses from its peasant populations.

It is therefore not only in capital and market relations that external economic pressures on peasants can arise. To be sure the state often plays a role oriented to the interests of particular representatives of capital, for example by altering the legal basis of tenure in order to make land available for large scale production, by creating marketing channels which favour some purchasers above others, or by acting as intermediary in contracts between external corporations and internal peasants, but this is not the only guise in which the state may operate.

It is also possible, and indeed common, for the state to override or substitute for market forces. It does this when, for example, it fixes the prices itself of the inputs and outputs of farm production, establishes exclusive state marketing channels for the handling of farm commodities, insists on peasants growing particular export crops, or encourages them to use more purchased inputs financed by state loans.

Summary

1 This chapter concerns concepts in political economy which are useful for thinking about the larger social processes within which peasant production takes place.

2 The neoclassical and Marxian theoretical approaches to the study of the capitalist economy are contrasted. Neoclassical economics begins with the individual economic unit and emphasises freedom of choice and social harmony. Marxian political economy begins with society as a whole and emphasises social constraints on individual action and contradiction in the relations between social classes.

3 A number of Marxian concepts are introduced including social relations of production, mode of production, simple versus expanded reproduction and surplus value. The distinction is also made between production for direct use (use value production) and production for exchange in the market.

4 The application of these concepts to peasant production is

considered. It is observed that peasant household production is never a mode of production in itself, it is always located within a dominant mode, and for most contemporary peasants this dominant mode is the world capitalist economy.

5 The long run survival of peasant production involves an interplay between opposing forces; some contributing to its disintegration, and others contributing to its stability and persistence.

6 Disintegration may occur for several reasons associated with the spread of capitalist relations of production. Increased reliance on market exchanges (e.g. specialisation in cash crop production, borrowing to finance cash inputs, emergence of a land market) creates more risk of ruin and places more economic power in the hands of landowners, moneylenders, and traders. The process by which rural society tends to polarise between an emerging landless class, the rural proletariat, and an emerging class of labour-hiring capitalist farmers is referred to as 'social differentiation'.

7 However, there are also factors which work in opposition to this disintegration. Amongst these the partial engagement of peasants in market relations, their capacity to intensify the use of labour in farm production, and flexibilities they possess in the use of family resources, are considered important reasons for their persistence as market relations become more pervasive.

8 An alternative transition for peasants is towards commercial family farming in fully developed markets. The family farm is a persistent feature of agricultural production in advanced capitalist economies.

9 The chapter examines various concepts of 'surplus expropriation' from peasants, and it sets out seven mechanisms by which part of the product of peasants is captured by other social groups. These are: unwaged labour service; rent in kind; rent in cash; wage labour; relative price shifts; usury; and taxation. With the exception of wage labour none of these mechanisms correspond to 'exploitation' of peasants in the strict Marxian sense of that term.

10 In contemporary agrarian economies the state can have a major influence on the short and long term prospects of peasant production. This is not just because the state may be allied to large private capital rather than small, but often more directly because the state attempts to supplant the market by regulating the prices and marketing channels of farm inputs and outputs.

Further reading

Perhaps the easiest introduction to the concepts of political economy used in this chapter is Chapter 3 of Wolf (1982). The application of Marxian concepts to peasant agriculture is found in many papers contributed to the *Journal of Peasant Studies*. Papers which were found especially clear and helpful in the preparation of this chapter were Bernstein (1979), Friedmann (1980), and Mann & Dickinson (1978). Another useful paper related to the concerns of this chapter is Deere & de Janvry (1979). A collection of relevant papers is contained in Harriss (1982), and de Janvry (1981) is also recommended.

Reading list

Bernstein, H. (1979). African peasantries: a theoretical framework. *Journal of Peasant Studies*, Vol. 6, No. 4.

Deere, C.D. & de Janvry, A. (1979). A conceptual framework for the empirical analysis of peasants. *American Journal of Agricultural Economics*, Vol. 61, No. 4.

Friedman, H. (1980). Household production and the national economy: concepts for the analysis of agrarian formations. *Journal of Peasant Studies*, Vol. 7, No. 2.

Harriss, J. (ed.) (1982). *Rural Development: Theories of Peasant Economy and Agrarian Change*. London: Hutchinson.

de Janvry, A. (1981). *The Agrarian Question and Reformism in Latin America*. London: Johns Hopkins.

Mann, S.A. & Dickinson, J.M. (1978). Obstacles to the development of a capitalist agriculture. *Journal of Peasant Studies*, Vol. 5, No. 4.

Wolf, E.R. (1982). *Europe and the People without History*. Berkeley: University of California Press.

Part II

The theory of the optimising peasant

Introduction

Part II contains five alternative theories of peasant household economic behaviour. It is entitled 'The theory of the optimising peasant' after the seminal paper by Michael Lipton (1968). Each theory assumes that the peasant household maximises one or more household objectives.

Each theory is based on a set of assumptions about the working of the larger economy within which peasant production takes place. Many of these assumptions are shared by more than one theory, and some of them are shared by all the theories. All theories also share the same theoretical method. The alteration of certain key assumptions is what distinguishes one theory from another, but it should not be deduced from this that the theories are entirely different, and competing, explanations of household behaviour. A comparative summary of the assumptions, predictions, and policy implications of the theories is given at the end of this part of the book.

These five chapters follow a similar format which includes a statement of the theory, variants and extensions, approach and results of empirical validation, and wider interpretation. The balance between these components varies according to matters of emphasis pertinent to each theory.

Certain important topics in peasant economic analysis are introduced in the context of the household theory to which they most closely relate; for example the topic of interlocked agrarian factor markets is treated in Chapter 8 on share tenancy. The same is also true for extensions of basic economic theory beyond that given in Chapter 2; for example the simple economics of consumer choice is introduced in Chapter 6, and the theory known as neoclassical home economics is introduced in Chapter 7.

The theories have certain limitations in common. The most obvious one is that the household or family is treated as a single decision making unit. This means, as discussed much later in Chapter 9, that the objectives of the household head are assumed to represent the goals of all household members. The orthodox approach is to assume that the household is ruled over by a patriarch, and to refer to peasant decisions by the male pronoun, 'he'. These theories neglect the social basis of the division of labour between women and men in the household, and also the differences in their command over resources and income. These omissions are rectified in Part III.

Reading list

Lipton M. (1968). The theory of the optimising peasant, *Journal of Development Studies*, Vol. 4, No. 3, pp. 327–51.

4

The profit maximising peasant

Peasants and economic efficiency

It is over two decades since the American economist, T.W. Schultz, advanced the celebrated hypothesis that farm families in developing countries were 'efficient but poor', and thus that 'There are comparatively few significant inefficiencies in the allocation of the factors of production in traditional agriculture.' (Schultz, 1964: 37–8). This hypothesis had a lasting influence on the perceptions of economists about peasant decision making. Its plausibility, limitations, and policy implications remain of central interest to peasant economics.

The proposition that peasants are efficient ascribes to the peasant household the motivation of profit maximisation. Efficiency and profit maximisation are two sides of the same coin, at the level of the individual production unit you cannot have one without the other (see Chapter 2). The strict definition of economic efficiency also requires a competitive market, since neither the individual production unit nor the sector can attain efficiency if different producers face different prices or if some economic agents can influence the prices and returns of other economic agents.

At first sight these conditions would seem to rule out the discussion of efficiency in the context of peasants. By our very definition of peasants – their partial engagement in usually imperfect markets – strict economic efficiency is ruled out.

There are, however, several valid reasons for examining what is meant by economic efficiency in the study of peasants. There are virtually no aspects of peasant economics which are not touched in one way or another by considerations of efficiency and these include:

  (a) The household theories which are the subject of this part of the book;

(b) ideas about the contribution of peasant agriculture to economic growth;

(c) arguments in political economy about the persistence of peasant production and its ability to compete with capitalist enterprises in farming;

(d) a parallel argument in neoclassical economics concerning farm size and economic efficiency (Chapter 10 below);

(e) most short and medium term economic policies designed to increase output in the peasant sector.

In this chapter we consider various facets of the theory of the profit maximising peasant. We begin by looking more closely at what is meant by economic efficiency at the microeconomic level. This then leads into the methods used to substantiate the efficient peasant hypothesis from sample surveys of peasant farmers. The results and limitations of research into peasant efficiency are examined and the policy implications of the efficient peasant hypothesis are considered. Finally the topic is placed in certain wider perspectives of the economic study of peasants.

Three points of initial clarification must be made. First, the profit maximising hypothesis does not require the existence of profit in the form of a sum of money. What it requires is for there to be no adjustment of inputs or outputs which would give the household a higher net income whether measured in money or physical terms, and this applies equally to a near subsistence household as to a fully monetised one. For practical investigation inputs and outputs must be assigned market prices, and at that point there may be problems with the degree to which such prices represent competitive market conditions.

Second, profit maximisation has both a behavioural content (motivation of the household) and a technical–economic content (farm economic performance as a business enterprise). Most work in the area of efficiency infers the nature of the former by investigation of the latter. It is therefore concerned less with the way the farm household reaches its decisions than with the outcome of those decisions for the efficiency of the farm as a firm.

Third, even if the nature of peasant economy inhibits the attainment of efficiency in its strict neoclassical sense, this does not mean that a strong element of economic calculation cannot exist in the context of the multiple goals and constraints of the farm household. The existence of such an element is, in fact, virtually an axiom of most agricultural policy and planning in developing countries. Thus partial or constrained profit maximisation may exist even if strict efficiency is not observed.

Allocative, technical, and economic efficiency

The profit maximising model is already set out in Chapter 2. It is not intended to repeat its propositions here. However, its earlier treatment ignores by assumption an important aspect of efficiency which requires sharper definition for the consideration of peasant efficiency. The assumption in question is the one that states that farms operate on, rather than within, the production possibility frontier (PPF) available to them. Another way this is expressed is that farms are assumed to operate on the *outer bound production function*, i.e. the technically most superior production function available to them.

The problem with this assumption is that it overlooks those kinds of inefficiency that result from operation on an inferior production function. In effect the profit maximisation model tends to focus on only one aspect of efficiency, which is the adjustment of output and inputs to their relative prices. And the same is true of the efficient peasant hypothesis advanced by Schultz.

In order to perceive this problem, consider the simple production functions shown in Figure 4.1. These describe two possible relationships

Figure 4.1. Technical and price efficiency.

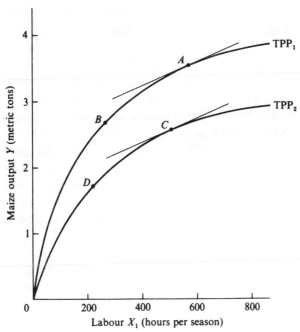

between a single output and a single variable input. The top one of these, labelled TPP_1 in the diagram, displays higher output for all positive levels of input use than the lower one, TPP_2. TPP_1 is clearly technically superior to TPP_2 in this diagram. A farm operating at any point on TPP_1, say at point B, is more efficient technically than a farm operating at any point on TPP_2. This is because any point on TPP_1 represents a higher level of output for a given level of the variable input.

This, then, is what defines *technical efficiency* as applied in the microeconomics of production. It is *the maximum attainable level of output for a given level of production inputs*, given the range of alternative technologies available to the farmer.

The concept of *allocative efficiency*, by contrast, refers only to the adjustment of inputs and outputs to reflect relative prices, the technology of production already having been chosen. These adjustments are the familiar marginal conditions for profit maximisation set out in Chapter 2, i.e. that marginal value product (MVP) should equal marginal factor cost (MFC) for any single variable input, and that MVP per unit of an input should be equal across different outputs (the principle of equi-marginal returns). Some writers prefer to use the term *price efficiency* to describe allocative efficiency, and this serves to emphasise its focus on the correct adjustment to relative prices.

The distinction between technical and allocative efficiency gives rise to four possible alternatives for describing the relative success of farms in achieving efficiency and these are shown on Figure 4.1. First, a farm might display both technical and allocative inefficiency as given by a point such as D on TPP_2 where neither of the efficiency conditions are met. Second, a farm might show allocative efficiency but technical inefficiency as shown by point C. Third, a farm might display technical efficiency but allocative inefficiency as shown by a point such as B on TPP_1. Fourth, a farm may have achieved both technical and allocative efficiency, as shown at point A.

The term *economic efficiency* is reserved for this last situation of both technical and allocative efficiency. Thus the achievement of either one of the efficiencies may be seen as a necessary but not sufficient condition to ensure economic efficiency. The simultaneous achievement of both efficiencies provides the sufficient condition to ensure economic efficiency.

The same distinctions can be illustrated equally well on an isoquant diagram, as in Figure 4.2(*a*), or using production possibility curves, as in Figure 4.2(*b*). In both these cases the subscript 1 indicates the technically superior set of production conditions, the point D displays both technical and allocative inefficiency, C displays allocative efficiency but technical inefficiency, B displays technical efficiency but allocative inefficiency, and A defines the point of *economic efficiency*.

Thus in the isoquant diagram, Y_1 is the isoquant which minimises the level of inputs required to produce a given output, say 100 units. Point A is the allocative efficient point on this technical efficient isoquant, and is thus economically efficient. Similarly in the PPF diagram, it is PPF$_1$ which represents the maximum combinations of output obtainable from a given

Figure 4.2. (*a*) Isoquants and efficiency. (*b*) Production frontier and efficiency.

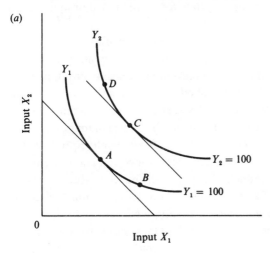

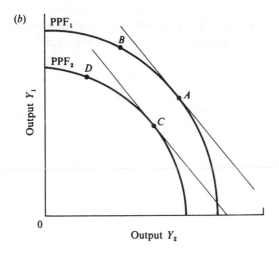

set of inputs. Point A is the allocative efficiency position on this technically efficient production possibility curve, and is thus economically efficient.

In pursuit of the efficient peasant

Our concern here is with the investigation of peasant efficiency as a general hypothesis. In other words it is with the quest to obtain supporting evidence for a theoretical proposition with wide applicability, not with observations about partial aspects of individual peasant farms. This focus is stressed because the methods used for such a general proposition differ from those which would be appropriate for more limited or more practical purposes.

It should be clear by now that in order to investigate the efficiency attributes of peasant farmers two main kinds of information are required. The first is their varying degree of success at maximising output from given levels of inputs. This is the technical efficiency dimension, and it might be indicated, for example, by the observation of different yields or productivities between farms as discovered by a farm management survey. The second is their judgement with respect to the relative prices of inputs and outputs. This is the allocative efficiency dimension and it requires that the marginal physical products (MPPs) of the main productive resources are known since the MPPs are required in order to examine whether the conditions of allocative efficiency are being met.

The main method which has been used for tackling both these dimensions of peasant efficiency is to estimate a *production function* for peasant farms i.e. to obtain an equation which links farm output in a specific way to a series of inputs. This is not a textbook in econometrics (the branch of economics concerned with the statistical estimation of economic relationships), but in order to proceed with this topic the student requires a rudimentary idea of what is involved in obtaining a production function from a sample of peasant farms.

Consider, for example, obtaining a production function which relates paddy yields, Y, to the labour time per hectare put into production, L. Data are collected from a sample of farms on paddy yields in kilograms per hectare and on labour input in days per hectare over a crop season. Thus each farm in the sample gives two pieces of information – a level of yield associated with a level of labour input – and these could be plotted on a graph as is shown by the crosses in Figure 4.3. In what follows we refer to the paddy output and labour input in Figure 4.3 without restating their per hectare basis which is taken as given.

Figure 4.3 displays a hypothetical scatter of points for a sample of 10 farms. For example farm No. 4 produced 2500 kg paddy with 140 days of labour, farm No. 6 produced 3400 kg paddy with 300 days of labour, and so on. The graph also shows the solid curve which describes the best average position between these scattered observations. And this is precisely what is involved in the statistical procedure, called regression analysis, used for estimating a production function. It finds the line which minimises the deviations between the scattered observations for a sample of farms.

An estimated production function like that shown in Figure 4.3 is used to discover the marginal physical product (MPP) for each resource used in production. As explained in Chapter 2 the marginal physical product is the *slope* of the production function, and it diminishes as resource use increases. The level of the marginal physical product which is of interest for the peasant efficiency hypothesis is the *average* level at which farms in the sample are operating, and this is shown in Figure 4.3 at point A on the estimated production function.

At point A the average farm in our sample uses 150 days of labour to obtain 2700 kg of paddy. The average physical product of labour at this point is thus 18 kg of paddy, and the marginal physical product (of labour,

Figure 4.3. Estimating a production function from sample farms.

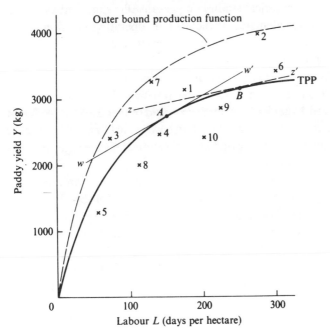

MPP_L), is 7 kg at this point i.e. one more day of labour in the vicinity of point A would yield a 7 kg increase in paddy output.

Given data on the price of the input (the wage rate per hour) and the price of output, we are then in a position to see whether our average farmer in the sample achieves allocative efficiency. This follows from the allocative efficiency rule we described in Chapter 2 which states that the slope of the production function (i.e. the MPP) should equal the inverse ratio of input price to output price at the profit maximising point:

$$MPP_L = w/p,$$

where w is the wage rate and p is the price of paddy.
Alternatively, by cross-multiplying:

$$\frac{MVP_L}{w} = 1$$

i.e. the marginal value product of a variable input divided by the input price should equal one if allocative efficiency is being observed. This ratio is often referred to as the *allocative efficiency ratio* (k) for a single input, where:

$$k = MVP_X/P_X,$$

for any variable resource, X.

Thus the focus of empirical studies on peasant efficiency centres on the estimated value of k, calculated at the average operating position of the sample of farms, and on whether this value seems to be close enough to 1 for the efficiency hypothesis to be substantiated.

Returning now to the example, the allocative efficiency condition would be exactly satisfied if, say, the market wage rate was $1.05 per day and the paddy price was $0.15 per kg. The ratio w/p would be then $1.05/0.15 = 7$, and this is the same as $MPP_L = 7$ kg. The relative wage cost line, ww' in Figure 4.3, is then exactly tangent to the operating position of the average farmer at point A on the production function.

Any other input–output price ratio would not give the same point of tangency, and the average farmer at point A would then be allocatively inefficient. Thus if the observed market wage was $1.05 per day, but the paddy price was $0.30, then the ratio w/p would be 3.5, and this corresponds to the relative wage cost line zz'' with tangency at point B on the production function. The MVP at point A (7 kg $\cdot$ $0.30 = $2.10) is in this case twice the wage rate ($1.05), the allocative efficiency ratio is $k = 2$, and the 'average' farmer operating at point A is inefficient.

Note that even if the allocative efficiency condition is satisfied at point A, it requires something of an act of faith to assert that this 'proves' that the peasant farmers in the sample are efficient. This act of faith is that all farmers in the sample are considered to have been striving, with varying degrees of success, to reach point A. As described by one writer: 'Our test is mainly a test of whether individual firms *attempt* to be efficient ... Having found that "on the average" they *succeed* in being efficient, we may assign a high probability value to the extent that individually they *attempt* to be efficient.' (Yotopoulos, 1968: 34).

The procedure we have described in Figure 4.3 has been used in a number of studies aimed to test the hypothesis of the profit maximising peasant. These include a series of sample investigations in India in the 1960s (e.g. Hopper, 1965; Chennareddy, 1967; Sahota, 1968; Saini, 1968), and many conducted elsewhere (e.g. for Africa, see Norman, 1974; 1977). These and other studies reach the conclusion that peasant farmers are allocatively efficient since they tend, on average, to equate the marginal value product of each variable input to its market price.

Agreement on this finding is not unanimous, however. Doubts of a statistical nature surround the range of the allocative efficiency ratio, k, taken as 'proving' efficiency. A re-examination of several of the studies cited above found that MVPs differed, on average, by more than 40 per cent from the factor prices to which they were supposedly equated (Shapiro, 1983). Moreover other researchers have come up with different findings. For example in their study of the economy of Palanpur, an Indian village, Bliss & Stern (1982: 273–6) found the MVPs for three wheat production inputs to be more than three times above their market prices. The reasons for this seemed to be the high cost of credit and uncertainty. The authors concluded: 'farmers were not doing the best that they can do given their resources. But one should not, and we did not, expect the world to be that simple' (Bliss & Stern, 1982: 293).

Conflicting evidence apart, there are two other reasons for caution about the validity of the procedure outlined for testing the efficiency hypothesis. The first is that it obscures varying levels of technical competence between farmers by its emphasis on the 'average' production function. The second is that its finding of allocative efficiency at a single point on the production function involves a rather dubious leap in the dark from a viewpoint of statistical interpretation.

Technical inefficiency

The production function approach to testing the efficiency hypothesis ignores the technical efficiency aspect of the overall concept of economic efficiency. This is because it averages out the vertical distances between sample farmers as shown graphically in Figure 4.3, and these vertical differences represent variations in the yield per hectare achieved by different farm households for given amounts of labour input.

The vertical spread of the scatter of sample farms suggests an implicit *outer bound production function*, shown in Figure 4.3 as a broken curve, which represents the true efficient frontier for the sample of farms. It is implausible to argue that farms which lie on or near this outer curve are trying, but failing, to locate themselves on the technically inferior 'average' production function. It is more likely that some farmers are more technically competent than other farmers in the sample.

Technical efficiency has been investigated using a linear programming method to 'push' the production function to its outer position. Studies which have done this find, not surprisingly, that technical inefficiency is rife in samples of peasant farmers. In a study of peasant cotton farms in Tanzania, Shapiro (1983) found that the output of the sample could have been 51 per cent higher if all farms had achieved the technical efficiency level of the best farms in the sample. A similar result is reported by Ray (1985) for a sample of farms in West Bengal, and Lingard *et al.* (1983: 170) found that the best farm produced over three times as much as the worst farm in a sample of 32 peasant farms in the Philippines.

Mention may also be made here of the 'yield gap' work undertaken by the International Rice Research Institute (IRRI) in the Philippines in the 1970s (Herdt & Mandac, 1981; Barker, Herdt & Rose, 1985). The concept of a 'yield gap' covers both allocative and technical inefficiency. The maximum technical yield under farm (*not* research station) conditions was found by cultivating trial plots on sample farms using optimal agronomic practices. This was then compared to actual average yields on the same sample farms, and the difference (the yield gap) was divided into the three components of (a) downward adjustment to reflect correct profit maximising behaviour, (b) incorrect allocation decisions, and (c) technical inefficiency. The research found a yield gap of about 25 per cent, of which 14 per cent was attributed to technical inefficiency, 10 per cent to allocative inefficiency, and 1–2 per cent to 'profit seeking'.

Allocative efficiency and improper averaging

A similar problem surrounds allocative efficiency. The average operating position for all farms in the sample shown at point A in Figure 4.3 need not coincide with the operating position of any single farm in the entire sample. If point A then turns out to be efficient ($k = 1$), then all points away from A are inefficient by definition: the average farm proves to be efficient, only when the scatter of actual farms are all inefficient for the single input price which they all supposedly confront (Rudra, 1973; 1982).

The problem here is the double averaging involved in the assumption that all farmers in the sample are seeking to operate at the single point A. There is the first averaging which finds the production function by minimising the vertical distances (variations in yield) of farmers from the estimated curve, and this is acceptable as a statistical exercise. However, point A also involves a second averaging, which is the collapsing of the horizontal differences (variations in labour use) between farmers to the single point. This is doubtful since no statistical relationship between input and output is proposed which gives grounds to suppose that horizontal departures from this point represent failed attempts to reach the average position.

These difficulties stem from a logical problem inherent in the neoclassical concept of economic efficiency (Yotopoulos & Nugent, 1976: 74). If all farms in the sample really did (a) possess the same production technology, (b) face the same prices for inputs and outputs, and (c) follow profit maximising behaviour, then all farms would operate with identically the same inputs and outputs. There would be no variation between farms from which a production function could be estimated. At the same time the existence of variation which does permit a production function to be estimated implies that one or more of the above three conditions are being violated by the farms in the sample.

If condition (a) is violated it really throws the baby out with the bathwater because one cannot talk about relative success at achieving either technical or allocative efficiency of farms using different technologies (i.e. operating on distinct production functions). If condition (b) is violated then markets are deemed not to be working properly and differing patterns of inputs and outputs between farms would reflect the different prices confronting farmers rather than their relative degrees of efficiency. If condition (c) is violated then one is talking about varying, partial, or unsuccessful efforts to profit maximise implying that the pure profit maximisation model is an incomplete explanation of farm household behaviour.

In summary, the proposition that peasant farmers are efficient in a pure neoclassical profit maximising sense is neither proven as a general hypothesis, nor is it insightful of variation and its causes in the peasant economy. It requires such strict assumptions about the homogeneity of production and resource conditions confronting all farmers in a sample, as well as about the competitivity of the markets in which peasant farms operate, that these are rarely likely to pertain in the peasant populations from which samples are drawn. By obscuring variation and its causes between farms it also does a disservice to the economic analysis of peasants: if the average peasant is efficient, then the problems of farm households which depart from the average are overlooked. Finally the pursuit of the averagely efficient peasant is at odds with the conception of peasant economy as involving complex forms of interaction between households of varying economic status in imperfect markets.

To reject the efficiency hypothesis in its pure form is not, however, to throw away entirely the theory of the profit maximising peasant. A great deal of indirect evidence, especially on the responsiveness of peasants to changes in relative market prices between crops, reveals a strong element of economic calculation on the part of peasant farm households everywhere. More relevant perhaps than the pure efficiency hypothesis is some notion of *constrained profit maximisation*. Apart from short term resource rigidity, constraints may be of various kinds. The existence of risk and uncertainty is one (see Chapter 5). Trade-offs between profit maximisation and other household goals is another (see Chapters 6 and 7). Unequal relationships of power and coercion between households is a third (see Chapter 8). Pervasive market imperfections in output, credit, and input markets are a fourth.

Considered in retrospect the Schultzian hypothesis derives its importance not from its accuracy as a description of resource allocation in peasant agriculture, but from its success in placing peasant economic rationality firmly on the agenda. Prior to Schultz the literature on 'traditional' agriculture was permeated by stereotypes of laziness, perversity, lack of motivation, and, in short, irrationality, on the part of peasants as economic agents. His hypothesis was the point of departure for taking much more seriously the logic of peasant farm systems, and, from there, for seeking to discover the underlying logic of peasant farm practices instead of dismissing them out of hand as 'backward'.

Policy aspects

Perhaps the most basic policy implication which follows from the theory of the profit maximising peasant is that peasant farm households make predictable adjustments to changes in the prices of farm inputs and outputs. This applies even if the proposition of constrained profit maximisation is substituted for the full efficiency hypothesis, though the speed and extent of adjustment then depends on the severity of the constraints. Policies which seek to increase the output of the peasant sector by raising farm output prices or by lowering the cost of variable inputs are predicated on profit maximisation as a behavioural trait of peasant farm households.

More generally the implications for economic policy of the theory of the profit maximising peasant depend on the degree of acceptance of the various components of the efficiency hypothesis. We can distinguish several strands of policy conclusion as follows:

(a) If the hypothesis is accepted in its pure form, i.e. profit maximising peasants are efficient in competitive markets, within the limitations of their existing technology, then the only way of achieving increases in the output of peasant agriculture is to change massively the farmers' inputs and technology. It is this implication which led Lipton (1968: 329) to call Schultz's hypothesis 'a doctrine of revolutionary pessimism': it excludes the potential for low cost adjustments leading to improved output and incomes for peasant farm families.

The view that only dramatic shifts in farm technology could transform peasant agriculture (the 'transformation approach') manifested itself in many rural development programmes of the 1960s and 1970s. Examples are large scale irrigation projects, tractorisation schemes, and ambitious attempts to impose complete technical 'packages' (seeds, fertilizers, insecticides, credit, etc.) on members of peasant communities. In practical terms the bias was towards purely technical solutions – the 'quick technical fix' – rather than on social or market constraints to increased output.

(b) If the efficiency of peasants is constrained only by imperfect markets, including lack of knowledge of the best technologies available, then the emphasis of policy shifts to improving the working of markets, and diffusing information on production technologies as widely as possible. This interpretation was not very popular in the 1960s and 1970s, but came into its own with the general resurgence of free market economics in the 1980s (see also the first part of 'wider perspectives' below).

(c) An alternative to the 'transformation approach' is to engineer price changes, which because peasants are deemed allocatively efficient, will cause them to change their production methods and to innovate. The prevalence of policies like credit schemes and subsidised fertilizer prices result from this thinking, which plays on *prices* as the stimulus to adoption of improved technologies. This also, of course, involves a consideration of the relative costliness (in social welfare and/or to the government) of this against alternative (a) above.

(d) If the allocative efficiency part of the hypothesis is accepted but the technical efficiency part is rejected then there exists scope for improving the technical efficiency of individual farms up to the level of the best farms in the community, or to some other defined standard. The emphasis here is on *farmer education* and *extension work* as relatively low cost methods of achieving increases in productive efficiency. This is sometimes referred to in the literature as the 'improvement approach'.

These are the main links between elements of the efficiency hypothesis and specific policies. If the strict hypothesis is dropped and replaced by the notion of partial or constrained profit maximisation, the emphasis switches to identification and removal of the constraints. Many small farm economic policies, and many rural development books, are based in some sense on a notion of removing constraints to improved efficiency. So too is the routine work of the farm management economist and the extension worker. By the same token these policies and interventions are designed, whether consciously or not, whether successfully or not, to de-peasantise the peasants and to convert them into family farm enterprises in a competitive market system.

Wider perspectives

The theory of the profit maximising peasant does not, of course, possess only an economic aspect; ideology and politics also enter its domain. As a household level proposition about economic motivation it also has limitations which need to be recognised. Here we consider briefly three wider aspects of the profit maximising peasant: its ideological dimension; its relationship to Marxian theories of peasantry; and its neglect of the internal relations of the household.

The profit maximising peasant conveniently fits a free market view of the world. According to this peasant farmers already approximate the perfect market ideal, and if left more or less to their own devices will do so even more with gratifying consequences for economic growth and social welfare. In this vision state intervention is enemy number one, and the role of government should be strictly limited to providing the infrastructure necessary for improving the working of markets.

This view has become prevalent in recent times as a reaction to the disasters of post-independence state interventions in African agriculture (see e.g. Bates, 1981). Its beguiling reasoning notwithstanding, however, it has evident shortcomings. First, it is just too glib, defining away the problems of peasants as if there were none of the extreme poverty, inequality, insecurity, and deprivation which characterise peasant life in most parts of the world. Second, it falsely assumes a classless peasantry everywhere in which no conflicts of access to resources etc. arise in the pursuit by individual households of market gain. Third, it ignores the major social upheavals which often lie at the heart of success stories of peasant farming (e.g. the significance of land reform in South Korea, as described by

Lee (1979)), and falsely presents such success as entirely the work of the market place. Fourth, it even neglects the commonplace reasons (food security, price stability) for market intervention as practised in all the industrial free market economies.

From a different perspective, Marxian theory would tend to see profit maximisation as a question of the tension between the relative autonomy of peasants and their integration into capitalist markets. The more deeply enmeshed in market relations, the more competitive peasants must become, and those who fail to adopt more efficient production may lose the basis of their livelihood to those who do. In this view, then, efficiency is not something which can be defined in isolation and held aloft as having a character of its own. Efficiency always has a context in space and time, and is relative to the intensity of competitive pressures both near and far, to innovation and cost reduction in the wider capitalist economy, and to the demands of outsiders who may have direct or indirect influence on the conditions of peasant survival.

Where there is disagreement within this perspective it is on the durability of peasant autonomy and on the end result of the competitive process. As we have seen in Chapter 3, one sequence sees the independence of peasants crumbling rapidly under the advance of capitalist relations. Another sees peasants being gradually, and unevenly, transformed into competitive family farms, rather than capitalist farms, and thus surviving as farm households shorn of their transitional features.

An important gap in the theory of the profit maximising peasant is any sense of the relations internal to the household which ensure this single purpose. Two alternative assumptions are common. One is that the household is ruled over by a patriarch who makes the decisions on the part of other household members. The other is that decisions comply with 'The primitive communism rule governing the allocation of work-load and the distribution of consumption ... within the household.' (Saith & Tankha, 1972: 351). Neither assumption is satisfactory as we shall consider in more detail in Chapter 9. The first is not because there exist countless examples, especially in Africa, where cultivation decisions are made by women notwithstanding their social subordination to men. The second is not because it neglects conflicts of interest which result from the unequal distribution of tasks and gains in the typical peasant household.

Summary

1 This chapter examines the twin and inseparable hypotheses that peasants are profit maximising economic agents who are thus efficient producers in the neoclassical sense.

2 The distinction is made between technical efficiency and allocative efficiency as two components in the overall neoclassical concept of economic efficiency.

3 The chapter outlines the approach which has been used to try to substantiate peasant efficiency as a general hypothesis. It is shown, with an illustrative example, that this approach focuses only on allocative efficiency and that it does this by imputing a single desired operating position to the variable economic behaviour of individual farms.

4 The evidence and problems of this approach are briefly reviewed. It is concluded that the pursuit of the averagely efficient peasant is elusive and not very meaningful. However, ideas of partial or constrained profit maximisation make sense given the widespread evidence of economic calculation on the part of peasant farmers.

5 The policy implications which are drawn from different stances on the efficiency question are examined:

(i) if peasants are efficient within the constraints of existing technology, then only dramatic change in technology will do ('transformation approach');

(ii) on the assumption that farmers are allocatively responsive to price changes, then manipulation of input and output prices (e.g. credit schemes, subsidised fertilizer) may have the same effect at lower cost;

(iii) if inefficiency results from market imperfections then the working of markets should be improved;

(iv) if farmers are technically inefficient then farmer education and extension has a major role ('improvement approach').

6 The chapter concludes with certain wider perspectives on the theory of the profit maximising peasant including its relation to free market ideology; aspects of it as seen from the viewpoint of the Marxian analysis of peasants; and its gaps with respect to the internal relations of the household.

Further reading

A descriptive review of some aspects of peasant economic rationality is given in Adams (1986). Much of the neoclassical literature on this topic is difficult with respect to its mathematics and statistics. A manageable introduction to concepts of economic efficiency and their measurement is given in Yotopoulos & Nugent (1976: Ch. 5), and the paper by Yotopoulos (1968) on the investigation of efficiency for a sample of

Greek peasant farms is about the easiest to follow of its kind. Norman (1974, 1977) is excellent for the rationality of peasant farming systems, especially mixed cropping, at a rather more concrete level of description than is common. Readable and still pertinent to many aspects of farm household economic analysis is the critical review of Schultz's book by Lipton (1968). And of course there is Schultz (1964) itself, although this is going back to the very origins of this literature.

Reading List

Adams, J. (1986). Peasant rationality: individuals, groups, cultures, *World Development*, Vol. 14, No. 2.

Lipton, M. (1968). The theory of the optimising peasant, *Journal of Development Studies*, Vol. 4, No. 3, pp. 327–51.

Norman, D.W. (1974). Rationalising mixed cropping under indigenous conditions: the example of northern Nigeria, *Journal of Development Studies*, Vol. 11.

Norman, D.W. (1977). Economic rationality of traditional Hausa dryland farmers in the north of Nigeria, in Stevens, R.D. (ed.) *Tradition and Dynamics in Small-Farm Agriculture*. Ames: Iowa State University Press.

Schultz, T.W. (1964). *Transforming Traditional Agriculture*, Yale University Press.

Yotopoulos, P.A. (1968). On the efficiency of resource utilization in subsistence agriculture. *Food Research Institute Studies*, Vol. 8, No. 2.

Yotopoulos, P.A. & Nugent, J.B. (1976). *Economics of Development: Empirical Investigations*. New York: Harper & Row.

5

The risk-averse peasant

Uncertainty and peasants

It is widely recognised that a high level of uncertainty typifies the lives of people in peasant farm households in developing countries. This uncertainty is more pervasive and serious for them than for farm families in temperate zones for several reasons. Variations of climate are more unpredictable and tend to be more severe in their impact on crop yields in the tropics than in temperate zones. Also markets are more unstable where information is poor and other imperfections abound. Insecurity of poor peasant families due to low social and economic status is important in some countries; insecurity due to the vagaries of state action is important in others. And looming above all these kinds of uncertainty is the sheer poverty of so many peasant families meaning that the outcome of uncertain events can often make the difference between survival and starvation.

The pervasiveness of various kinds of uncertainty in peasant production has important implications for its economic analysis and for the interpretation of its future prospects. The following points summarise some of the propositions and arguments which surround uncertainty:

(a) it results in sub-optimal economic decisions at the microeconomic level of the unit of production (absence of profit maximisation);

(b) it results in unwillingness or slowness to adopt innovations (peasant conservatism);

(c) it is the reason for various farming practices, like mixed cropping, which represent successful adaptations to uncertainty by ameliorating its effects;

(d) its impact is more severe for poor than for better off farm households, implying that it reinforces social differentiation;

(e) it is reduced by increasing market integration due to improved information, communication, market outlets etc.;

(f) it is exacerbated by greater market integration since the safety of subsistence is replaced by the insecurity of unstable markets and adverse price trends.

The purpose of this chapter is to examine these and other aspects of the impact of uncertainty on the livelihood of peasants. It covers, first, the main different kinds of uncertainty confronting peasants; second, the definition of the terms uncertainty and risk; third, the microeconomic analysis of the impact of risk on production decisions; fourth, the underlying basis of risk analysis in utility maximisation; fifth, research into the impact of risk and its results; sixth, some main policy implications of risk and uncertainty; and seventh, wider perspectives on risk in the context of the peasant household and the peasant economy.

Types of uncertainty

Uncertainty is a condition which in varying degrees surrounds all forms of activity in a market economy. It is considered more of a problem for agricultural production than for industrial production due to the influence of climate and other natural factors on output, and the length of the production cycle. Moreover peasant agriculture in developing countries is subject to kinds of uncertainty which are not so prevalent in the organised production structures of industrial countries. Different types of uncertainty are summarised under four main headings as follows:

Natural hazards

This refers to the unpredictable impact on output of weather, pests and diseases, and other natural calamities. Note that adverse weather may affect the outcome of planting decisions at any stage from cultivation through to final harvest, and is not restricted only to the catastrophic impact of long term drought. Note also that the capacity to combat pests and diseases may depend on the ability to purchase relevant cash inputs, and this can vary widely between different households within a peasant community. Natural hazards may also be described as yield or output uncertainty.

Market fluctuations

The lengthy lag between the decision to plant a crop or to start up a livestock enterprise and the achievement of an output means that market prices at point of sale are unknown at the time decisions are made. This is common to agriculture everywhere and is a major reason for state intervention in agricultural markets in many countries. The problem is more severe where information is lacking and markets are imperfect, features which are prevalent in developing country peasant agriculture. It is also acute for perennial tree crops (like cocoa or coffee) with a lag of several years between planting and first harvest. Market fluctuations may also be described as price uncertainty.

Social uncertainty

This refers in the main to insecurity caused by differences of control over resources within the peasant economy and the dependence for survival of some peasant households on others through such devices as crop sharing or usury. This occurs where there is unequal ownership of land in peasant communities, and it typically expresses itself in a high level of uncertainty concerning land access for some households but not for others. It is more prevalent in some parts of the world than others.

State actions and wars

The peasant household is not only uncertain about the weather, the market, and the local behaviour of the landlord or moneylender. Peasant economy as a whole is susceptible to the vagaries of decisions by agencies of the state which may chop and change greatly from one moment to the next, one coup to the next, one visit by the IMF to the next. Peasants are often caught up in guerilla wars, occasionally as protagonists, more often as bystanders subjected to marauding expeditions by either side in an armed struggle. The level of such uncertainty obviously varies unevenly across space and time, but rarely can it be overlooked entirely in the economic study of peasants. Also relevant here, and of increasing importance worldwide, is the insecurity of refugee peasant families who typically have very few social or legal rights in their countries of adoption.

Definitions of risk and uncertainty

The reader may have noted that the word 'risk' has largely been avoided so far. This is because the terms risk and uncertainty are not strictly interchangeable in the context of economic analysis; risk has a rather precise meaning which is distinct from the descriptive sense of uncertainty. Textbooks in agricultural economics typically make the following distinction between risk and uncertainty:

Risk is restricted to situations where probabilities can be attached to the occurrence of events which influence the outcome of a decision-making process; for example, if drought occurs on average in two years out of five, the probability of a drought occurring is 0.40. In this context it is worth reminding the reader that probability means the expected frequency of occurrence of an event or a set of events, and is always expressed out of one. Hence the probability of obtaining either 'heads' or 'tails' on the toss of a coin is 0.50 in each case, summing together to 1 since in this case only two events can occur.

Uncertainty refers to situations where it is not possible to attach probabilities to the occurrence of events. The likelihood of their occurrence is neither known by the decision maker nor by anyone else.

This distinction, while not entirely redundant for some purposes, has been superseded in the economic literature. Its underlying basis is a notion of risk as an *objective* matter, i.e. it assumes that provided enough information were available it should always be possible to attach objective probabilities to the incidence of events. Thus it might be argued that historical patterns of rainfall are known from weather station records, permitting the calculation of an objective probability for the incidence of drought.

Current practice in the economic analysis of risk is not based on this notion of objective risk. It is pointed out that in most decision situations what is relevant is not the spurious assumption of superhuman knowledge concerning the likelihood of uncertain events, but rather the decision maker's *personal* degree of belief about the occurrence of events. Thus in the example of patterns of rainfall what is important is not the known past average occurrence of drought (which may anyway be a most unreliable indicator of its future incidence) but rather the farmer's personal view about the likelihood of drought. It is this personal view which determines the course of action taken by the farmer to cope with the incidence of drought. This changes the analysis of risk and uncertainty from an objective to a *subjective* matter, with the following changes in the definitions of risk and uncertainty:

Risk still refers to probabilities, but these are now the *subjective* probabilities attached by farm decision makers to the likelihood of occurrence of different events. The analysis of risk involves not just these probabilities but also the way they enter economic decisions. Hence the term 'risk' is used to describe the entire mechanism by which farmers make decisions with respect to uncertain events.

Uncertainty does not refer to probabilities or their absence at all. It refers in a descriptive sense to the character of the economic environment confronting peasant farm households, an environment which will contain a wide variety of uncertain events to which farmers will attach various degrees of risk, according to their subjective beliefs of the occurrence of such events.

Analysis of risk behaviour

Within the above definition of risk there are two distinct approaches to subjective probability. One is to treat probability, and hence risk, as variance either side of the expected average outcome of uncertain events. Hence reference is often made in the context of farm production to risk as the 'income variance' which results from uncertain events. Variance is of course a concept of statistics which measures the average deviation of a set of figures from their mean. Thus risk in this approach is the probability of events occurring which result in incomes above or below the average expected income in a succession of crop seasons.

The second approach is to treat risk as the probability of disaster i.e. the probability that the variable outcome of uncertain events will take on a value less than some critical minimum or disaster level. This is closer to the dictionary definition of risk than the other approach, and also accords with the normal idea of risk from the perspective of insurance against loss or damage. Insurance companies almost always approach risk by assessing the probability that the event which is being insured against will occur. For the analysis of the impact of risk on the situation and behaviour of poor peasant families this definition has obvious merits. It focuses on avoidance of disaster as the possibly central goal of peasant families rather than the profit maximisation under certainty which was the hypothesis of the previous chapter.

The implications of risk for the neoclassical model of farm production can be examined with the aid of a graph as given in Figure 5.1. This is just another simple production function graph, with which the reader should now be familiar, showing three different response curves of output to a single variable input, units of purchased nitrogen fertilizer. The response curves are in value terms, they are total value product (TVP) curves, so that features of profit and loss are shown. Any reader who has difficulty in understanding the basic format of this graph is referred back to Chapter 2, especially Figure 2.2.

Figure 5.1 is designed to explore the 'income variance' approach to risk. However, it also serves to illustrate the principle of the 'disaster avoidance' approach. The risk situation which it describes is one of uncertainty about the weather in which there are only two events which can occur: the weather may be 'good' with the pattern of rainfall etc. being just what is required to obtain the best crop yields; or the weather may be 'bad' signifying lack of rainfall and poor crop yields. The graph contains alternative output response curves to describe the outcome of these two events as well as the farmer's subjective assessment of the balance between them according to the following definitions:

TVP_1 = *the total value product response to increasing the level of nitrogen input in a 'good' year;*

TVP_2 = *the total value product response to increasing the level of nitrogen input in a 'bad' year;*

$E(TVP)$ = *the expected total value product given the farmer's subjective views about the likelihood of occurrence of 'good' and 'bad' seasons.*

In this example the farmer expects 3 years out of every 5 years to be 'good', and 2 years out of 5 years to be 'bad'. Hence the probabilities and calculation of the expected total value product, $E(TVP)$, are as follows:

p_1 (probability of a 'good' season) = 0.60

p_2 (probability of a 'bad' season) = 0.40

$E(TVP) = 0.60(TVP_1) + 0.40(TVP_2)$

Figure 5.1. Production decisions under risk.
Notes: TVP_1 = total value product in 'good' years
TVP_2 = total value product in 'bad' years
$E(TVP)$ = expected total value product
$= p_1 \cdot TVP_1 + p_2 \cdot TVP_2$ where p_1 and p_2 are the probabilities of 'good' and 'bad' years occurring
$= 0.60 \cdot TVP_1 + 0.40 \cdot TVP_2$.

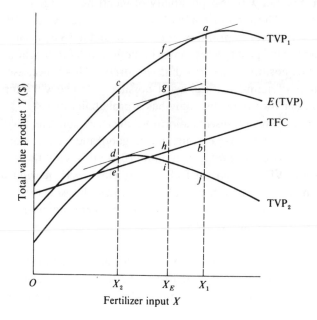

In risk analysis TVP_1 and TVP_2 are described as the *outcomes* of events or *states of nature*. In this example the shapes of the curves reflect the impact of 'good' and 'bad' weather conditions on the response of output to varying levels of nitrogen fertilizer. Lack of rainfall results in the very poor output response depicted by TVP_2. The subjective probabilities attached by the farmer to the occurrence of 'good' and 'bad' years are p_1 and p_2. These probabilities must sum to 1 since the example only recognises two states of nature, and one or other of these must occur. $E(TVP)$ is a weighted, or if you like balanced, average of the two outcomes, TVP_1 and TVP_2, where the weights are the probabilities, p_1 and p_2.

With the addition of a Total Cost (TFC) line representing the increase in total production costs as more nitrogen fertilizer is purchased, the impact of risk on the efficiency calculation of the farmer can be examined. Figure 5.1 displays three alternative operating positions, X_1, X_E, and X_2, each of which is allocatively rational depending on the farmer's subjective preferences with respect to risk:

(a) *Input use* X_1. This is consistent with allocative efficiency on TVP_1. It means that if TVP_1 occurs the largest possible profit, *ab*, is obtained. On the other hand if TVP_2 occurs, a substantial loss, *bj*, is incurred. A farmer choosing to operate at this position is described as *risk-taking*. This is because she prefers to take a chance at the largest possible profit, even though it only has a probability in her own mind of 0.60 of happening, than taking a safer position with less possibility of incurring a large loss.

(b) *Input use* X_2. This is consistent with allocative efficiency on TVP_2. It means that if TVP_1 occurs a profit, *ce*, is obtained; and if TVP_2 occurs the farm still makes a small profit, *de*, as shown in the graph. A farmer choosing to operate at this position is described as *risk-averse*. This is because she prefers the safety of acting as if the worst possible outcome will happen, even though in her own mind this only has a probability of 0.40.

(c) *Input use* X_E. This represents allocative efficiency consistent with a balanced assessment of the average outcome of 'good' and 'bad' seasons. It means that if TVP_1 occurs a profit, *fh*, is obtained but this is not the largest profit possible on TVP_1. Similarly if TVP_2 occurs a loss, *hi*, is incurred, and this is not the smallest loss possible on TVP_2. A farmer choosing to operate here is described as *risk-neutral*. The choice of operating position is consistent with the average outcome of 'good' and 'bad' years taken together.

We have described the alternatives in Figure 5.1 in terms of the 'income variance' approach to risk. TVP_1 and TVP_2 represent the variation either side of the average response curve of output to fertilizer, and their position on the graph is defined in terms of the level of subjective probability attached to each of them. Risk aversion occurs here as a matter of personal choice between several alternatives. The diagram can also be used, however, to illustrate the idea of risk aversion as a response to the probability of disaster.

Disaster avoidance is what Lipton (1968) means by the 'survival algorithm' of peasant farmers. Lipton's argument is that poor small-farmers are of necessity risk-averse. They cannot afford not to cover their household needs from one season to the next since if they fail to do so they will starve to death. In terms of Figure 5.1 the incurring of a loss may be considered a disaster; for a poor family existing at a bare subsistence level of production a loss means starvation. In order to avoid disaster the farmer must operate with input use in the vicinity of X_2, no other operating position will do.

The notion of disaster avoidance is sometimes referred to as the safety first principle. In formal terms it is rather more complicated than we have described it, though this does not mean that the picture given of it with respect to Figure 5.1 is inaccurate in so far as it goes. More precisely it means that decision making is constrained by the farmer's unwillingness to risk obtaining a net income below a given level, unless the probability of it falling below that level is very low indeed. Thus if the minimum level in the farmer's mind were \$500 she might be prepared to accept no more than a 0.10 chance of her net income falling below that amount in making farm decisions. Both the minimum income level and the maximum acceptable risk of it not occurring are referred to in the literature as safety first 'rules of thumb'. The reader interested in more detail of the safety first approach to risk analysis is referred to Roumasset (1976).

The consequences of risk aversion for optimum resource use, whether as a matter of choice or of survival, is illustrated in Figure 5.2. Economic rationality in the pure neoclassical sense demands that the farmer should operate at the point where:

$$E(\text{MVP}) = \text{MFC}$$

The expected marginal value product of fertilizer should equal the price of fertilizer. This is the profit maximising position, taking good years with bad over a run of seasons.

Instead the risk-averse farmer operates at the position where $\text{MVP}_2 = \text{MFC}$. This ensures that household consumption needs are covered in all seasons, even though profit is not being maximised except in 'bad' seasons. The consequence is that the expected marginal value product

(MVP_E), shown at point A on the $E(MVP)$ curve, is well above marginal cost: the optimum level of resource use is not being followed and profit is not being maximised. The proposition that risk aversion causes a situation in which, on average, $MVP > MFC$ is, in principle, a testable one which forms the basis of some of the empirical research into the impact of risk on farm household behaviour.

Expected utility and decision theory

The treatment of risk as being 'based on the decision maker's *personal* strengths of belief about the occurrence of uncertain events and his *personal* evaluation of potential consequences' (Anderson *et al.*, 1977: ix) is firmly rooted in the economic concept of personal utility maximisation. The meaning of 'utility maximisation' is that individuals are considered to make decisions consistent with their personal objectives, and therefore to maximise their personal 'welfare' or 'happiness'. This idea is basic to the method of neoclassical economic theory, and it is given fuller treatment in later chapters of this book, especially in the context of the consumption goals of farm households (Chapters 6 and 7). Here it is sufficient to note that confronted by a choice between alternative actions, the utility maximising individual will select that alternative which yields the highest personal happiness.

In the case of the subjective assessment of uncertain events the individual maximises *expected* utility, referred to as $E(U)$, given her beliefs about events and outcomes. Expected utility theory also gives rise to a formal economic approach to risk analysis called decision theory.

Figure 5.2. Marginal value product under risk.

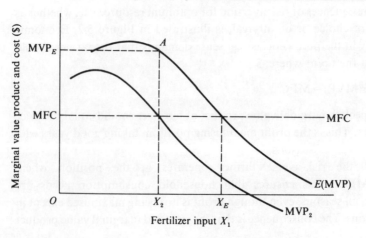

In keeping with standard utility theory, expected utility requires that the individual holds consistent preferences between various alternatives which confront her. At the core of the theory is a concept called certainty equivalence (CE). This is what enables less and more risky alternatives to be compared and placed in a scale of personal preferences by the decision maker. It is introduced here with a simple example before setting out expected utility more fully.

Say you face a choice between (a) being given a definite sum of money, $500, or (b) taking a chance (say, on the toss of a coin) to obtain the much larger sum of $1200 or sustain a loss of $100. The alternative you choose says a lot about your subjective attitude to risk. Most people would accept the $500 and, in doing so, would reveal themselves to be risk-averse. This is because the objective average of the chance, called the Expected Money Value (EMV) is, at $550, larger than the certain amount, $500. The EMV is the weighted average of the two outcomes of the chance: it is $(0.50 \cdot \$1200) + (0.50 \cdot (-\$100)) = \$550$. If you waver between the two choices i.e. you would be happy to take either, then the certain amount, $500, is termed your *certainty equivalent*: it is the amount that would make you just as happy, or indifferent, to taking the chance on two widely differing outcomes.

These ideas can now be placed rather more formally in the context of utility maximisation, and this is done with reference to Figure 5.3. This graph describes the relationship of utility (vertical axis) to income (horizontal axis). It thus displays the simplest possible utility function of the form $U = f(I)$, or, put another way, happiness (U) is a function of money income (I).

The straight line DC on the graph represents a simple linear relationship between utility and income, and it has a positive slope (more money yields greater happiness). I_1 and I_2 are two different risky income levels which have different probabilities of occurrence attached to them, p_1 and p_2, which sum to 1. In order to make this graph compatible with the Figures 5.1 and 5.2, we make $p_1 = 0.60$ and $p_2 = 0.40$. We then have the following definitions and positions with respect to risk:

Expected utility: $E(U) = p_1 \cdot U(I_1) + p_2 \cdot U(I_2)$

In other words expected utility is the sum of the utilities derived from incomes I_1 and I_2, weighted by the respective probabilities of their occurrence.

Expected money value: $\text{EMV} = p_1 \cdot I_1 + p_2 \cdot I_2$

This is the income which could be expected on average, given a run of chances at I_1 and I_2. It is also sometimes called the actuarial value of I_1 and I_2 taken jointly.

Risk-averse: Say there is a certain income $I_A <$ EMV which yields the same utility (happiness) as EMV to a person i.e. the person is *indifferent* between I_A and risky income EMV. This implies that she is prepared to forego an amount of income equivalent to EMV minus I_A in order to achieve certainty, and is thus said to be *risk-averse*. It also means that her utility function over the relevant range has the shape given by DAC, displaying diminishing marginal utility of income within this range. Another way this is sometimes expressed is that the income foregone, EMV $- I_A$, is the *insurance* premium the person is prepared to pay in order to achieve certainty.

Risk neutral: Where the person is indifferent between a certain income I_E and the expected money value of two risky incomes, EMV, i.e. when $U(I_E) = E(U)$, or the utility of a certain income level I_E is the same as the expected utility of the two uncertain incomes, then she is said to be *risk-neutral*. This means that her utility function is the straight line DC.

Risk taking: Some people might have a preference for taking the chance on obtaining the higher income, I_1, even though it is one of two risky outcomes, the second of which might make them worse off than before. Clearly if asked what level of certain income would make her as happy as the gamble, this person is not going to reply with either I_A or I_E, neither of which

Figure 5.3. Utility theory of choices involving risk.

Note: $\text{EMV} = p_1 I_1 + p_2 I_2$
$E(U) = p_1 U(I_1) + p_2 U(I_2)$
$p_1 = 0.60$
$p_2 = 0.40$.

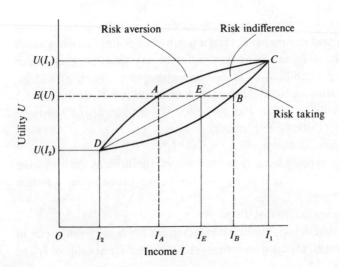

are high enough to induce her not to take the gamble. In fact the amount this person would accept in order to be indifferent between the certain sum and the chance is going to be higher, say at I_B, than the EMV of the chance. Such a person is described as a *risk-taker*. Another, less flattering, but accurate description is that the person is a *gambler*, and the amount I_B – EMV is the premium she is prepared to pay for the opportunity to gamble. The utility curve of such a person would be as given by *ADC*, displaying rising marginal utility of income over the relevant range.

The concepts contained in the expected utility approach to risk are obviously relevant to the decision-making behaviour we considered in Figures 5.1 and 5.2. They also form the basis of a more structured approach to risk analysis in the farm enterprise called decision theory. Since the basic components of decision theory tend to consolidate the material we have covered so far in this chapter, it is useful to set them out in brief here. This is a simplified version of the treatment of this topic given in Dillon & Hardaker (1980).

Obtaining a grasp of decision theory is facilitated by a device called a *decision tree*, and also by the use of an example. A simple decision tree is set out in Figure 5.4, and it contains example figures which are compatible with the earlier analysis of a production decision in Figure 5.1. The components of the decision theory approach are as follows:

Acts: This is the set of alternative actions between which a choice must be made. Acts a_1, ..., a_j should be mutually exclusive and exhaustive of alternatives available. Continuous variables (e.g. fertilizer rates) are represented by a finite set of discrete acts. In Figure 5.4 there are two acts: (a) apply fertilizer in full up to recommended agronomic practices – act a_1, and (b) apply a token amount of fertilizer – act a_2. These are the discrete equivalents of courses of action X_1 and X_2 in Figure 5.1. The two acts branch off from a single *decision node* (a square symbol) in the decision tree.

States: These are the uncertain *events* or *states of nature* which may occur and influence the outcome of whatever decision is taken. States S_1, ..., S_i are mutually exclusive and exhaustive of the range of events which can occur. Some state variables are continuous (e.g. rainfall) but in decision theory these are given a discrete representation (e.g. good, average, poor). In Figure 5.4 there are two states (a) 'good' weather, and (b) 'bad' weather. These states may occur with either act, and hence they are duplicated from the *chance node* (a circle symbol) of each act. They are the same as the states underlying TVP_1 and TVP_2 in Figure 5.1.

Probabilities: These are the degrees of belief held by the decision-maker about the likelihood of each state occurring. They are subjective probabilities, $p_1, \ldots, p_i$. The probability of the ith state must be between 0 and 1. The probability of at least one of the states occurring must be 1, i.e. the sum of the probabilities for all states must equal 1. In Figure 5.4 the probabilities p_1 and p_2 are 0.60 and 0.40 corresponding to states S_1 and S_2 respectively; and these of course are the same as in Figure 5.1.

Outcomes: The decision between two or more choices or acts leads to specific outcomes of payoffs, the level of which depend on which of the uncertain states occurs. The outcome associated with the jth act and the ith state is C_{ij}. For practical purposes outcomes should be specified as *net* money payoffs, otherwise they cannot be compared. In Figure 5.4 these payoffs are shown down the right-hand side of the decision tree: act a_1 (plenty fertilizer) has the two possible payoffs of a profit of $2000 in the event of good weather or a loss of $375 in the event of bad weather; act a_2 (token fertilizer) has the two possible payoffs of $1300 in the event of good weather or a profit of $300 in the event of bad weather. These payoffs correspond, respectively, to the gaps ab, bj, ce, and de in Figure 5.1.

Choice criterion: The criterion for choosing between acts is the maximisation of expected utility. As we have seen this is the sum of the utilities associated with each payoff weighted by the subjective probability of their occurrence. This criterion means choosing the act which best meets personal preferences about payoffs, while at the same time taking account of personal perceptions of the risks involved.

Solution procedure: The solution method for a decision tree problem begins from the right-hand side and works backward towards the decision

Figure 5.4. Decision tree analysis of a risky decision problem.

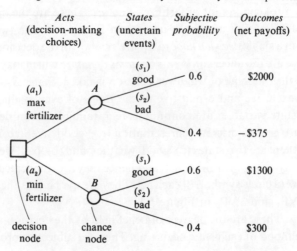

node(s). It consists of:

(a) calculating the EMV of the outcomes of each chance node: in this example the EMVs are \$1050 for chance node A and \$900 for chance node B;

(b) eliciting from the farmer the *certainty equivalent* net income which corresponds to the risky outcomes of each act: in this example the farmer has a risk-averse CE for a_1 of \$850 ($<$\$1050), and a risk-neutral CE for a_2 of \$900 ($=$\$900);

(c) rejecting the alternative which has the lower certainty equivalent: in this example act a_1 is eliminated and the farmer would maximise utility by choosing act a_2.

This exercise shows how the outcome of risk-averse decision making is different to profit maximisation. The profit maximising alternative in the above problem is act a_1 (EMV = \$1050), but risk aversion means that act a_2 is chosen. Act a_2 maximises the utility of the farmer with respect to uncertainty, it does not maximise profit.

Research into peasant risk behaviour

The view that uncertainty has a serious impact on the economic behaviour of the peasant household provides much scope for empirical research into the risk question. This research is designed to discover whether and to what degree peasants are risk averse, the impact of risk on farm efficiency and on agricultural growth, the major sources of risk, and ways that the adverse effects of risk might be ameliorated. Within an area of enquiry which covers almost all aspects of the livelihood of peasant families, a few main propositions have received most of the attention of research. These are:

(a) Peasants are risk-averse. This results in inefficient levels of resource use at the farm level (MVPs $>$ factor prices). Moreover the extent of this departure from efficiency increases the more risky (i.e. the higher variance) is the output for a given resource. For example, if a given resource, labour, can produce crops A, B, C in descending order of output variability, then $MVP_A > MVP_B > MVP_C$, rather than the equimarginal returns which efficiency demands (see Chapter 2).

(b) Peasant risk aversion results in cropping patterns designed to increase family security rather than maximise output or profits. This may take the form of allocating a higher proportion of land to subsistence food crops than is warranted by relative net returns between food and cash crops. Or it may consist of cultivation practices, like mixed cropping (see below), which achieve security at the expense of lower returns than could be achieved by cropping in pure stands.

(c) Peasant risk aversion inhibits the diffusion and adoption of innovations which could improve the output and incomes of peasant farm families. This point closely ties the concept of risk to lack of information or its inadequacy. Peasant scepticism about innovation is thought to be largely related to imperfect knowledge of innovations and the agronomic practices appropriate to them. Also important are other constraints to adoption such as the high cost or lack of credit.

(d) Risk aversion declines as wealth or income rises. Higher income or wealthier farm households are better able to withstand the losses which might result from taking risky decisions. It follows that higher income farmers might be expected to be more efficient, more prepared to specialise in cash crops, and more willing to innovate. They are also likely to be better informed and have greater access to credit. Since these factors are cumulative an implication is that the more uncertain the decision-making environment, the more advantaged are better off farmers compared to poor ones, and the greater the likelihood of emerging and deepening inequalities between households.

These propositions have been investigated using various techniques. These include the production function approach (see Chapter 4) used to investigate efficiency conditions, and programming methods based on the income variance or disaster avoidance concepts of subjective risk. Most research, even though based in the subjective theory of risk, has used objective indicators of risk (e.g. variation in prices, variation in yields across seasons, variation in incomes obtained from different crops) in order to derive conclusions about peasant risk behaviour. A few studies have confronted the subjective theory head on by asking sample farmers questions designed to discover their certainty equivalence of uncertain outcomes (see Dillon & Scandizzo, 1978; Binswanger, 1980; Binswanger & Sillers, 1983).

The results of various empirical studies seem to support the above propositions at least with respect to the elements of them which are susceptible to measurement. Peasants are risk-averse (Schluter & Mount, 1976; Dillon & Scandizzo, 1978; Binswanger & Sillers, 1983). This results in sub-optimal resource allocation (Wolgin, 1975; Bliss & Stern, 1982: 273). Many communities and households follow cultivation practices, and choices of crops, designed to increase security rather than income (Wolgin, 1975; Norman, 1974, 1977). Risk creates barriers to innovation related to lack of information (de Janvry, 1972; Hiebert, 1974) and to imperfections in credit and land markets (Lipton, 1979). Risk aversion declines as income rises (Hamal & Anderson, 1982).

Of course not all studies concur in these conclusions. Like the efficiency hypothesis, the risk-averse hypothesis suffers in part from the attempt to generalise the non-generalisable: some peasants are more risk-averse than others; some peasant communities display more conservatism towards change than others, both within and between countries; some poor farmers are prepared to take an enormous gamble by which they either prosper or end up as penniless landless labourers. Using the disaster avoidance (safety first) approach Roumasset (1976) found not very strong evidence for risk aversion and some evidence of preparedness to gamble amongst a sample of peasant households in the Philippines. Binswanger & Sillers (1983) using the certainty equivalent approach conclude that level of wealth does not affect degree of risk aversion.

An important problem in the empirical study of risk is wrongly attributing to risk aversion all the departures from economic efficiency which are observed. This applies especially to those studies which use variations in objective data, like prices or rainfall patterns, as the basis for drawing conclusions about the subjective behaviour of farmers. The certainty equivalence approach, used by Binswanger (1980) and others, is designed to overcome this difficulty. However, these studies experience another problem: by equating farm decision making with the result of gambling experiments conducted with farmers (Binswanger & Sillers, 1983) they are in danger of drawing false inferences. It seems commonsense that many farmers would treat gambling experiments as a game, not related to the business of survival. People the world over will take a bet if one is offered to them (especially if they cannot lose, as was the case in the studies cited) but this may show little or nothing about risk attitudes to their livelihood.

The problem of incorrect attribution applies with particular force to cultivation practices, like mixed cropping, which are frequently cited as risk averse production strategies. Mixed cropping is widely prevalent in the tropics, especially in Africa, and was in the past considered a deplorable farming practice by agricultural officers and extension workers. It refers to the intermingling of a variety of crops, commonly between two and five, but sometimes up to eight or nine, in a single field.

Norman (1974) and others have demonstrated numerous advantages of mixed cropping, of which security through diversification is only one. Some of these are:

 (a) superior use of light, water, and nutrients due to the differing spacing, height, and nutrient requirement of the different crops;

 (b) beneficial effects of the growth of some plants on other plants (e.g. nitrogen fixing pulses on other plants);

(c) reduction of susceptibility to pests and diseases because spread between plants is inhibited;

(d) protection of the soil from leeching or drying out due to the overlapping periods during which leaf cover and root systems are in place;

(e) evening out the labour requirements of weeding and harvesting over the year;

(f) ensuring variety and nutritional balance in food supply;

(g) higher returns in general, or to the limiting factor of production;

(h) security of food supply, or of income, in the face of adverse weather or market prices.

Note that only the last of these corresponds directly to risk avoidance as a production objective. Most of the rest relate to production efficiency, and one of them (reason (f)) refers to utility maximisation in consumption. Norman (1977: 88) finds that 'growing of crop mixtures provides an outstanding example of a practice meeting both the profit-maximisation and security criteria'. Thus risk avoidance strategies are not of necessity in conflict with efficiency criteria, nor can all economic behaviour not consistent with profit maximisation be attributed to risk.

Policy aspects

The theory of the risk-averse peasant, like that of the profit maximising peasant, is associated with government interventions designed to remedy the adverse impact of risk aversion on agricultural productivity and growth. As in the profit maximising case these policies are premised on the implicit assumption that the aim is to bring the peasant economy closer to the perfect competition model. There is a somewhat contradictory aspect of this, since a role for government is assumed which is not necessarily only of a minor or corrective nature. Alternative policy implications of risk aversion may be grouped broadly in line with the categories of hazard they are designed to overcome as follows:

Natural hazards

Irrigation Perhaps the most obvious policy response to natural uncertainty is that of *irrigation* as an answer to rainfall variability. Note that irrigation can serve both (a) to alleviate the risk of drought between one season and the next, and (b) to smooth out within season fluctuations of water supply to plants. In addition it can permit higher productivity cultivation practices, such as multiple cropping (sequential cropping in the same year), with a direct impact on the volume of output and farm incomes.

In this sense irrigation is not just a risk strategy, it also has a major impact on output via its complementarity with multiple cropping, increased fertilizer use, and improved seeds. Irrigation does not of necessity require state intervention, indeed a great proportion of tubewell irrigation takes the form of private investment by individual farm households. On the other hand large scale irrigation schemes involving dams, canals, flood control etc. are infrastructural investments of a size which are most unlikely to attract private investment. Moreover governments may wish to pursue active irrigation policies for reasons of coverage and equity which are unlikely to occur on a private basis.

Crop insurance The most theoretically consistent and comprehensive proposal for alleviating the adverse impact of natural hazards is *crop insurance*. Insurance is logical within a neoclassical framework (see earlier) as a method of achieving income security in the face of potential disasters. People pay risk premiums, representing the average social degree of risk aversion, and are thence protected against the incidence of uncertain events. However, insurance for crop production faces almost insuperable practical problems. Average risk aversion needs to be demonstrably high for the benefit of crop insurance to outweigh the formidable administrative costs of operating an insurance scheme (Roumasset, 1976). A major difficulty is posed by the fact that crop disasters tend to be catastrophic over a wide area, implying that a workable insurance scheme would require the capacity to meet enormous fluctuations in claims from one year to the next. Crop insurance has not got very far as a risk policy in agrarian societies, but this is not through want of serious consideration (see Hazell *et al.*, 1986).

Resistant varieties. More practical and relevant, because of the much lower cost in relation to potential benefits, is *plant breeding* or *selection* designed for resistance to pests, diseases and drought, and stability of yields. There are of course trade-offs here. Stable yields may not be consistent with the highest attainable yields. Research station breeding of disease resistant strains may not be that much more successful than traditional varieties, or agronomic practices, which achieved the same ends in the past. Moreover there may be sacrifices in palatability, storability etc. which are not foreseen when new varieties are released.

Market risks
Price stabilisation. The most popular policy response to market price instability is *price stabilisation*. Indeed this is the main economic basis underlying agricultural price policies worldwide, including in all the

developed industrial countries. Price stabilisation may take many forms, implying varying degrees of state intervention, from minimum floor prices for key strategic staples through to fixed producer prices across a wide range of crops. Where crop yields remain highly variable, price stabilisation may serve to exacerbate rather than reduce income variance. This is because, under the market, prices rise in low yield years (lack of supply) and fall in high yield years (oversupply), resulting in some smoothing out of annual incomes. With stable prices this does not occur and income variation follows yield variation.

Information. Where risk aversion is attributed to inadequate information (about prices, about input use, about new seeds etc.) then *information provision* is considered a useful component of risk policy. Diffusion of information to peasants can take many forms: extension work, training and visit programmes, the radio, bulk leaflets, farm education in schools, and so on. The difficulty with these lies not so much in their basic provision as in ensuring the quality, timeliness, and relevance of the information with respect to location, latest alternatives etc. This is more costly than might appear at first sight.

Credit subsidies. The provision of *subsidised credit* is often cited as a risk related policy, even though it has wider connotations. Where risk aversion is related to disaster avoidance, and this prevents the poor peasant from adopting higher productivity technologies (new seeds) and the variable inputs to go with them (fertilizer) then easier credit is seen as a means of overcoming this barrier. Subsidised credit schemes have a long history of problems (default on repayment etc.) but wide scope still exists for general availability of finance for poor farm families on terms which are better than those in highly imperfect rural money markets (Lipton, 1979).

Social and state hazards

These are large questions to which there are no single 'policy' solutions, but rather they are matters of politics. The relationships between landlords and peasants in agrarian communities characterised by great inequalities of access to resources is a complex one to which we return in Chapter 8. That these relationships increase the uncertainty of poor peasants there is no doubt, but their alteration (e.g. through land reform) is not a purely economic matter even if sound economic arguments are put forward for the change. As for hazards which originate from the state itself, the important point is to recognise that these can occur and to relate them to the underlying social position of peasants. They often point to the need for greater political participation by peasants themselves in decisions which affect their welfare and their future.

Wider perspectives

The theory of the risk-averse peasant, like that of the profit maximising peasant in Chapter 4, assumes that the peasant farm household is an individual optimising economic unit. It differs from the profit maximising theory only in so far as the household is thought to modify the efficiency goal to take into account the risk it attaches to uncertain outcomes. Aspects of risk and uncertainty relatively neglected in this theory relate to the social relations of peasant production.

In Chapter 1 it was suggested that one of the features which makes a particular kind of farm household a peasant household rather than a 'family farm enterprise' is the continued prevalence of non-market forms of economic interaction between households within peasant communities. Some of these non-market transactions are measures for coping with disaster, and it has been argued that they constitute part of a 'moral economy' of peasant society which may transcend individual self interest (Scott, 1976).

The policies described above for alleviating the adverse impact of risk do not take account of, nor attempt to build on, existing social mechanisms for coping with risk. Perhaps this is not surprising. The spread of market relations inevitably exposes peasants to new risks because it erodes non-market social interactions, reduces the subsistence basis of survival, and increases competitive pressures. At the same time these processes increase the efficiency of peasant production due to the discipline of the market. Preservation of non-market measures for coping with risk is incompatible with improving the working of markets for economic efficiency.

The mainstream literature on the economics of risk in peasant agriculture virtually ignores the impact of uncertainty on intra-household matters. Given the social subordination of women in most peasant societies, and their key role in the subsistence and reproduction of the household, it seems plausible that they might take a different view of risky actions than men. In many, but not all, circumstances women have good reasons to defend the subsistence basis of family survival while men often stand to make personal gains from activities, however risky, which generate cash over which they have spending power. This is a case where the interests of the two sexes may deviate, and it becomes relevant for economic analysis as soon as women's concerns are placed more firmly on the agenda (see Chapter 9).

Summary

1 This chapter examines the impact of uncertainty on the economic decision-making of the peasant household. Four main categories of uncertainty confronting peasant farmers are identified, and these are:
   (a) natural hazards or yield uncertainty;
   (b) market fluctuations or price uncertainty;
   (c) uncertainty deriving from social relations in the rural economy;
   (d) uncertainty of state actions and wars.

2 Uncertainty is distinguished from risk, taking the contemporary economic view of risk as the *subjective* probability attached by the individual to uncertain events. Uncertainty is a descriptive term concerning the environment surrounding farm decisions. Risk refers to the probability of occurrence of alternative outcomes in decision making.

3 The terms risk aversion, risk neutrality, and risk taking are defined by reference to the subjective preferences between certain and uncertain alternatives. The chapter sets out the basis in utility maximisation of these attitudes to risk, and it shows how this is applied in farm decision analysis.

4 It is shown how risk aversion results in different farm decisions from profit maximisation. Risk-averse behaviour results in the sub-optimal use of variable inputs, such that the expected marginal value products (MVPs) of variable inputs are above the input prices. Too little variable inputs are used so that profit and output are below their profit maximising levels.

5 The results of research into the risk behaviour of peasant households is summarised, and the policy implications of risk aversion are set out. Policies to alleviate yield uncertainty include irrigation, plant breeding for yield stability, and crop insurance. Policies to cope with price uncertainty include output price stabilisation, improved market information, and improved credit delivery to farmers.

6 The chapter concludes with wider issues surrounding the economic analysis of risk. The individual household focus of much writing on risk tends to neglect non-market social measures for coping with adversity which may exist in peasant societies. These non-market mechanisms of social security are typically ignored by economists

and are in any case eroded by the spread of market relations in the peasant economy. Finally, it is noted that most risk analysis ignores differences in the intra-household impact of risk between women and men.

Further reading

The best introduction to the impact of uncertainty on peasant decision making remains Lipton (1968). A useful collection of papers, though many of them rather difficult for the non-specialist, is Roumasset *et al.* (1979). Papers in this collection by Roumasset (Ch. 1), Lipton (Ch. 18), and Binswanger (Ch. 20) are recommended. The expected utility approach to risk analysis is set out in full in Anderson *et al.* (1977), though a rather easier and much shorter version is given in Dillon & Hardaker (1980). The safety first approach is examined in Roumasset (1976) where it is also subject to empirical test. The investigation of risk aversion via the subjective approach of certainty equivalence is examined in Dillon & Scandizzo (1978) and Binswanger & Sillers (1983). For peasants' own security strategies see especially Norman (1974) and Walker & Jodha (1986). The latter is part of a collection which looks at risk issues from an insurance perspective (Hazell *et al.*, 1986).

Reading list
Anderson, J.R., Dillon J.L. & Hardaker J.B. (1977). *Agricultural Decision Analysis*. Ames: Iowa State University Press.

Binswanger, H.P. & Sillers, D.A. (1983). Risk aversion and credit constraints in farmers' decision-making: a reinterpretation. *Journal of Development Studies*, Vol. 20, No. 1.

Dillon, J.L. & Scandizzo P.L. (1978). Risk attitudes of subsistence farmers in northeast Brazil: a sampling approach, *American Journal of Agricultural Economics*, Vol. 60.

Dillon, J.L., & Hardaker, J.B. (1980). *Farm Management Research for Small Farmer Development*, FAO Agricultural Services Bulletin 41, Rome: FAO.

Hazell, P., Pomareda C. & Valdes A. (eds.) (1986). *Crop Insurance for Agricultural Development*. Baltimore: Johns Hopkins.

Lipton, M. (1968). The theory of the optimising peasant. *Journal of Development Studies*, Vol. 4, No. 3, pp. 327–51.

Norman, D.W. (1974). Rationalising mixed cropping under indigenous conditions: the example of northern Nigeria. *Journal of Development Studies*, Vol. 11.

Roumasset, J.A. (1976). *Rice and Risk: Decision-Making Among Low-Income Farmers*. Amsterdam: North Holland.

Roumasset, J.A. *et al.* (1979). (eds.) *Risk, Uncertainty and Agricultural Development*. New York: Agricultural Development Council.

Walker, T.S. & Jodha N.S. (1986). How small farm households adapt to risk. In Hazell P., Pomareda C. and Valdes A. (eds.) *Crop Insurance for Agricultural Development*. pp. 17–34, Baltimore: Johns Hopkins.

6

The drudgery-averse peasant

Peasants as consumers and producers

The theories of peasant household behaviour examined so far, profit maximisation and risk aversion, take no account of the consumption side of peasant decision making. This is a rather large gap. It brings us back to the observation by Wolf (1966: 2) that the peasant 'runs a household, not a business concern'. In fact the dual character of the peasant household as both family and enterprise, consumer and producer, was stated earlier to be a most important facet of the definition of the term peasant. Moreover there exists the proposition, which must be properly examined, that the interaction of consumption and production within the household causes a unique form of decision making which sets peasants apart from any other kind of production unit under capitalism.

A central consideration in the construction of more complete theories of household behaviour is to achieve a more accurate representation of the multiple goals of the household, the interaction between goals, and the impact these have on the response of the household to changing circumstances. In the profit maximising theory there is only a single goal, and economic responses are predictable provided that the assumptions of the theory are roughly met. In the risk-averse theory this single goal is modified, but not abandoned, and again responses are predictable subject to the impact on them of subjective responses to uncertainty. In the full household theory the pursuit of various different goals in consumption may result in variable or unpredictable responses to different kinds of economic or social change. Thus a major aim of such theory is to clarify as far as possible the links between goals, actions, and the outcomes of such actions.

In this and the next chapter we set out two main ways in which the consumption goals of households are incorporated into microeconomic models of peasant decision making. The first of these, dealt with in this chapter, is the theory of peasant economy put forward by Chayanov in the 1920s which emphasises the influence of family size and structure on household economic behaviour, via the subjective valuation of labour within the household. This theory has implications for the concept of peasant household production which go beyond the mere mechanics of its working as a microeconomic model, and these are considered towards the end of the chapter. The second, dealt with in Chapter 7, is farm household theories of more recent origin which draw on the Chayanov formulation but alter its assumptions, expand its scope, and extend its predictive powers in different directions.

Revision of indifference curve analysis

It is helpful for the graphical exposition of the farm household models described in this and the next chapter if the reader is reminded of the way personal utility maximisation is represented in neoclassical economics using indifference curves. In particular we revise here the simple example of consumer choice between leisure (in hours free from work) and income (in money) where both these contribute to the happiness of the individual. The graphical procedure for describing the combination of leisure and income which maximises individual utility is similar to that used in Chapter 2 to describe cost minimisation between two inputs in production. Consumer theory uses the concept of *an indifference curve* to describe a given level of utility (personal happiness) for different combinations of leisure and income (both treated as items of consumption).

The basic approach is shown in Figure 6.1(*a*). A set of indifference curves, I_1, I_2, I_3, describe successively higher *given* levels of personal happiness which can be met by alternative combinations of leisure and income. These indifference curves are convex to the origin because the consumer is assumed to experience diminishing marginal utility as consumption of either leisure or income rises. Thus if a given level of utility like I_2 is considered, a relatively large amount of leisure (H) would be sacrificed for a small gain of income (Y) towards the top-left of the curve (low marginal utility of leisure, high marginal utility of income), and only a small amount of leisure would be sacrificed for a large gain of income towards the bottom-right of the curve (high marginal utility of leisure, low marginal utility of income).

The slope at any point on one of these indifference curves represents the marginal rate of substitution (MRS) of income for leisure. This slope is negative: the indifference curve slopes downwards from left to right, and the slope can be expressed either as the amount of leisure which would be foregone for a small increase in income $(-dH/dY)$ or as the inverse ratio of the marginal utilities of income and leisure (MU_Y/MU_H). Thus in simple notation:

$$MRS_{Y,H} = -\frac{dH}{dY} = \frac{MU_Y}{MU_H}$$

Given a line, AB, which describes the rate at which leisure hours can be

Figure 6.1. (a) Indifference curve analysis of the choice between leisure and income. (b) Impact of an increase in the wage rate.

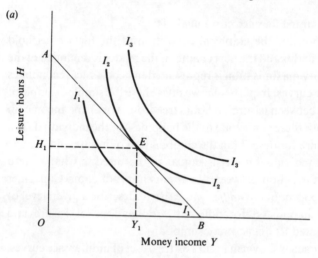

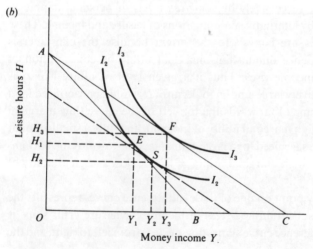

converted into money income at a given wage rate per hour (this is the *income constraint* and is the equivalent of the *budget line* when the choice is between two goods), then the consumer maximises utility at the point of tangency of this line with the highest attainable indifference curve. In Figure 6.1(*a*) this is given by point E, implying a leisure level of H_1 hours and a total income level of Y_1 units of money.

The slope of the income constraint is given by the inverse of the wage rate, $1/w$. As seen on the graph it is given by OA (vertical distance) over OB (horizontal distance). But OB is simply OA multiplied by the wage if all available hours are used for work instead of for leisure, hence the slope is $OA/(OA \cdot w) = 1/w$. The utility maximising position occurs where the slope of the indifference curve and the slope of the budget line are equal i.e. where:

$$\frac{MU_Y}{MU_H} = -\frac{dH}{dY} = \frac{1}{w}$$

Figure 6.1(*b*) considers the effect on utility maximisation of an increase in the level of the wage. A wage increase has the effect of increasing the amount of income which can be obtained for each hour worked, hence it changes the slope of the income line from AB to AC, implying a maximum income of C if all available hours were devoted to work rather than leisure. This places the consumer in tangency with a higher indifference curve, I_3, at point F.

An important feature of this analysis is that it is not possible to infer on *a priori* grounds the precise position of the new optimum point F. As drawn in Figure 6.1(*b*) it happens to display both higher leisure at H_3 and higher income at Y_3, implying that the individual has chosen to work fewer hours while still achieving an increase in money income because of the wage rise. This outcome would give a backward sloping supply curve for this person's labour: an increase in the wage rate results in lower hours of work.

Following standard textbook practice, the movement from E to F can be divided between a 'substitution effect' and an 'income effect' of the wage increase. The 'substitution effect', which is shown at S on the old indifference curve, tangent to a line parallel to the new wage line AC, unambiguously reduces hours of leisure and increases income as a response to the increase in wage rate. However, the 'income effect' of the wage increase (the movement back onto AC) works in the opposite direction. An increase in income raises the demand for leisure, unless leisure is an inferior good (an 'inferior' good is one for which consumption falls as income rises, like potatoes). Thus the 'income effect' normally tends to counterbalance the 'substitution effect', and depending on how far it does so the indifference curve, I_3, could be located so that the new level of leisure at H_3

were either lower or higher than the old level at H_1.

If the quantity of leisure taken is higher as in our diagram, i.e. if the 'income effect' outweighs the 'substitution effect', then an increase in wage rate results in a lower number of hours worked than before the change and we have a backward sloping supply curve of labour.

The Chayanov farm household model

The economic model of household decision making considered in this section is consistent in most respects with the analysis of peasant household behaviour first advanced in the 1920s by the Russian agricultural economist, A.V. Chayanov (Thorner *et al.*, 1966). Its form of presentation follows versions of a Chayanov-type microeconomic analysis put forward in the 1960s by Mellor (1963), Sen (1966), and Nakajima (1970), but in its discussion here we concentrate mainly on the emphases and insights found in Chayanov's own work.

The Chayanov peasant model is a theory of household *utility maximisation*. It focuses especially on the subjective decision made by the household with respect to the amount of family labour to commit to farm production in order to satisfy its consumption needs. This subjective decision is seen as involving a trade off between the drudgery or irksomeness of farm work (disutility of work) and the income required to meet the consumption needs of the household (utility of income). Another way this may be stated is that the household has two opposing objectives: an income objective which requires work on the farm, and a work-avoidance objective which conflicts with income generation. Hence the characterisation of the theory in this chapter as the theory of the 'drudgery-averse' peasant.

The main factor influencing this trade off is the size of the peasant household, and its composition between working and non-working members; in other words, the *demographic structure* of the household. This factor is summarised by the ratio of consumers to workers in the household, called the c/w ratio. For example if a household consisted of just two adults with no children, its c/w ratio would be 1.00; but two adults with an elderly parent and four children (say, two of which each make half an adult's work contribution) would have a c/w ratio of $7/3 = 2.33$.

We shall see shortly that the predictive power of the Chayanov model rests almost entirely on its demographic aspects, making it, in effect, a demographic model of household decision making. In the meantime, however, its key assumptions as a microeconomic theory of peasant household behaviour can be listed as follows:

(a) there is no market for labour, i.e. no hiring of labour by the household nor wage work by family members outside the household;

(b) farm output may be retained for home consumption or sold in the market, and is valued at the market price;

(c) all peasant households have flexible access to land for cultivation;

(d) each peasant community has a social norm for the minimum acceptable income per person, and thus, by implication, the household as a unit has a minimum acceptable consumption level.

The central elements of Chayanov's theory of peasant household behaviour are depicted graphically in Figure 6.2. The gross output of the peasant farm, which equals gross farm income, is measured on the vertical axis. Since there exists a market for output this income is expressed in money terms. The horizontal axis measures the total labour time available to the household, which is determined by its number of workers. This total time can be allocated either to farm work or to other activities ('leisure'). Thus the number of days committed to farm work is measured from left to right, OL, and the number of days engaged in other pursuits is measured in the opposite direction from work, from right to left, LO.

Figure 6.2. Chayanov model of the farm household.

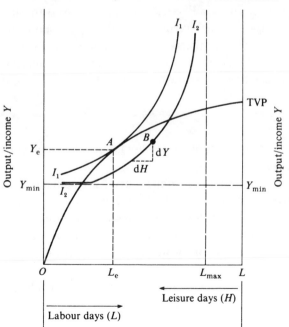

The model contains both production and consumption aspects of household decision making. The production aspect is handled by a production function describing the response of output to varying levels of labour input. This production function (TVP curve) displays the property of diminishing marginal returns to labour. Moreover since output and income are synonymous the TVP curve can be described as a *family income curve*. In production function notation:

$$Y = P_Y \cdot f(L)$$

Or, in words, the total income of the family is a function only of the market price of output and the labour input.

As set out in the graph this production function does not capture the flexible land access which is an important part of Chayanov's theory. The impact of flexible access to land is to defer the onset of diminishing returns as labour use increases, since extra labour is combined with additional rather than fixed land. In other words the production function may have a linear or near linear portion (constant marginal returns) before diminishing returns set in (Low, 1986: 30–5). While this aspect should be kept in mind for interpreting Figure 6.2 it does not affect the logic of what follows.

The consumption side is represented by a set of indifference curves, I_1, I_2, describing given amounts of total *utility* provided by alternative combinations of leisure and income. These indifference curves are convex towards the origin at L since leisure is measured from right to left along the horizontal axis. They are precisely the same in meaning as the income–leisure indifference curves of Figure 6.1, but are here relocated through 90° to reflect the changed position of the relevant axes. In utility function notation:

$$U = f(Y, H)$$

Or, in words, the utility or happiness of the peasant household is a function of income (Y) and leisure (H).

Any point on an income–leisure indifference curve, say point B on I_2, describes the subjective value placed by the household on work at that point. The slope of the curve at a point like B describes the amount of income, dY, which the household would need to gain in order to compensate for the loss of one unit of leisure, dH: in other words it is the household's *subjective wage level*.

The range and relative level of this subjective wage, as indicated by the slope and position of the indifference curves, is constrained, on the one hand, by the requirement that the farm household meets its minimum acceptable standard of living (given by Y_{min}) and, on the other hand, by the maximum number of full working days which it is physiologically feasible for worker members of the household to perform (given by L_{max}). Both these are again determined by the *demographic structure* of the household – the first by family size, and the second by the number of workers in the family.

The existence of these constraints affects the shape of the indifference curves at the extremes. Towards the bottom left any indifference curve hitting the minimum consumption curve will become horizontal at that level: the marginal utility of leisure becomes zero (no amount of leisure could compensate for a fall in income below this level). Similarly, although perhaps less plausible for poor peasant households, towards the top right the indifference curves will tend to become vertical: the marginal utility of income tends to zero (no amount of income could compensate for a further fall in leisure as the maximum labour constraint is approached).

The equilibrium position of the farm household is given by the point of tangency of the production function to the highest possible indifference curve of utility which can be achieved given the technology of production. This occurs at point A, with labour input L_e and income level Y_e. At this point the marginal product of labour (MVP_L) equals the subjective value of family labour time (dY/dH), i.e. the amount of income required to compensate for the loss of one unit of leisure.

Thus the way the economic problem of the peasant household is formulated in the Chayanov model is to maximise utility subject to three constraints (a) the production function, (b) the minimum acceptable income level, and (c) the maximum number of working days available. In simple notation:

$$\max U = f(Y, H)$$

Subject to: $\quad Y = P_Y \cdot f(L); Y \geqslant Y_{min}; L \leqslant L_{max}$

And assuming that it is the production function rather than one of the other constraints which is binding, the solution to this problem occurs where the marginal rate of substitution of leisure for income (the subjective wage) equals the marginal value product of labour:

$$MU_H MU_Y = dY/dH = MVP_L$$

Note that this theory is not the same as a target income hypothesis, which crudely supposes *fixed* aspirations on the part of the household. The Chayanov model does not involve a fixed consumption target, but it does embody the notion that *at the margin*, when the consumption norms of the family have been met, the disutility of additional work is high relative to the utility of additional income. By the same token the Chayanov model, although consistent with the observation of a backward bending supply curve of labour, does not of necessity predict such a result.

One further interesting feature of this model is that the degree of subsistence of the household, i.e. the proportion of farm output which is retained for household consumption, has no influence either on the slope of the income–leisure curve or on the equilibrium output and labour use of the household.

The importance of family size and family composition for this theory of peasant decision making is evident. Between them they define both the minimum and maximum level of output, and thus for the peasant community as a whole their average levels determine the lower and upper limits of the volume of economic activity. They are also the determinants of the relative weight attached to leisure versus income in the household utility function, and thus the level of the household subjective wage. And it is in this subjective nature of the microeconomic equilibrium of the household that Chayanov detected what he regarded as a *unique economic calculus* of peasant households which made them quite distinct from capitalist enterprises. In effect this model means that the marginal product of labour in peasant production is variable between households according to their demographic structure. And this contrasts with profit maximisation in capitalist enterprises, across which, of course, marginal labour products should be the same and equal to the market wage.

The demographic character of the Chayanov model is also emphasised if we consider the impact on equilibrium output and labour use of a change in the production function. The production function, or family income curve, may be altered by (a) changes in other resources which combine with labour to produce output, (b) a change in the technology of production, or (c) a change in the market price of output. These changes (when they involve increases or improvements) will tend to shift the family income curve upwards, and thus place the household on a higher indifference curve than before. Their impact on labour use is, however, *indeterminate*. This is because, as discussed already in relation to Figure 6.1(*b*), the positive 'substitution effect' of such changes is offset by a negative 'income effect' and the final balance of these cannot be predicted from within the logic of the simple model.

The Chayanov model thus has no predictive power concerning the response of the household to factors which affect the production function. But it does have predictive power concerning the impact of factors of family size and composition which affect the slope and position of the indifference curves. There are several changes which can be considered here, starting for the sake of convenience from a position where the household consists of just two adult workers without children (c/w ratio of 1.00).

First, the household grows in size as children are born, raising the minimum consumption level, and raising the c/w ratio perhaps up to a maximum of around 2.50 when children are small and their work contribution is low.

Second, children grow up and contribute increasingly to the work of the household, causing the c/w ratio to fall from its peak, and also meaning that the number of person-days of labour available to the household rises. This has the impact, with respect to Figure 6.2, of lengthening the horizontal axis towards the right.

Third, adult children begin to form families, and farms, of their own, thus reducing the family size once more, lowering the minimum consumption level, and reverting eventually towards the original demographic structure of the household.

In a rather abbreviated form these stages describe the *demographic cycle* of the peasant farm household which is a central feature of Chayanov's theory of peasant economy.

Figure 6.3 contains the graphical analysis of the first of these changes in

Figure 6.3. Impact of higher consumer worker ratio.

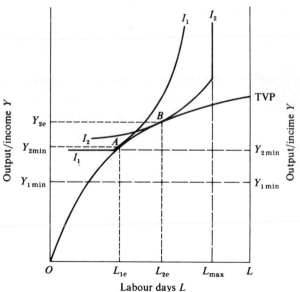

family size and structure. Once this is grasped there is no difficulty in perceiving the effects of subsequent phases in the demographic cycle, and these will not be pursued. The various aspects of relevance to be drawn from Figure 6.3, and comparisons with the previous equilibrium, are as follows:

(a) The number of workers (total person-days available) and the TVP curve stay the same.

(b) The minimum consumption constraint is raised from Y_{1min} to Y_{2min}, reflecting the increased consumption needs of the larger family.

(c) The shape and position of the income–leisure indifference curve changes. The curve has a shallower slope because the marginal utility of income has increased and the marginal utility of leisure has decreased for all points on the curve. In other words the *preferences* of the household change due to the need to feed a larger family. This means that the household is prepared to accept a smaller rise in income (dY) in order to compensate for the loss of one unit of leisure (dH) than before, at all points on the curve, or, put another way, there is *a fall in the subjective wage*.

(d) A new equilibrium is established at higher output Y_2e and higher labour input L_2e than was formerly the case. On the given production function this also implies that the marginal product of labour (MVP_L) is lower at B than it was at A, consistent with optimisation at a lower subjective wage. This capacity of the farm family to intensify labour use by lowering the subjective wage Chayanov termed the capacity of the peasant household for 'self-exploitation'. And again here there is a contrast being made between the 'self-exploitation' of the peasant household and the 'exploitation' of labour by capital in the capitalist enterprise, thus reinforcing the idea that the peasant household has a distinct mode of economic calculation.

(e) As already noted with respect to Figure 6.2, this analysis neglects the ease of access to extra land which Chayanov assumed. The effect of flexible land access is to widen the range of labour input levels across which the marginal product of labour remains roughly constant. It means that a rise in the minimum income line, Y_{min}, is less likely to push the household into the area of zero marginal returns to labour than would be the case with rigid land access.

In summary, then, the Chayanov model sets up a theory of the peasant household containing both consumption and production components. The key elements of this theory are the size of the peasant family, its consumer/ worker ratio, the absolute number of workers in the family, and the social norm of a minimum acceptable standard of living. These elements lead to a distinctive type of economic calculation on the part of peasants – equating the MVP of labour to the subjective wage – which is different from that followed by capitalist enterprises. In essence the model is a demographic explanation of household motivation which yields the following testable propositions:

(a) The marginal and average products of labour should vary significantly between households according to their demographic structure. This emphasis on *variation* in labour efficiency contrasts with the profit maximising hypothesis (Chapter 4) where the focus of empirical work was on *average* efficiency, *not* on variation and its explanation.

(b) The number of days (or, more accurately, hours) devoted to farm work per family worker should vary directly with the consumer/worker ratio. As the c/w ratio rises, so the amount of time devoted to farm labour by each worker should increase.

(c) The size of the area sown should vary directly with family size. Note that there might be problems of causality here – according to Chayanov increasing family size causes a larger area to be sown, but in a land-scarce peasant economy the size of farm might impose limits on family size.

(d) The lower the c/w ratio, the higher the average income per person in the household. This is because a low c/w ratio means a higher subjective wage, placing the family in a position on the production function with high marginal returns to labour.

Due to various peculiarities of the Chayanov model like (a) an implicit assumption that the labour of women and men is substitutable in farm work, (b) flexibility of access to land, and (c) absence of, or at least limited engagement in, a labour market, it has been found more useful for explanatory purposes in the African context than elsewhere (Levi & Havinden, 1982: Ch. 4). Both Hunt (1979) and Low (1986) provide evidence from African peasant communities which seem to corroborate the demographic predictions of the model. The implication of such studies is that peasant households vary in their economic performance according to household size and structure. Low (1986) is of special interest in this respect because it deals with a situation in which household demography is affected by off-farm wage work by household members. Since this involves abandoning Chayanov's assumption of a non-existent labour market, a closer examination of Low's model is deferred to the next chapter.

Policy aspects

The Chayanov model has not, generally, been found very useful for policy purposes except in dictating some caution about the degree of responsiveness of peasant households to exogenous changes in technology or prices. This is due to the ambiguity which surrounds the impact on household decisions of changes in the production function. Some thoughts were given in earlier policy analysis (e.g. Mellor, 1966: 167–73) to ways of influencing the income–leisure trade off so as to raise the marginal utility of income, decrease the slope of the utility function, and thus provoke peasant households to operate at a higher output and lower MVP_L on their production functions. Some suggested methods were:

(a) Taxation of marketed output (crop taxes), with the effect of reducing the cash income obtained per day of work, reducing the subjective wage, and resulting in a higher labour input at lower MVP_L (reminiscent of the colonial approach to peasant production);

(b) Increasing the range and availability of consumer goods in rural areas thus provoking a rise in the marginal utility of income;

(c) Land redistribution from large to small peasant farms, on the basis that small farmers have to operate further out along the production function in order to survive, and tend to have a higher marginal utility of income relative to leisure than larger farmers who can meet their minimum subsistence more easily.

However, in a context of seeking to improve the economic motivation of peasant households these ideas have flaws. They pander to the purported leisure preference of the household rather than creating active conditions in favour of output growth.

Chayanov himself (Thorner *et al.* 1966: 264–9) envisaged the institution of farmer *cooperatives* as the way forward to altering the social context of peasant production and hence, ultimately, the economic motivation of individual peasant households. He stressed what he called 'vertical cooperation' in the supply of farm inputs, delivery of improved technology, and marketing of farm output. This would increasingly bind farm households together with common goals and practices leading to higher output and increased intensity of production. Likewise other writers have emphasised the need to create a vigorous climate of social and economic change in the peasant economy in order to stimulate desired changes in the behavioural responses of the peasant household.

Wider perspectives

Chayanov's work on peasant economy possesses a rather wider significance than is indicated alone by the microeconomic model we have described in preceding sections. His notion of a unique economic calculus on the part of peasant households distinct from that of capitalist enterprises gives rise to a theoretical debate concerning the existence or not of a peasant mode of production. In addition his concept of a farm household demographic cycle led him to put forward the idea of the demographic differentiation of the peasantry in opposition to the Marxist concept of their social differentiation. We shall discuss these matters briefly here, beginning with the question of differentiation.

We have already noted that the emphasis of Chayanov's theory, in contrast to the efficient peasant hypothesis, is on variation between peasant households and its causes. The origin of this emphasis was a voluminous quantity of data which had been collected on peasant farm households in Russia over several decades around the turn of the twentieth century. These data revealed strong correlations of the kind which his model, as we have set it out, would predict; i.e. increasing farm size with family size, increasing days worked with a rise in the consumer/worker ratio, and so on. Demographic differentiation thus follows from the demographic cycle of the farm household. It refers to the variation in the size, output, and incomes of farms according to the size and structure of the households that work them.

In posing such variation as being the result of demographic differentiation Chayanov set himself in opposition to the Marxist orthodoxy of his time (Chapter 3), that its cause was social differentiation i.e. that it resulted from the progressive emergence in agriculture of the two social classes of capitalist farmers and a rural proletariat, leading to the concomitant disintegration of the peasant economy.

It is plain that the distinction between demographic and social differentiation was far more than a matter of academic controversy about the interpretation of data. Chayanov considered that capitalism had made few inroads into Russian agriculture, that the peasant economy represented a stable form of production subject to the cyclical fluctuations of its farm households, and that the peasantry could be drawn into socialist development via his ideas of vertical cooperation. Lenin and others, by contrast, argued that capitalism had already deeply penetrated agriculture, that the peasant economy was not stable but disintegrating, and that the role of the peasantry in socialist construction was severely problematical for those reasons. Thus vital matters of the strategic role and future of the peasant form of production in socialist economic development were at the core of this distinction. And the same issue tends to arise whenever broad perspectives on the future of the peasantry are debated with respect to the agrarian economies of contemporary developing countries.

The other wider issue arising from the Chayanov theory of peasant economy concerns the theoretical merits of a separate peasant *mode of production* distinct from the capitalist mode. The idea of a distinct peasant or household mode of production appears in various different guises in the literature. Two examples in non-Marxist writing are the domestic mode of production (DMP) put forward by Sahlins (1974) and the family mode of production (FMP) advanced by Lipton (1984). In the former the DMP is envisaged as a special economic theory applicable to precapitalist societies. In the latter the FMP is oriented especially to capturing the flexibilities of resource use in household forms of production whether in agriculture or in non-farm economic activities.

Notwithstanding the often valuable insights into household production yielded by such concepts the word *mode* to describe domestic or family economic behaviour has theoretical problems. No one would deny that household production possesses great differences in the uses it can make of labour time and other resources compared to the pure capitalist firm with hired wage labour. And these differences may permit both the survival and competitive advantage of household production in economic spaces within a capitalist economy. But household production does not occur independently of the dominant capitalist mode except in the extreme (and entirely theoretical) case of pure subsistence agriculture. As soon as households buy or sell in the market place they confront prices and costs which are established in the larger capitalist economy. Moreover unless they are pure subsistence farmers they have to engage in such transactions for family survival and their economic actions can no longer be considered independent of the wider system.

A second objection to the notion of a peasant mode of production concerns the deduction of a larger economic system from the subjective decision making of its individual participants. As we discussed in Chapter 3, a mode of production like capitalism comprises a comprehensive set of economic forces and social norms governing the way people relate to each other for the purposes of material production. There may be a great variety of ways in which individual producing units function within this comprehensive system, but they only do so on the terms established by the system as a whole. It is the wider system which governs the success or failure, in material terms, of individual decisions.

The aggregation upwards of subjective decisions of the Chayanov type does not result in a mode of production in this sense. Such an economy would be entirely stagnated in every sense: no markets, no exchanges, no wider social forces causing movement and change in any direction. It is not the sum of infinitely variable individual decisions which make a mode of production, it is the mode of production which sets the limits on the viability of individual decisions.

Summary

1 This chapter describes a farm household theory which integrates the consumption and production decisions of the peasant family. The aim of such theory is to achieve a more accurate representation of the totality of economic behaviour encompassed in household production.

2 Of special interest is the extent to which consumption decisions might alter the production responses of the household. In this connection the hypothesis that peasant production possesses a special kind of economic motivation, different from other enterprises in the market economy, is given due consideration.

3 The theory examined is that advanced in the 1920s by the Russian agricultural economist, A.V. Chayanov. We refer to this as the theory of the 'drudgery-averse' peasant because it centres on the choice between farm work and leisure, where farm work is considered irksome or toilsome by the household.

4 The assumptions of the Chayanov theory are:
(a) no hiring in or hiring out of labour by the household (absence of a labour market);
(b) flexible access to land by each household;
(c) farm output may be consumed or sold in the market, and is valued at the market price;
(d) household motivation follows, in part, a social perception of the minimum acceptable level of material income.

5 The first assumption makes the value of labour time, and hence the optimum level of labour use, a subjective matter which varies across households according to their demographic structure.

6 The first assumption also restricts the predictive power of the theory to the influence of family size and structure on labour time and output. Predictions include:
(a) higher labour input per worker as the consumer/worker ratio rises;

(b) marginal product of labour varies inversely with the consumer/worker ratio;

(c) more land cultivated as family size increases;

(d) average income per person in the household varies inversely with the consumer/worker ratio.

7 The uniqueness of household decision making in the Chayanov model is solely attributable to the lack of a labour market, and disappears when a labour market is introduced.

8 The chapter concludes with some points concerning the concept of a peasant mode of production. Notwithstanding the flexibility of resource use which household production may possess, this does not provide grounds for defining a domestic or family mode of production in opposition to the capitalist mode of production.

9 It remains more useful to consider peasant households in terms of their only partial integration into the market economy and the incomplete markets – in the Chayanov case, the non-existent labour market – within which they operate.

10 Chayanov's theory, like other theories we have examined so far, makes no distinction concerning the separate roles of men and women in the peasant household. For Chayanov male and female labour is perfectly substitutable in farm production, and the household is run by the male household head, or patriarch.

Further reading

An accessible and concise summary of Chayanov's theory of peasant economic behaviour is given in Hunt (1979), who also tests various aspects of the theory with data from a Kenyan case study. A useful collection containing a number of theoretical and empirical explorations of the theory is Durrenberger (1984). The graphical representation of the theory used in this chapter originates in Mellor (1963; 1966: Ch. 9), Sen (1966) and Nakajima (1970; 1986: Ch. 3). Low (1986: Ch. 4) contains a model which retains some components of Chayanov while adding a labour market to its working (see next chapter). The works of Chayanov translated in Thorner *et al.* (1966) are readable, and give a more ample perspective on the drift of his thought than any amount of secondary material. For critiques of Chayanov from the Marxian perspective see for example Harrison (1975, 1977), Littlejohn (1977), Patnaik (1979), and Kitching (1982). Finally for a thought provoking discussion of the special attributes of household production, under the description 'family mode of production', Lipton (1984) is recommended.

Reading list

Durrenberger E.P. (ed.) (1984). *Chayanov, Peasants, and Economic Anthropology.* New York: Academic Press.

Harrison, M. (1975). Chayanov and the economics of the Russian peasantry. *Journal of Peasant Studies,* Vol. 2, No. 2.

Harrison, M. (1977). The peasant mode of production in the work of A.V. Chayanov. *Journal of Peasant Studies,* Vol. 41, No. 4.

Hunt. D. (1979). Chayanov's model of peasant household resource allocation and its relevance to Mbere division, Eastern Kenya. *Journal of Development Studies,* Vol. 15.

Kitching, G. (1982). *Development and Underdevelopment in Historical Perspective.* London: Methuen.

Lipton, M. (1984). Family, fungibility and formality: rural advantages of informal non-farm enterprise versus the urban-formal state. in Amin, S. (ed.) *Human Resources, Employment and Development Vol 5: Developing Countries.* London: Macmillan.

Littlejohn, G. (1977). Peasant economy and society, in Hindess, B. (ed.) *Sociological Theories of the Economy.* London: Macmillan.

Low, A. (1986). *Agricultural Development in Southern Africa: Farm Household Theory & the Food Crisis.* London: James Currey.

Mellor, J.W. (1963). The use and productivity of farm family labor in the early stages of agricultural development. *Journal of Farm Economics,* Vol. XLVIII.

Mellor, J.W. (1966). *The Economics of Agricultural Development.* Ch. 9. New York: Cornell University Press.

Nakajima, C. (1970). Subsistence and commercial family farms: some theoretical models of subjective equilibrium. in Wharton, C.R. (ed.) *Subsistence Agriculture and Economic Development.* London: Frank Cass & Co.

Nakajima, C. (1986). *Subjective Equilibrium Theory of the Farm Household.* Amsterdam: Elsevier.

Patnaik, U. (1979). Neo-populism and Marxism: the Chayanovian view of the agrarian question and its fundamental fallacy. *Journal of Peasant Studies,* Vol. 6, No. 4.

Sen, A.K. (1966). Peasants and dualism with or without surplus labour. *Journal of Political Economy,* No. 74.

Thorner, D., Kerblay, B. & Smith, R.E.F. (1966). *Chayanov on the Theory of Peasant Economy.* Homewood, Illinois: Richard D. Irwin.

7

The farm household peasant

Household decisions with a labour market

Like all microeconomic models the logic and predictions of Chayanov's theory discussed in the previous chapter are dependent on its initial assumptions. Amongst these the absence of a labour market is the key assumption which leads both to the prediction of variable average and marginal products of labour across households and to the mainly demographic (household size and structure) explanation of household economic performance. The assumption of flexible land access is also important for deferring the onset of diminishing marginal returns to labour. It permits the farm family flexible adjustment to changing domestic circumstances, and it allows successive generations to obtain a livelihood from farming.

Subsequent development of the farm household model has focused on the impact for the logic of the model of altering these key assumptions, while extending its capacity to handle simultaneous consumption and production decisions. Before entering into the detail of such changes, it is useful to consider, first, the impact of allowing for a competitive labour market on the model as we have so far set it out.

Figures 7.1(a) and (b) show what happens to the Chayanov model when the household is permitted either to hire labour from outside to work on the family farm or to engage in off-farm work at the market wage rate. In both cases the existence of a competitive labour market means that a wage cost line (ww') is introduced into the economic calculus of household decision making (any reader confused by the meaning of this line should refer again to the description of profit maximisation for a single variable input in Chapter 2). This wage cost line represents the *opportunity cost* to the household of alternative uses of family labour time, namely, 'home' activity (i.e. household non-farm activity), farm work, or wage work off the farm.

The first of these alternative uses of time is referred to as 'home' activity rather than 'leisure' since this avoids the dubious connotation that the only use of time apart from work is indulging in idle pursuits. 'Home' time

Figure 7.1. (*a*) Farm household hiring in labour. (*b*) Farm household hiring out labour.

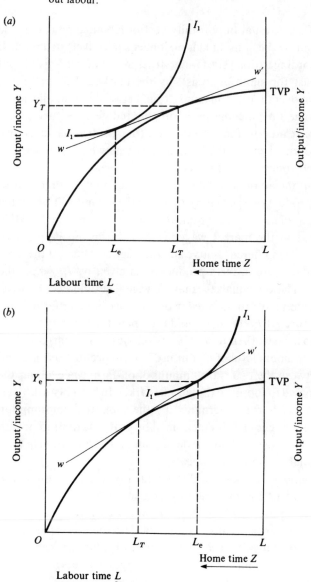

includes the entire range of activities associated with the daily maintenance of the household i.e. food processing and preparation, house building and repair, water and fuel carrying, childcare, and so on which are part of satisfying the consumption needs of the household. These goods and services produced within the household for direct use rather than for market exchange are referred to in the neoclassical literature as Z-goods (see below).

The impact of an external opportunity cost of labour time is that the valuation of labour by the household is no longer subjectively determined, and variable, according to domestic family structure. Rather it is given, and invariable (at least for static analysis), by the market. This permits a separation, within overall utility maximisation, between labour allocation related to the home time/income trade off (the indifference curve), and labour allocation related to farm production (the production function). This separation occurs because the household can now hire in or hire out labour at its opportunity cost which is the market wage.

In Figure 7.1(a) the amount of labour which the family is prepared to commit to farm production is given by L_e where the income (Y) which the household is prepared to sacrifice for one more hour of home time (Z) (i.e. dY/dZ) is equated to the market wage. This is shown by the point of tangency between the indifference curve and the wage cost line. At the same time optimum labour use in farm production is given by L_T where the marginal product of labour equals the market wage. The difference between L_T and L_e is the amount of labour hired in by the household for farm work.

Similarly in Figure 7.1(b) the household is prepared to commit L_e hours of labour either to farm work or to wage work off the farm. In this case L_e is greater than the optimum level of labour use in farm production, L_T, and the difference between the two is the amount of off-farm wage labour the household is prepared to supply to the labour market. In both cases the level of farm output is no longer determined by the subjective consumption preferences of the household, it is determined by profit maximisation with respect to the market wage. So, too, the demographic determination of farm output and farm labour input disappears.

The existence or not of a labour market is evidently crucial to how a farm household model works and the kind of predictions it provides. It can be shown (Barnum & Squire, 1979: 26–36) that no matter how complete the specification of the various consumption and production alternatives confronting the farm household, in the absence of a labour market the response of output and labour use to external changes in prices and costs is either indeterminate or negative (as in the Chayanov model). On the contrary when a labour market is introduced production decisions become *independent* of consumption decisions, and the response of the household to a change, say, in the price of output becomes predictable and positive (i.e. a higher output price increases production and labour use).

New home economics

As well as drawing on Chayanov's farm household theory, the models of farm household decision making which we examine later in this chapter are based on a branch of neoclassical economic theory often referred to as the 'new home economics'. In fact this branch of neoclassical economics is no longer that new. It originates in a seminal journal paper by Becker (1965) on time allocation within the household, complemented by several related theoretical contributions in the 1960s. The simplified account of the approach given here follows a summary provided by Michael & Becker (1973).

A central feature of the new home economics is that the utility function is redefined in several ways. In conventional theory the individual consumer has a utility function which represents her preference ordering between the range of market goods and services which she can purchase. The utility or happiness resides in the goods or services themselves. In the new home economics the household has a utility function which represents its preference ordering between a range of final characteristics of home-produced goods and services. In this approach the household is seen as a *production unit* which converts purchased goods and services, as well as domestic resources, into a set of final use values yielding utility in consumption. Thus it is not carrots, potatoes, and beans which yield utility, but the vegetable soup made from them which possesses utility-giving attributes. Moreover the consumption level of this vegetable soup is determined not only by the relative market prices of its ingredients, but also by the relative cost of its production to the household in terms of the time required for its preparation. The main features of the new home economics can be summarised thus as follows:

(a) The household, not the individual (unless the two coincide), is the relevant unit for analysing utility maximisation;

(b) Utility is not only, or even generally, derived directly from market commodities, it is obtained from the objects of final consumption (we shall call them 'use values') produced within the household;

(c) These use values are referred to in the theory as Z-goods to distinguish them from purchased commodities (X-goods), and hence the utility function takes the form:

$$U = f(Z_1, Z_2, \ldots, Z_n);$$

(d) The production of Z-goods within the household requires inputs of household time as well as purchased goods and services, hence a major emphasis of the theory is on the time allocation of the household between Z-goods production and wage work;

(e) The household produces Z-goods from market inputs (x_i) and time spent on them (T_i), hence the home production function takes the form:

$$Z = f(x_i, T_i);$$

(f) The household maximises utility, not subject to a simple budget constraint, but subject to its production function, a total time constraint, and a money income constraint;

(g) The total time constraint (T) is given by work time outside the household (T_w) and the sum of the times allocated to Z-good production (ΣT_i):

$$T = T_w + \Sigma T_i;$$

(h) The money income constraint (Y) is determined by the market wage rate multiplied by the time allocated to wage work (wT_w). In equilibrium this money income must equal the value of x-goods (market commodities) used as inputs into Z-good production $(\Sigma p_i x_i)$, where the p_i are the prices of the x-goods:

$$Y = wT_w = \Sigma p_i x_i;$$

(i) By valuing all units of the household's time, T, at the market wage rate the time constraint and money income constraint can be collapsed into a single constraint, defined as the household 'full income' (F):

$$F = wT = w\Sigma T_i + \Sigma p_i x_i;$$

(j) It can be shown, and is intuitively in keeping with other microeconomic theory, that the equilibrium of the household is given where the ratio of the marginal utilities of any pair of Z-goods (the marginal rate of substitution between them) equals the ratio of their full marginal costs of production (MC_i/MC_j). Here the full marginal cost of any Z-good, say Z_i, is the sum of, *first*, the wage rate multiplied by the marginal product of the household time allocated to its production, and, *second*, the market prices multiplied by the marginal products of the market commodities used in its production.

The logical structure of the new home economics is no different from that already used to describe farm household models in this and the preceding chapter. There is nothing intrinsically new or difficult in the theory provided it is kept in mind that it consists of maximising utility subject to a production function and other constraints. Indeed if we construct a simple example where (a) the household produces only one Z-good referred to simply as Z, (b) the utility function contains only Z and leisure, and (c) a single price, p, is used to value the market inputs, x_i, used in Z production; then the theory can be described in a graph (Figure 7.2) which is similar in most respects to earlier graphical analysis.

The components of Figure 7.2 are described briefly as follows. The household has a total time available for all activities given by T. This time is divided into the three components of home work time (T_Z), wage work time (T_w), and leisure (T_H). The opportunity cost of time is given by the real market wage w/p, where w is the money wage, and p is the general price level of purchased goods. The line OF, with slope w/p, describes the rise in total real income as hours increase (recall from Chapter 2 that the slope of the real total cost line was given by the inverse ratio of factor price/product price). Hence the point F represents the full opportunity cost of household time obtained by valuing the total hours available (T) at the real wage. It equals wT/p.

Figure 7.2. The home production model.

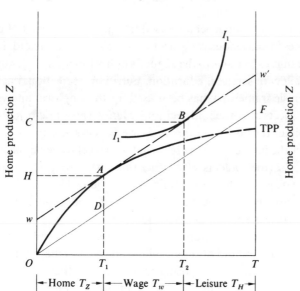

Figure 7.2 also contains a production function, representing the transformation of home work time into final home output, Z; an indifference curve, representing a given level of utility obtained by different combinations of leisure and Z, and a shifted real wage line, ww', representing the opportunity cost of time in terms of market prices.

The equilibrium of the household in the *production* of Z is given at point A, where the MPP of home work equals the real wage:

$$\text{MPP} = w/p \ \ or \ \ \text{MVP} = w$$

This is of course the same as in the theory of the farm as a firm, and it gives the 'home' component of the total cost of Z at H.

The equilibrium of the household in the *consumption* of Z is given at point B, where the marginal rate of substitution of leisure for Z (MU_L/MU_Z) equals the ratio of the opportunity cost of leisure to the market price of the ingredients of Z (w/p).

Note how the diagram satisfies the various constraints on utility maximisation of the home economics model. The time constraint is satisfied by the sum of the three components of total time along the horizontal axis. The money income constraint is satisfied provided that the cash outlay on market purchases (distance CH on the graph) equals the market wage, w, multiplied by wage-labour time, T_w. Household 'full income' is given by point F shifted upwards to w' to take into account the net product of labour in home production (distance AD – the 'profit' of conventional production theory).

The home economics model can be used to explore the impact of many different changes in exogenous variables confronting the household. It also allows many things to be put into the Z-goods utility function – e.g. number of children, childcare services, education, nutrition, recreational activity etc. – and its basic framework has been used for the empirical analysis of wide ranging aspects of household decisions. Here we note briefly just some of the more direct results of the theory as we have set it out:

(a) Consider the impact of an increase in the market wage on the model given in Figure 7.2 (the reader is left to trace this out). A wage rise increases the slope of the wage cost line, ww'. A first effect will be to lower the home production component of the production of Z and raise its market component, because the marginal cost of home time increases relative to the marginal cost of purchased inputs. A second effect is that full income is increased and the household attains equilibrium on a higher indifference curve. A third effect, with two opposing components, is that the extra time now available may be used either for more wage work, or for more leisure, or for a combination of both.

(b) It is seen that a rise in wages, or a fall in market prices, involves several different substitution and income effects. There is a pure substitution effect in home production which results in lower home work time and higher market purchases. There is a pure substitution effect in consumption which results in lower leisure and more time available either for home work or for wage work. There is an income effect in consumption which results in higher leisure, but unless this income effect is very large it is unlikely to negate the double impact on the time available for wage work of the two substitution effects.

(c) More generally it has been found useful to distinguish between different kinds of Z-goods: those which are home-time intensive (time-intensive goods) but which require low market inputs, and those which require high market inputs (money-intensive goods) but require little or no home time in their preparation for final use. The consumption mix of these two types of goods will obviously depend on the cost of market inputs (the prices of commodities and services) relative to the opportunity cost of time (the market wage). If the market wage rises then money-intensive goods will be substituted for time-intensive goods (this is a 'substitution effect') but whether the additional time then available is used for wage work or for leisure depends on an 'income effect' which is uncertain.

(d) As applied to the tasks surrounding childcare (nursing, cooking, washing etc.), which are time-intensive goods, the model suggests that a rise in wages, and especially of the wages and work opportunities of women, should act as a powerful incentive to have fewer children and thus incur less time-intensive chores (Evenson, 1981). This, however, is a very complicated issue because it depends *inter alia* on (a) the extent to which children are regarded as consumption rather than investment with future family income-earning potential, and (b) the nature of the roles of men and women within the household, and the degree to which women have any real choice to undertake wage work.

It is not intended to pursue the application of home economics in the areas of childcare, nutrition, education, and population in this book. But the reader should be aware of its many applications in this area, and we do return to the economic analysis of women in the peasant farm household in Chapter 9.

Several models of farm household behaviour have been developed and tested using the new home economics approach. We examine two of these models in the following sections.

The Barnum–Squire farm household model

Barnum & Squire (1979) develop and apply a model of a farm household which has its roots partly in the new home economics and partly in a paper by Hymer & Resnick (1969). This model is an important one since it provides a framework for generating predictions about the responses of the farm household to changes in domestic (family size and structure) and market (output prices, input prices, wage rates, and technology) variables. The account of the model given here is of necessity simplified for reasons of space, and so that it can be understood in terms of the graphs already presented. The assumptions of the Barnum–Squire model are as follows (contrast them with those of the Chayanov model):

(a) There exists a market for labour so that farm households are able to hire in and hire out labour at a given market wage;

(b) Land available to the farm household is fixed, at least for the duration of the production cycle under study;

(c) 'Home' activity (production of Z-goods) and 'leisure' are combined and treated as the same consumption item for the purposes of utility maximisation;

(d) An important choice for the household is that between own consumption of output (C) and sale of output in order to purchase non-farm consumption needs (M for manufactures);

(e) Uncertainty and behaviour towards risk are ignored.

The structure of the model closely follows the logic of the new home economics. The main difference is that here we are dealing with a farm (a production unit in the conventional sense) as well as a household. This means that the production function refers to farm output which can be traded, not just to 'home' production for direct use. Moreover the farm household has the option of hiring in labour at the market wage as well as hiring it out. There are now three items in the utility function; time for the production of Z-goods and for leisure combined (T_Z), home consumption of output (C), and purchased goods (M). The utility function is thus:

$$U = f(T_Z, C, M)$$

The preferences between these are influenced by the size of the household and its composition between workers and dependants. The production function is:

$$Y = f(A, L, V)$$

where A is land under cultivation (presumed fixed), L is total labour (both household and hired) used in production, and V is other variable inputs into production.

Utility is maximised subject to the production function, a time constraint, and an income constraint. The time constraint is of the familiar form:

$$T = T_Z + T_F + T_w$$

Where T_Z is time allocated to Z-goods and leisure (combined), T_F is time allocated to farm work, and T_w is wage work which may be positive or negative – if labour is hired in ($T_w > 0$) this increases the total time available, if it is hired out ($T_w < 0$) it reduces total time, T. For convenience we shall refer to the sum of the household's own time, i.e. T_Z and T_F, as G.

The income constraint states that net household earnings should equal expenditure on market goods:

$$p(Q - C) \pm wT_w - vV = mM$$

Here p is the output price, $(Q - C)$ is the quantity of total output (Q) sold rather than consumed, w is the market wage and wT_w may either represent an addition to income (if labour is hired out) or a subtraction (if labour is hired in), v is the price of variable inputs, V, and m is the average price of market purchases, M.

As in the home economics model these last two constraints may be collapsed into a single expenditure constraint, F', which is an augmented form of the 'full income' concept:

$$F' = wT_Z + pC + mM = \Pi + wG$$

Where wT_Z is the opportunity cost of the time spent in Z-goods production, pC is the market value of home consumption of output, and mM is the value of market purchases. This must equal net farm income or profits, Π, plus the implicit value of total household time, wG.

The equilibrium conditions of this model follow the standard microeconomic results for production and consumption, as we have seen variously in Chapter 2 and elsewhere in this book. They are:

(a) that the marginal product of labour (MVP_L) should equal the wage rate (w);

(b) that the marginal product of other variable inputs (MVP_V) should equal their average price (v);

(c) that the marginal rate of substitution between home time (T_Z) and purchased goods (M) should equal the wage/purchased goods price ratio (w/m);

(d) that the marginal rate of substitution between home consumption

(C) and purchased goods (M) should equal the output price/ purchased goods price ratio (p/m).

The existence of two pairs of consumption trade-off and three resources in the production function means that this model cannot be shown in a single graph. Nevertheless part of its working can be shown by a graph which combines elements of Figures 7.1 and 7.2. In Figure 7.3 we illustrate those components of the model which involve:

(a) the choice between higher consumption of farm output (C) and more time to spend on non-farm activities (T_Z);

(b) the production function for a single farm output with labour as a single variable input;

(c) the case when labour is hired in rather than hired out by the farm household.

In Figure 7.3 the farm household utilises a total quantity of time given by T along the horizontal axis. This time is divided between the farm work of family members, T_F; hours of hired labour, T_w; and the home time of household members, T_Z. The opportunity cost of time is given by the relative market wage w/p, where w is the money wage, and p is the farm output price. The line OF, with slope w/p, describes the rise in the total cost of labour as its use increases. The point F represents the total implicit cost of

Figure 7.3. Part of the Barnum–Squire farm household model.

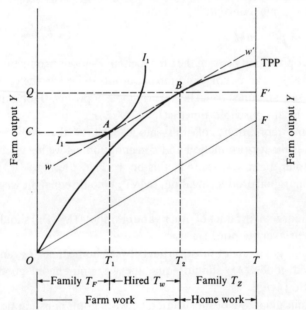

all units of time available to the household, no matter whether family or hired.

The graph also contains the production function of farm output (TPP), the indifference curve for a given level of utility derived from different combinations of home time and home consumption of farm output, and the shifted wage line, ww', representing the relative wage cost of farm production. The equilibrium of the farm household in *production* is given at point B, and this also determines the augmented version of 'full income', F', for the production model. The equilibrium of the farm household in *consumption* is given at point A, and this defines the level of own consumption of farm output, C, and the level of marketed supply, Q minus C. Since market purchases do not enter this simplified model, the expenditure constraint is satisfied provided that income from market supply $p(Q-C)$ is sufficient to pay for hired labour (wT_w).

Even in this simplified form the model possesses considerable predictive power concerning the impact of changes in the wage level or output price on farm household decisions. Here we will consider briefly, and leave for the reader to trace out, the separate and opposing effects of a rise in wages or a rise in prices:

(a) A rise in the market wage rate increases the price ratio, w/p, and makes the shifted wage cost line, ww', steeper in slope. This causes:

(i) a fall in output and corresponding fall in 'full income';

(ii) a rise in farm work by the household, and a decline in the use of hired labour;

(iii) an increase in home consumption, and a fall in market sales.

(b) A rise in the market price of output reduces the price ratio, w/p, and makes the shifted wage cost line, ww', shallower in slope. This causes:

(i) a rise in output and a rise in 'full income';

(ii) a decrease in farm work by the household, and a rise in the use of hired labour;

(iii) a decrease in home consumption, and an increase in supply to the market.

With reference to the full model, a similar set of predictions can be derived concerning the relative preference of the household between home time and market commodities. This refers, of course, to the slope of an indifference curve, and it may be observed:

(a) that if the household displays a relatively high preference for home activities, then more labour must be hired, farm cash profits are reduced, and there is less income to purchase consumer goods;

(b) that if the household displays a relatively high preference for market commodities, then less labour is hired, farm cash profits are higher, and the household has more income to purchase consumer goods.

The independence of production and consumption decisions in the Barnum–Squire model allow it to be solved, for practical purposes, in a sequential way:

First, the production function is estimated, and this is used to generate the output and net farm income available to the household.

Second, the demand functions for the three consumption choices in the utility function are estimated. These demand functions contain the several variables (wage rate, prices, size and composition of family) which have an impact on the consumption decisions of the household. They are constrained in the model by the need to meet minimum consumption levels of own output, home time, and purchased items respectively. In other words, variations are only permitted above the provision of basic needs, and this may be termed the discretionary choice open to the household. The demand functions yield estimates of the elasticities of demand with respect to the exogenous variables.

Third, the interaction between the production and consumption decisions can be traced on the basis of the individual responses which have been estimated.

Once calibrated with information from a sample of farm households this model permits the response of the average farm household to both domestic (family structure) and market changes to be examined. Barnum & Squire (1979) do this for a sample of paddy growing farm households in the Muda River Valley in Malaysia. Table 7.1 reproduces some of their results which

Table 7.1 *Household response elasticities*

Variables	Total paddy output	Marketed paddy output	Own paddy consumption	Household farm labour input	Demand for hired labour
Market					
Price of paddy	0.61	0.66	0.38	-0.57	1.61
Wage Rate	-0.47	-0.55	-0.08	0.11	-1.47
Domestic					
No. workers	–	-0.09	0.44	0.62	–
No. dependants	–	-0.50	0.23	0.12	–

Source: Barnum & Squire, 1979, Table 16, p. 88

are in the form of elasticities i.e. they give the percentage response of various household decisions to a one per cent increase in an exogenous variable. These responses are in directions which the logic of the farm household model would predict. What is interesting is for the size of them to be quantified. Taking the price of paddy as an example, it was found that a 10 per cent increase in the paddy price would result in a 6.1 per cent increase in total paddy output, a 6.6 per cent increase in marketed supply of paddy, a 3.8 per cent increase in own consumption of paddy, a 5.7 per cent decline in the labour input of the household itself, and a 16.1 per cent increase in the demand for hired labour. It is left to the reader to trace the other responses shown and the way they fit into the logic of the farm household model.

The responses set out above refer to the way that an individual farm household would respond to a specified change in a single variable. This reveals only part of the analytical power of the model, and represents the first stage of its application for policy purposes. The second stage is to examine how these responses interact in the larger economic system. For example, a rise in the output price is observed to increase greatly the demand for labour. If hired wage labour is in short supply this will raise the market wage, and it is seen in the above table that a wage rise reduces total paddy output and, even more, its marketed supply. For policy purposes it is the market, rather than household, responses to a change in policy variables which are relevant. The market response elasticities of the Malaysia study corresponding to the household data given above are reproduced in Table 7.2.

The significance of tracing through the market interactions of farm household decisions is immediately apparent. Taking the impact on market supply of a 10 per cent rise in the paddy price as an example, it is seen that the predicted household level of response of 6.6 per cent translates into a

Table 7.2 *Market response elasticities*

Variables	Total paddy output	Marketed paddy output	Own paddy consumption	Household farm labour input	Demand for hired labour
Market					
Price of paddy	-0.02	-0.08	0.27	-0.41	-0.36
Domestic					
No. workers	0.15	0.09	0.46	0.58	0.47
No. dependants	0.03	-0.47	0.24	0.11	0.09

Source: Barnum & Squire, 1979, Table 17, p. 90

market level response of -0.8 per cent. This is due to the impact of the price increase on rural wages in a situation of scarce wage labour: not given in the table is a result which shows that a 10 per cent rise in the paddy price indirectly increases rural wages by 13.4 per cent.

The analytical power of the Barnum–Squire model thus resides in its capacity to pursue the impact of joint production and consumption decisions within the household into the larger economic system. In other words it provides the basis for a *general equilibrium* analysis of the peasant economy, in addition to the partial equilibria of the various components in the individual household.

The Low farm household model

Allan Low (1986) develops and applies a farm household model which differs in some interesting ways from the one just described. Again the roots of this model are partly in Chayanov and partly in the new home economics, but Low's model has different assumptions and emphases from the Barnum–Squire model.

The situation which Low tackles is that of agricultural production in African countries bordering South Africa. A dominant feature of economic life in those countries is the proximity of a highly developed market for wage labour. The conditions which concern Low are:

(a) The existence of a labour market in which wage rates vary for different categories of labour, and especially between men and women. This differs from the single market wage rate assumed in the Barnum–Squire model.

(b) An indigenous land tenure system which permits flexible access to land for farm households according to their family size. This is the same as in the Chayanov model, and differs from the fixed land assumption of the Barnum–Squire model.

(c) Semi-subsistence farm households for which the farm-gate price of food differs from the retail price at which food can be purchased back from the market. This contrasts with the single food price assumed in the Barnum–Squire model.

(d) The widespread occurrence of food-deficit farm households with hiring out of family labour. This contrasts with the conditions informing the Barnum–Squire model of food-surplus farm households which, mainly, hire in more labour than they hire out.

The first of these conditions implies that different household members have different potential for earning wage income. In other words some members have a greater *comparative advantage* in wage work than others.

The second condition means that the land input can be increased in parallel with the labour input, thus deferring the onset of diminishing returns. Low assumes that the marginal physical product of labour (MPP_L) can be taken as constant over the relevant range for economic analysis. The third and fourth conditions mean that for food-deficit households the amount of labour to commit to subsistence food production depends not on the farm-gate price of output, but on the ratio of wages to the retail price of purchased food.

The working of Low's model for a food-deficit farm household is shown in Figure 7.4. This has real income on the vertical axis, and time on the horizontal axis, as in previous graphs. For illustrative purposes we assume that the household contains three individuals of working age, the labour times of which are given by the gaps A, B, and C along the horizontal axis. These individuals each have the same productivity in farm subsistence production, but they command different wage rates in the labour market.

The graph contains a total product curve (TPP) for subsistence output which is *linear*: the marginal product of labour is constant and is the same for each household member. The line OW traces out the rise in total wage income (or opportunity cost of labour) which occurs as the labour time of each member is valued by the real wage that they could earn in the labour market. The 'real wage', w/p, is given by the nominal wage rates (w) divided by the *retail* price of food (p). This is because for the food-deficit household

Figure 7.4. The Low farm household model.

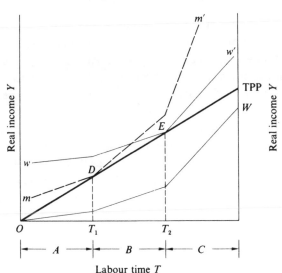

what is relevant is the purchasing power of wages over the retail price of food.

Corresponding to segmented line OW is the parallel opportunity cost of labour line, ww', which touches the TPP curve at point E. Visual inspection of the graph confirms that point E defines the 'profit maximising' level of labour input for this household (the gap between TPP and OW is much the widest at this point). The implication is clear: only those family members whose real opportunity cost of time, w/p, is lower than their MPP_L engage in work on the farm; family members, such as C, whose real opportunity cost of time is higher than the MPP_L on the farm should engage in off-farm wage work in order to maximise household income. In terms of the graph what is relevant is the *slope* of the real wage line, w/p, compared to the slope of the production function. Where $w/p < MPP$, then that household member should engage in subsistence production; where $w/p > MPP$, then the household member engages in off-farm wage work.

The significance of using the retail price of food as the deflator is revealed if one considers the impact of a fall in retail food prices or a rise in wage rates on the division of labour within the household. A fall in the retail price of food, holding wage rates constant, results in the opportunity wage cost line switching to mm' in Figure 7.4. Household member B should now join C in off-farm work, leaving only member A in subsistence production. The same result occurs for an across-the-board rise in wages, holding food prices constant. In this variant of the farm household model the production behaviour of the food-deficit household is determined by the purchasing power of wages in terms of the retail price of food.

Although Figure 7.4 simplifies Low's model it does convey its essential features. Given the relationships between wage levels and retail food prices in southern Africa, Low found that the model seemed to provide a plausible explanation of agricultural stagnation in the region. This is not solely due to the wage-price mechanism illustrated in Figure 7.4. It is also because those family members who have a comparative advantage in wage work tend to be the able-bodied males of the household, so that subsistence production is carried out by women, children, the old and the infirm. The farm productivity of adult women may well be as high as that of men, but they also have innumerable other tasks to perform (the daily maintenance of the household discussed in Chapter 9) which constrain the hours they can spend in farm work.

Low's model demonstrates the flexibility of farm household theory to adapt to alternative assumptions, and to yield predictions pertinent to the varying circumstances which farm families may confront. Even though

Low's assumptions differ in almost every respect from those used in the Barnum–Squire model, the same basic idea of optimum time allocation in the context of a household production function is common to both models and is found to provide a powerful tool of microeconomic analysis.

Policy aspects

Farm household models of the kind just described do not generate policy implications which are independent of the findings of empirical investigation. Although the internal logic of such models can yield predictions about the direction of various responses at the household level, aggregate behaviour is dependent on the exact size of response elasticities and their interaction in the larger economy. These are likely to vary from one community, region, or country to another depending on the extent of market imperfections, the degree of land scarcity or abundance, and the nature of the market for labour.

This point is illustrated by the findings of an Indonesian case study using the Barnum–Squire model (Hardaker *et al.*, 1985). In this case the market level supply response to a 10 per cent increase in the output price was only slightly lower, at 6.3 per cent, than the household level supply response of 9.0 per cent. The reason for this was a relative abundance of hired wage labour (a high supply elasticity of labour), implying that the output price increase had only a minor effect on the wage level.

Wider perspectives

The models we have just described, in which joint consumption and production decisions are made in the context of an active labour market, would seem to dispel rather definitively any notion of a unique economic calculus on the part of peasant households distinct from that of capitalist enterprises. The purported uniqueness of peasants which is the cornerstone of the Chayanov model is seen to be entirely dependent on the assumed absence of a labour market. As soon as a labour market is permitted the production decisions of peasant households revert to the same economic calculus as other enterprises in the capitalist mode of production.

This result seems to confirm that what is distinctive about peasant forms of production is not a unique economic rationality common to all of them, but rather their partial integration into markets, and the degree of imperfection of those markets. What the Chayanov model describes is nothing more nor less than a singular market imperfection; that of no labour market.

The Barnum–Squire model tends to err, if anything, in the opposite direction to Chayanov. It assumes fully working factor and product markets. On the one hand, this brings the model close to describing a commercial *family farm enterprise* rather than a peasant farm household. The residual peasant element of the model is the choice the household exercises over home consumption of farm output. On the other hand, the capacity of the household to hire in labour brings the model close to describing a *capitalist farm enterprise*. And again the residual peasant element is the variable extent to which hired labour is used. In both cases the peasant aspects of the model reside only in the partial degrees of integration into markets, not in market imperfections.

The assumption of working markets restricts the application of the Barnum–Squire model to circumstances in which markets are fully formed and reasonably competitive. Where markets are non-existent, incomplete, or otherwise highly imperfect the model becomes much less useful because choices come to depend on the variable rather than uniform prices confronted by individual households. Situations of highly imperfect markets are examined in the next chapter.

Summary

1 This chapter begins by examining the impact on the Chayanov farm household model of relaxing the assumption of a non-existent labour market. The household is now allowed to hire in or hire out labour.

2 This has a dramatic impact on the logic of farm household theory, since it permits optimum production decisions with respect to labour use to be separated from optimum consumption decisions with respect to income versus alternative uses of time.

3 The chapter gives an introductory account of the new home economics, a branch of microeconomic theory concerned with the links between time allocation and utility maximisation in the home. The new home economics provides the logical structure on which many farm household models are based.

4 The new home economics treats the household as a production unit, in which the time of household members is combined with purchased goods or services to produce items of final consumption. All units of time, whether in housework, wage work, or leisure, are valued at their opportunity cost in terms of the market wage.

5 The Barnum–Squire farm household model is outlined. This model

contains three goals in the household utility function – home time, own food consumption, market purchases – giving three pairs of trade-offs between goals. An example of its predictions is that a rise in the market wage causes a fall in total farm output, a rise in farm work time by the family, a decline in hired labour use, and a rise in the proportion of output consumed at home.

6 A particular strength of this model is its capacity to generate general equilibrium analysis of the wider peasant economy from the outcome of peasant decisions in output and input markets. A possible weakness of the model is its dependence on an assumption of competitive markets for the applicability of its results.

7 The farm household model put forward by Low to explain farm output stagnation in southern Africa is summarised. This model has different market wage rates for different household members, such that those members for whom $w > MVP_L$ do off-farm wage work, while those for whom $w < MVP_L$ stay on the farm. Wage rates are measured in real terms, i.e. in terms of their purchasing power over retail food. Thus the proportion of household labour working outside agriculture is a function both of money wage levels and the consumer price of food.

8 Both the Barnum–Squire and Low models stress the significance of a labour market for the working of the peasant economy. The presence of a labour market alters the internal logic of the household model and the way the household interacts with the larger economy. One aspect is that the unique mode of economic calculation proposed by Chayanov disappears. Another is that the effects of an output price increase must be traced through both product and labour markets in order to gauge their impact on market supply.

9 Low's model explains the division of labour between women and men by reference to 'comparative advantage' in wage earning versus farm productivity. Whether the comparative advantage principle provides a satisfactory account of the social relations between women and men within the peasant household is explored in Chapter 9.

Further reading

A descriptive introduction to the new home economics is given in Evenson (1981). Also useful, but more difficult, is the summary of the theory given in Michael & Becker (1973). Both Barnum & Squire (1979) and

Low (1986) contain extensive treatment of the application of the new home economics to farm household theory. While some readers may find the mathematical logic of these models difficult to follow, both sources contain descriptive accounts which are clear and helpful. Further applications of the Barnum–Squire model are Hardaker *et al.* (1985), and Ahn, Singh & Squire (1981) which extends the model to farm households with more than one main output. Finally two new books became available after this chapter was written. One of these contains an extended theoretical treatment of farm household models (Nakajima, 1986), and the other provides a collection of papers on extensions and applications of the Barnum–Squire model (Singh, I. *et al.*, 1986a). An overview of the latter and survey of the field is given in Singh, I. *et al.* (1986b).

References

Ahn, C.Y., Singh I. & Squire L. (1981). A model of an agricultural household in a multi-crop economy: the case of Korea. *The Review of Economics and Statistics*, Vol. LXIII, No. 4.

Barnum, H.N. & Squire L. (1979). *A Model of an Agricultural Household: Theory and Evidence*. World Bank Occasional Paper No. 27, Washington DC: World Bank.

Evenson, R.E. (1981). Food policy and the new home economics. *Food Policy*, August.

Hardaker, J.B., MacAulay, T.G., Soedjono, M., & Darkey C.K.G. (1985). A model of a padi farming household in Central Java. *Bulletin of Indonesian Economic Studies*, Vol. XXI, No. 3.

Low, A. (1986). *Agricultural Development in Southern Africa: Farm Household-Economics and the Food Crisis*. London: James Currey.

Michael, R.T. & Becker G.S. (1973). The new theory of consumer behaviour. *Swedish Journal of Economics*, Vol. 75, No. 4.

Nakajima, C. (1986). *Subjective Equilibrium Theory of the Farm Household*, Amsterdam: Elsevier.

Singh, I., Squire L. & Strauss J. (eds.) (1986a). *Agricultural Household Models*. Baltimore: Johns Hopkins.

Singh, I., Squire L. & Strauss J. (eds.) (1986b). A survey of agricultural household models: recent findings and policy implications. *World Bank Economic Review*, Vol. 1, No. 1.

8

The sharecropping peasant

Peasants as share tenants

Sharecropping is a form of land tenancy in which the payment for the use of land, the rent, is a percentage of the total physical output obtained in the crop season. Since this proportion is fixed in advance of the crop season an important feature of sharecropping is that the absolute amount of rent varies with the level of harvest. Sharecropping differs in this from other types of farm tenancy based on fixed annual rents, whether in cash or in kind. As a form of livelihood based on access to land sharecropping also contrasts with (a) traditional land rights, (b) freehold land ownership, and (c) agricultural wage labouring. Sharecropping has occurred widely in history in many different parts of the world, and remains prevalent today especially in South and South-East Asia.

The economic decision making of the sharecropping peasant differs in significant ways from the theories examined so far. Sharecropping perforce involves *interaction between households* which differ in their command over land and other resources. At its simplest this interaction concerns land and is between households which possess land (the landowners) and those which do not (the landless share tenants). At its most complex it is an interaction with multiple levels of contractual obligation between households involving land, credit, consumption loans, input prices, access to markets and so on. In all cases it shifts the emphasis from the isolated decision making of the individual household to the nature of economic relationships between households. And in doing so it serves to highlight the wider village, community, or class dimensions of peasant production instead of downplaying them as in other microeconomic theories of peasant behaviour.

Sharecropping tends to be regarded as an interesting theoretical puzzle by neoclassical economists and as an oppressive form of exploitation by some Marxian economists.

The puzzle of sharecropping resides in the incapability of ordinary economic analysis to explain certain aspects of its existence as an institution, namely:

(a) the fairly strong grounds for suspecting that it may be less efficient and less open to innovation than other kinds of farm tenancy;
(b) its historical persistence and its coexistence, often in the same locations, with cash tenancy and capitalist farming;
(c) customary crop shares between landowner and tenant (e.g. fifty–fifty) which cannot be explained by optimising criteria alone.

The exploitation view of sharecropping stems from the way it concentrates economic power in the hands of landowners, and the control this gives them over the livelihood of tenants and landless workers.

The link between these two angles on sharecropping – the economic riddle and the exploitation – is found in the concept of interlocked (or interlinked) factor markets. This refers to the lack of independence (lack of arm's length prices) between different input markets when multiple transactions (e.g. for land, labour, consumption loans, input costs etc.) are tied together in a single tenancy contract.

The complexity in practice of sharecropping contracts needs to be stressed because its theoretical treatment inevitably involves simplification.

First, even in its simplest form it involves simultaneous transactions in two input markets, land and labour (the labour of the tenant household works on the land belonging to the landowner).

Second, sharecropping contracts are routinely a great deal more wide ranging than this and may involve consumption loans, credit for production, labour service by members of the tenant household for the landowner, cost sharing for variable inputs, and innumerable other special arrangements.

Third, sharecropping does not always imply a clear cut distinction between a class that owns land and a class that is landless. More typical is for land ownership to be variably distributed in the peasant community, for some owners of small parcels of land to sharecrop other land, even for complicated chains of tenancy and cross-tenancy to exist between households with varying command over land and other resources.

This chapter sets out the main components of the analysis of sharecropping and interlocked factor markets. It covers (a) the basic microeconomic models of sharecropping in a competitive environment, (b) the pursuit of the rationale of sharecropping into dimensions of risk aversion, bargaining theory, and market imperfections, (c) the analysis of interlocked factor markets, (d) the question of exploitation related to sharecropping, (e) policy implications which have been drawn from the economic study of sharecropping, and (f) some wider perspectives on share cropping deriving from the overall approach of this book.

Economic analysis of sharecropping

We begin by considering the simplest possible models of sharecropping, those which restrict the share contract to a transaction in the use of land (and thus, implicitly, labour too) and which assume a competitive environment. There are two opposing competitive models of sharecropping, one which views production behaviour from the viewpoint of the tenant, the other from the viewpoint of the landlord. The first originates in the treatment of share tenancy contained in Marshall's *Principles of Economics* (1890) and is thus often referred to as the Marshallian model. The second is attributed mainly to Cheung (1968; 1969). We examine each of these in turn before considering various modifications and extensions of them.

The tenant model

In this approach the share tenant is taken to be a profit maximiser in a competitive market subject to the output shares being fixed in advance. It is convenient to refer to the share of the output going to the landowner as S, and the share going to the tenant as $(1 - S)$. Thus if the shares were 60 per cent and 40 per cent then S would equal 0.60 and $(1 - S)$ would equal 0.40. The economic position of the share tenant is shown in Figure 8.1. The farm has a total output response to the input of tenant family labour as shown by the total product curve (TVP). However, the tenant only receives a proportion, $(1 - S)$, of the total product. Thus as perceived from the viewpoint of the tenant's economic interest the relevant output response to labour is given by $(1 - S)$TVP.

Given a competitive market wage which represents the opportunity cost of labour time to the tenant family, the profit maximising position with respect to the labour input can be examined. It is rational for the tenant to maximise with respect to $(1 - S)$TVP by operating at point A with labour input L_1. However, this gives a lower total profit (EC) and lower output (Y_1) than the profit (BD) and output (Y_2) which could have been obtained by maximising on TVP (labour input L_2). The use of the variable input, labour, is sub-optimal and sharecropping is *inefficient*.

The same result is demonstrated even more clearly in the graph of the

144   The theory of the optimising peasant

marginal product curves which correspond to the total products of Figure 8.1. The marginal product curves are shown in Figure 8.2 as MVP and $(1-S)$MVP. The tenant maximises at point A, with labour input L_1, where $(1-S)$MVP $= w$, the market wage. At this point the total MVP of labour at point E is higher than the market wage, w, and, once again, sharecropping is *inefficient*.

There are a number of aspects of this inefficiency model of sharecropping which are worth drawing out more fully, and these are set out below. For some of them it is helpful for the reader to appreciate that the area under a marginal value product curve, like, for example, the area $OHEL_1$ in Figure 8.2, represents the total product in value terms (or gross income) corresponding to the amount of input specified (the area under the curve is the sum of the MVPs over every successive unit of input, and it therefore equals the TVP). Thus different segments of this total area represent income flows either to landlords or to tenants.

(a) The analysis rests on an assumption that the tenant is free to choose the level of labour input supplied; there is no control by the landlord over the labour time committed to production.

(b) The same result obviously occurs for all variable inputs the use of which is left to decision of the tenant, since in each case the production

Figure 8.1. Sharecropping – the tenant model.

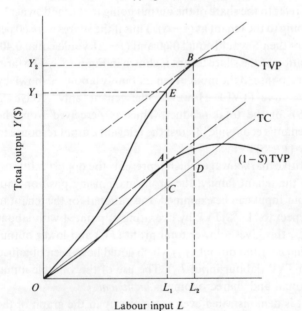

function for the tenant is the share $(1 - S)$ of the output response to any variable input.

(c) The economic waste of sharecropping (to the economy as a whole) is represented by the area AEB in Figure 8.2, which is the net income foregone due the sub-optimal level of input use at L_1. This loss is incurred by the landowner, not by the tenant, since it lies entirely within the landlord's share (S) of the total product.

(d) By the same token as the tenant equates $(1 - S)\text{MVP}$ to the price of any variable factor of production under her control, so the tenant would use land, if made available, up to the point where the marginal product of land were zero. This is because, as perceived by the tenant in this model, land has a zero price (the landowner's share, S, does not enter the decision making of the tenant as a price for land, but instead as a prior deduction from output which reduces the average and marginal products of all inputs).

(e) In this model the tenant obtains a higher income, and the landowner a lower income, than would be the case if the landowner used wage labour or leased out the land for a fixed cash rent. This is indicated by the area FGA in Figure 8.2, which, for the tenant, is an income above that which she could obtain as a wage worker $(OFAL_1)$ and, for the landowner, is a subtraction from the total profit, $FHEA$, which could have accrued by using wage

Figure 8.2. Marginal product of labour in the tenant model.

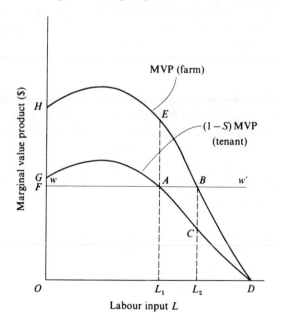

labour instead of share tenants to farm the land. Alternatively the landowner could create a cash tenancy at a rent level which would leave the tenant at the same income level as a wage worker.

These last two points mean that the inefficiency model does not describe a stable equilibrium. Point (d) implies that there would be excess demand for land by tenants and the need for some form of land rationing. Point (e) means that landlords would hardly be happy to continue sharecropping, given the alternative either of self-cultivation with wage labour or of cash tenancy, both yielding higher net incomes than sharecropping.

In this connnection it has been pointed out (Hsiao, 1975) that the extra income involved in moving from work effort L_1 to L_2 in Figure 8.2 should lend itself to bargaining between the two parties. The landowner stands to gain from receiving any proportion of the additional area AEB and the tenant should be happy to comply if compensated slightly above the extra wage cost incurred in the area ABC. The point B, at labour use L_2 (i.e. the efficient point), in fact represents a position of equality between the *net* MVP of the landowner and the *net* marginal labour cost of the tenant. Since the crop share is already fixed beforehand, this efficiency solution might be achieved by a side-payment (e.g. promise of bonus) from the landowner to the tenant.

A concise exposition of the various arguments concerning the tenant model of sharecropping is given in Basu (1984: Ch. 10). Although often treated as Marshall's only contribution, the tenant model in fact represented only part of his analysis of this subject much of which accorded with the landowner model set out below (see e.g. Bliss & Stern, 1982: 57–9).

The landowner model

In this model the landowner is a profit maximiser who can vary the amount of land at his disposal, decide the number and size of land parcels distributed amongst share tenants, decide the rent share, and stipulate in the share contract the amount of tenant labour input which is required. The only constraint on the landowner is the market wage: the tenancy contract must permit the tenant to obtain at least the same income as could be obtained by working as a wage labourer or no tenants will offer themselves as sharecroppers.

As set up in this way an entirely different conclusion about the efficiency of sharecropping is reached. Since the landowner now sets the labour input of the tenant, profit maximisation ensures that this occurs where the MVP of labour equals the wage i.e. at a labour input of L_2 in Figure 8.1 or 8.2. Further, the landowner will adjust the number of tenancies, tenancy size, and share rate so that the implicit rent per unit land is equal to the marginal product of land. With both these conditions satisfied sharecropping becomes *efficient* (Cheung, 1968; 1969).

In effect this model turns the landowner into a capitalist farmer. The income distribution resulting from the share tenancy is the same as if the landowner managed the land and hired in labour at the market wage. Gone is the advantage of sharecropping to tenants over wage labour implied by the 'extra' income FGA in Figure 8.2.

This result depends crucially on the assumed capacity of the landowner to vary the size and number of tenancies, to vary the share rate, and to stipulate the labour input of the tenant. These assumptions are not considered very satisfactory:

First, they seem to place the landowner in the position of a monopolist who can offer all-or-nothing choices to prospective tenants (Jaynes, 1982: 347), and this contradicts the intention of the model to demonstrate the neoclassical competitivity of sharecropping.

Second, it is thought unlikely that the individual landowner could use the share proportion as a variable in seeking efficient land use, because crop shares are subject either to custom or to competition between landowners (in which an individual landowner would be a price taker) which make them fixed in practice.

Third, the notion that the landowner can stipulate the labour intensity of the tenant is open to doubt. It assumes a zero enforcement cost to monitoring the labour process on the tenant farm.

However, in favour of the efficiency model is the consideration that under sharecropping motivation of work effort is more secure than for wage labour. The share tenant is at least self-motivated up to the efficiency point on the proportionate production function, whereas the wage worker requires constant supervision. The incentive is all the stronger given the typically short term (season to season) nature of crop share contracts which means that loss of contract hangs over the head of the tenant.

Moreover, efficiency for all other variable inputs can be achieved through the device of cost sharing i.e. if the landowner contributes to the cost of purchased inputs in the same proportion as the crop share then efforts by the profit maximising tenant to equate her share of MVP to her share of the input price will result in the efficient use of variable inputs. This is thought to be a lower cost way of monitoring input use than direct supervision.

Risk, information costs, and incomplete markets

Neither of the basic models of sharecropping provide a satisfactory explanation for its existence. The tenant based, inefficiency, model, does so even less so than the landowner based, efficiency, one since it works so clearly to the landowner's disadvantage and is socially inefficient compared to other forms of land tenure. However, the landowner model does not solve the riddle either. If the outcome for the landowner is no different from employing wage labour or leasing under a fixed cash rent, then why adopt sharecropping instead of one of the other production arrangements?

One way forward is to drop the assumption of certainty from the analysis. When uncertainty and *risk* are taken into account the adoption of sharecropping seems more plausible. This can first be posed in relation to the alternatives. Under a fixed rent tenancy the risks associated with production in an uncertain environment are borne entirely by the tenant; under self-cultivation with wage labour (capitalist farming) they are borne entirely by the landowner. Thus if either the tenant, the landowner, or both parties are risk-averse a risk-sharing arrangement may be preferred to one in which the risk is entirely borne by one or the other of them. With sharecropping this risk is shared between tenant and landowner in the same proportion as output is shared.

Thus one plausible explanation for sharecropping seems to be risk aversion in an uncertain environment. However, this explanation works better for tenants than for landowners, depending in part on other assumptions about the nature of markets surrounding production decisions. If these markets are competitive it can be shown for the landlord that there is some combination of cash rent tenancy and self-cultivation which would provide exactly the same degree of risk spreading as a given share contract, while at the same time avoiding the potential inefficiencies of sharecropping. Moreover this combination would result in the same income shares, between tenants and landlords, as in the Cheung solution to sharecropping efficiency (Newbery & Stiglitz, 1979).

The existence of uncertainty, and the subjective response to it in the form of risk-aversion, do not therefore on their own solve the riddle of sharecropping. It is the kinds of risk separately confronting tenants and landowners, the importance of imperfect information in creating those risks, and hence the imperfection of markets in this kind of peasant economy which in the end provide the explanations for sharecropping. As soon as the causes of sharecropping are sought in the range and nature of market imperfections in the peasant economy 'there is no unanswered puzzle as to the apparent absence of reasons for the common practice of sharecropping. On the contrary there is an embarrassment of riches.' (Bliss & Stern, 1982: 64). A number of such reasons are considered as follows:

Imperfect labour markets. Neither tenants nor landlords in practice face the competitive labour market alternative which is assumed in both the Marshallian and Cheung sharecropping models. For tenants supplying their labour the market is partial, uneven, and the costs of job search are significant; farm production requires labour unevenly through the year and there is no certainty that sufficient wage labour could be obtained for survival. For landowners seeking wage labour, hiring sufficient workers, with appropriate skills, at the correct time (for cultivation, for harvesting) is a problem, with recruitment costs, which sharecropping can help to avoid.

Incomplete or non-existent markets. It is observed that certain markets operate incompletely if at all in the kind of agrarian economy which gives rise to sharecropping. The most obvious of these is the market for credit which tends to be fragmentary because the information costs necessary to establish the creditworthiness of small farm households are too large for formal financial institutions to become involved, the risks of default are too high, and farmers are unable to provide sufficient collateral to offset such risks. Sharecropping contracts with credit provisions overcome these problems because the collateral for loans lies in the crop share (more on this below). Another market which sometimes does not work is that for bullock services, and sharecropping thus provides the only means by which the owner of a bullock team can obtain a sufficient area of land to make efficient use of the team.

Incentive and monitoring problems. It is argued that one of the chief reasons for sharecropping is providing sufficient incentive for work effort, monitoring the quality and effectiveness of work and the use of inputs, and avoiding loan defaults. These are sometimes referred to as 'moral hazard' problems; they relate, in the context of imperfect and incomplete markets, to a supposed high potential for non-fulfilment of exchange obligations whether these are in the markets for labour, for inputs, for credit, or for bullock services.

These various explanations of the advantages of sharecropping are drawn together by Stiglitz (1986) under the umbrella argument of imperfect information. The fragmentary nature of markets in an agrarian economy typified by variable and unequal ownership of land and poor communications means that landowners always have a highly imperfect picture of the state of the wider markets which surround them. Sharecropping is an arrangement for organising the production process which gives the most complete *local* information on the various inputs and outputs of the farm, especially with respect to the labour input.

However, the economic analysis of sharecropping remains incomplete at this point. Command over information is one facet of the control over fragmented markets which is obtained by locking together transactions in various different markets in the sharecropping contract. The efficient landowner argument interprets this interlocking of markets as a means of internalising external market imperfections, thus achieving greater efficiency of resource use than would otherwise occur. It is to this topic which we now turn.

Interlocked markets

The term 'interlinked factor markets' is often used to describe the simultaneous fixing of transactions in more than one market which is prevalent in the rural economy of many developing countries. However, it has been pointed out (Stern, 1986: 257) that markets, whether competitive or otherwise, are always interlinked in the sense that prices in one market (say, for a farm output) affect prices in other markets (for farm inputs). It is for this reason that this chapter employs the term 'interlocked markets' to describe the contractual tying of the terms of exchange in one market to that in other markets.

We have already described the potential range of transactions which might be contained either formally or informally in a sharecropping contract. To summarise again, they may include:

(a) the access to land via the crop share rent;
(b) the labour on the tenant farm;
(c) labour services to be rendered by the tenant household either on the landowner's farm or some other activity (including domestic service);
(d) the terms of consumption loans from the landlord to the tenant;
(e) the terms of production loans from the landlord to the tenant;
(f) the sale or cost share of farm inputs between the landlord and the tenant;
(g) the sale of consumption goods from the landowner to the tenant;
(h) the marketing of the farm output by the landowner, both the landowner's own share and sometimes that part of the tenant share to be marketed;

(i) possible provision of other goods and services, housing, water supply etc. from the landlord to the tenant.

While it is most unlikely that any single crop share contract would contain all these transactions, a good many of them appear in one situation or another and the simultaneous transaction of land, labour, labour services, and consumption credit is highly prevalent.

This interlocking of markets is open to two opposing interpretations, with various intermediate positions between them. The neoclassical interpretation tends to emphasise the increased efficiency and more rapid adoption of innovations, like higher yielding varieties, which it makes possible. In this interpretation interlocking of markets is the means by which profit maximising landowners overcome the inefficiencies of incomplete and fragmentary markets. They achieve this by internalising the adverse externalities (risk aversion, low work effort, loan default etc.) of imperfect markets, and in so doing they cause higher social welfare than would occur in the absence of such practices. Some of the main ways interlocking is thought to achieve this end are as follows:

(a) The interlocking of share tenancy with consumption loans to tenants can be used by the landlord to induce the tenant to work harder. The tenant must repay the debt from the tenant share of output, thus creating a treadmill in which ever more output is required to clear the debt of the previous season. Indeed many tenants are in a permanent cycle of indebtedness as a result of this practice, from which they cannot escape because they can never entirely clear the loan (a form of debt bondage). The penalty of default is loss of the share contract, which at best may result in a tenuous survival as casual wage labour and at worst starvation.

(b) The interlocking of share tenancy with production loans can ensure that the tenant carries out those investments and innovations which the profit maximising landlord considers most desirable. In this the landlord provides credit which would not otherwise be available to the tenant due to problems of default and collateral which the landowner is in a better position than anyone else to control.

(c) The interlocking of share tenancy with stipulated input supply, or with variable cost sharing for inputs, can induce the tenant to adopt the efficient level of input use. This also overcomes sub-optimal input use resulting from risk aversion on the part of tenants.

(d) The interlocking of share tenancy with labour service on the landlord's farm, with supply at fixed prices on consumption items to tenants, or with control over the marketing of farm output are all mechanisms which can be used by the profit maximising landlord to construct a set of penalties and incentives designed to extract the greatest work effort from the tenant and the members of the tenant household.

Thus this interpretation tends to make a virtue of the much greater control over the lives of tenants which interlocking markets permit compared to their absence. And the basis of this virtue is that greater efficiency, higher production, and more rapid innovation – in short, higher social welfare – occurs than would be the case given seriously flawed agrarian markets.

Sharecropping as exploitation

The alternative view, that sharecropping and interlocked factor markets ensure the persistent exploitation of tenant farm households, does not necessarily reject the higher output claims of the above argument. To be sure, considerable ambiguity surrounds the proposition that interlocked markets work better than the imperfect markets for which they substitute (proof either way is almost impossible to construct), but this is not the main point. Even conceding the drift of the neoclassical argument, the question can legitimately be posed, higher social welfare for whom?

The opposing argument is that the purported increase in social welfare is experienced entirely, and cumulatively over time, by the landowning class while the welfare of the tenant class is continuously forced back to the bare survival level. In other words there is a cumulatively unequal participation in the benefits, if any, which result from interlocked factor markets.

At the root of this interpretation is the view that sharecropping is a non-market (non-capitalist) form of surplus extraction by one class, the landowners, from another class, the landless tenants. This surplus extraction is direct, it is the physical crop share obtained by the non-producing landowner from the producing share cropper. It is not mediated by prices, and it is therefore closer to a feudal relation of production than a capitalist one. Sharecropping has been referred to as 'semi-feudalism' in this context (Bhaduri, 1973).

The various instruments we have discussed as increasing the efficiency of sharecropping are, in this vein, ways of improving the effectiveness of this surplus extraction. Moreover, to the extent that they succeed in simulating the relationship between capitalist and worker which typifies capitalist production, this merely serves to reinforce the idea that surplus transfer from the direct producer to the owner of the means of production is the central feature of sharecropping.

It is an inadequate response to this argument to suggest that if exploitation were the primary goal of landowners this could be achieved simply by increasing their crop share without recourse to interlocked markets (Braverman & Stiglitz, 1982: 695). By the logic of the efficiency argument itself an increase in crop share alone would reduce the marginal product of tenant labour, as well as of other inputs, and result in less efficient production and hence less potential surplus extraction for the landowner. The various arguments about the enhanced control and greater intensity of tenant labour provoked by interlocking markets are thus consistent with the exploitation hypothesis. Indeed the combination of instruments which result in virtual bondage of the tenant to the landlord allows for the much more comprehensive extraction of every ounce of surplus product above bare minimum subsistence than could any amount of varying the share rate alone.

The major arguments in the exploitation view of interlocked factor markets are set out in Bhaduri (1973; 1983; 1986). An important strand is that since the comparison is between interlocked markets and seriously defective markets, there is no competitive outcome with which the welfare results of interlocking can be compared. It cannot, therefore, be proven that interlocked markets are more efficient. Moreover, the compulsion exerted over tenants by interlocked contracts means that:

(a) tenants are not voluntary participants in arm's length exchanges, they are involuntary participants in enforced transactions;

(b) the function of exchanges is not to clear the market at an equilibrium price, but to give advantage to one party at the expense of the other party;

(c) what is 'efficient' from the landowner's point of view can in no way be equated with social efficiency as the outcome of competitive markets.

Further notes on interlocked agrarian markets

Interlocked agrarian markets are by no means unique to sharecropping contracts, even though this is the main guise in which they appear in this chapter. Just for the record, the reader may wish to note the following social relations which involve enhanced control by one party over another via interlocked transactions:

(a) the landowner/moneylender in a crop share and consumption loan contract with a farm tenant – this is typical of the sharecropping situation already described;

(b) the employer/moneylender in an employee and consumption loan contract with a labourer – this sometimes defines a bonded labour situation which the labourer and his family is locked into for life;

(c) the trader/moneylender in a crop sale and consumption loan contract with a small landowner – in this case the consumption debt gives the trader a lien over the output of the farm, and this may be perpetuated for years;

(d) the shopkeeper/moneylender in a triangular consumption loan arrangement with the landowner and his workers – the landowner acts as agent for the shopkeeper in the recoupment of consumption loans.

In all these cases moneylending and consumption debt (the credit market) are the levers which permit control over the terms of transactions in land, labour, or output markets. The interlocking of markets does not always rest on this mechanism, however. Outgrower schemes whereby small farmers – tenants or owners – are locked into exclusive sales contracts at fixed input and output prices are another, rather different, form of the same idea. Again in outgrower schemes, as in other cases, it is control over productive activity and command over information which are the motivations for the contractual locking together of markets.

Policy aspects

The policy conclusions which are drawn from theories of the sharecropping peasant evidently depend rather heavily on the positions taken with respect to (a) its efficiency or inefficiency as an organisational form of farm production, and (b) its impact on income distribution between landowners and tenants. Given that sharecropping is intimately connected with the unequal distribution of land ownership much of the policy emphasis in this area is on land reform. This and other policy aspects of sharecropping are summarised briefly here as follows:

Land reform

Land reform as a major instrument of policy follows both from the inefficiency theory of peasant decision making under sharecropping, and from concern over its impact on income distribution. Indeed if the inefficiency argument is even partially accepted, then land reform can be seen to promote both efficiency and equity goals at the same time.

Land reform is unlike most policy interventions which seek to alter the economic environment within which peasant production takes place. This is because it centres on property ownership and related issues of social status and economic power of an order quite different from typical 'market interventions' by governments. For one thing property owners usually predominate in the structures of political power in most countries, and are the least likely class to change the underlying basis of their own status. For another land reform is not a marginal or graded shift in relative prices or access to resources; it involves a major, once-for-all, change in the land ownership structure of a country.

For these reasons, and others, land reform has always proved an extremely difficult proposition, has seldom occurred except in conditions of severe social unrest or revolution, and usually fails in its objectives if it is only partial or restricted in scope. The evidence from countries where major land reforms have been carried out shows that it does greatly accelerate the transition of peasant agriculture either into capitalist farms or into commercial family farms.

Legal controls on crop shares and interest rates
These are interventions designed to evade the political difficulty of full scale land reform, while at the same time attempting to give tenant sharecroppers some protection against what are considered to be excessive crop shares and usurious interest rates. Evidence as to their efficacy is mixed, but a major drawback is the ease with which they can be avoided or offset within the context of interlocked factor markets. If a ceiling is placed on the landowner's crop share, then the interest rate on credit can be used as a substitute for surplus extraction; if a ceiling is placed on interest rates, then variations in the cost of inputs, or in labour service, or in countless other devices can be used to offset the control.

Subsidised credit schemes and others
The provision of alternative, low cost, credit to tenants via state credit schemes is another way of attempting to alter the balance of advantage in favour of tenants. The same is true of targetted inputs and similar devices. The problem with these is their high cost of administration, the risk of default on loans, and the impossibility in practice of controlling the final distribution of inputs. They may have some ameliorating effect on the situation of poor tenant farm families, but one cannot help feeling that where sharecropping is perceived as a serious barrier to improving the welfare of poor people bolder policy initiatives than these are required.

The conclusion concerning policy responses to the unequal economic power of landowners under sharecropping is that only land reform has any prospect of improving the welfare of tenants (Braverman & Srinivasan, 1981). Partial reforms are likely only to intensify the use by landowners of interlocked markets to evade them; and tenant credit subsidies end up as subsidisation of the welfare of landowners leaving tenant welfare unchanged.

Wider perspectives

The analysis of sharecropping, more so than any of the other decision making models examined in this part of the book, emphasises the importance and relevance of the interaction between the household and the wider economic environment for coming to grips with the economic situation of peasants. In this case this perspective is forced into the economic analysis because sharecropping involves interaction between households with varying command over productive resources. However, it serves to highlight that peasant decision making cannot be examined in isolation from wider economic relationships both near and far.

Recognition of the influence of agrarian social relations on farm production and resource use decisions is becoming more prevalent in neoclassical writing than was formerly the case. For example, a paper by Binswanger & Rosenzweig (1986) sets out a comprehensive array of relationships between property ownership, risk, collateral, and barriers to the existence of complete markets in the land-scarce economy. At their present stage of development these ideas yield mainly descriptive observations about directions of causality and response between different components. They are interesting, however, for their formal recognition of major departures from the competitive ideal for the working of the agrarian economy.

Like other household models, the theory of sharecropping tells us nothing about the impact of this form of production on internal relations within the household, and in particular on the situation of women. It seems plausible that sharecropping and interlocked factor markets impose more severe burdens on women than would occur in their absence. This is partly due to the incapacity of the tenant household to raise its standard of living above the survival level, and partly to the contingent clauses, such as labour service, of some sharecropping contracts.

Summary

1 This chapter sets out the microeconomic analysis of share tenancy, a type of peasant farming in which the rental payment for land is a percentage share of the physical output of the farm.

2 Share tenancy involves interactions between households with unequal command over land and other resources. Its initial economic analysis diverges according to whether it is the tenant or the landowner who is regarded as the principal decision-making agent in resource allocation.

3 The tenant model gives the tenant control over resource decisions, subject only to the payment of the agreed crop share (S) to the landowner. Since the tenant experiences total and marginal products which are only some fraction $(1 - S)$ of farm output, the equating of fractional marginal products to the market prices of inputs results in sub-optimal levels of resource use.

4 The landowner model gives the landowner control over resource decisions including the number, size, and crop share of each tenancy. This permits the landowner to approximate the operating position which would occur for a capitalist farm employing wage labour. Share tenancy becomes efficient, but its existence remains unexplained.

5 Explanations of sharecropping have been sought in uncertainty, labour motivation, monitoring, collateral, and information problems. These may be summarised under the general rubric of incomplete and fragmented factor and product markets.

6 Landowners can reduce these difficulties for themselves by interlocking factor and output markets within the tenancy contract. A typical example of interlocking occurs when the landowner advances loans to the tenant which must be repaid from the tenant's crop share. In this case the markets for credit, land, and labour are interlocked.

7 Interlocked agrarian markets have been interpreted as an efficiency response by landowners to market imperfections. Resource use, output, and adoption of improved technology are higher than would occur in the absence of interlocking.

8 Alternatively, interlocking can be viewed as a mechanism for the effective exploitation of tenants by landowners. The manipulation of personalised transactions gives landowners substantial power over the lives of tenants, and permits the extraction of every last ounce of surplus product above the bare survival needs of the tenant family.

9 Policy measures designed to redress the unequal economic power of share tenancy include land reform, legal controls on crop shares and interest rates, and special credit schemes for tenants. Since partial schemes and legal controls can be evaded via interlocked markets, land reform is the only meaningful instrument for altering social relations in the agrarian economy. It is also, however, the most politically difficult option to pursue.

10 The analysis of share tenancy highlights the inseparability of

household decisions from the social relations of production in the agrarian economy. This applies with equal force to other theories of peasant economic behaviour, but is not usually quite as obvious as in the landowner–tenant relationship in sharecropping.

Further reading

A number of useful surveys of sharecropping exist. Amongst these Quibria & Rashid (1984) is fairly accessible even to the non-specialist reader; Bliss & Stern (1982: 53–65) and Basu (1984: Part III) are excellent for the reasonably competent economist. The basic diagrammatic presentation of the so-called Marshallian model is contained in a number of sources, amongst which Hsiao (1975) and Cheung (1968; 1969) are particularly clear. Developments of the efficiency model in the direction of risk and market imperfections are given in Newbery & Stiglitz (1979). An excellent survey of interlocking factor markets is provided by Bardhan (1980), and, rather more difficult, by Braverman & Stiglitz (1982). A readable descriptive summary of the neoclassical position is Stiglitz (1986). For the view of sharecropping and interlocked markets as exploitation of tenants by landowners there is no substitute for Bhaduri (1973; 1983), and the summary paper by Bhaduri (1986). Also relevant in the latter context is the collection of theoretical and historical studies edited by Byres (1983). Policy aspects of sharecropping are contained in Braverman & Srinivasan (1981). Finally Binswanger & Rosenzweig (1986) is interesting as a neoclassical effort to deal with social relations and incomplete markets in the land-scarce agrarian economy.

Reading list

Bardhan, P.K. (1980). Interlocking factor markets and agrarian development: a review of issues. *Oxford Economics Papers*, Vol. 32, No. 1.

Basu, K. (1984). *The Less Developed Economy: A Critique of Contemporary Theory*. Oxford: Basil Blackwell.

Bhaduri, A. (1973). A study in agricultural backwardness in semi-feudalism. *Economic Journal*, Vol. 83.

Bhaduri, A. (1983). *The Economic Structure of Backward Agriculture*. London: Academic Press.

Bhaduri, A. (1986). Forced commerce and agrarian growth. *World Development*, Vol. 14, No. 2.

Binswanger, H.P. & Rosenzweig M.R. (1986). Behavioural and material determinants of production relations in agriculture. *Journal of Development Studies*, Vol. 22, No. 3.

Bliss, C.J. & Stern N.H. 1982. *Palanpur: The Economy of an Indian Village*. Ch. 3. Oxford: Clarendon Press.

Braverman, A. & Srinivasan, T.N. (1981). Credit and sharecropping in agrarian societies. *Journal of Development Economics*, Vol. 9.

Braverman, A., & Stiglitz, J.E. (1982). Sharecropping and interlinking of agrarian markets. *American Economic Review*, Vol 72.

Byres, T.J. (ed.) (1983). *Sharecropping and Sharecroppers*. London: Frank Cass.

Cheung, S. (1968). Private property rights and sharecropping. *Journal of Political Economy*, Vol. 76.

Cheung, S. (1969). *The Theory of Share Tenancy*. University of Chicago.

Hsiao, J.C. (1975). The theory of share tenancy revisited. *Journal of Political Economy*, Vol. 83.

Newbery, D.M.G. & Stiglitz, J.E. (1979). Sharecropping, risk sharing and the importance of imperfect information. Ch. 17 in Roumasset, J.A., *et al.* (eds.) *Risk, Uncertainty and Agricultural Development*, New York: Agricultural Development Council.

Quibria, M.G. & Rashid, S. (1984). The puzzle of sharecropping: survey of theories. *World Development*, Vol. 12, No. 2.

Stiglitz, J.E. (1986). The new development economics, *World Development*. Vol. 14, No. 2.

Comparative summary

Having examined in some depth five alternative theories of peasant economic behaviour, we are now in a position to compare and contrast their salient features. It is already apparent that the theories are not distinct in all respects. Moreover particular peasants or peasant communities may combine attributes from more than one theory. A comparative summary is helpful to trace the main lines of reasoning for any particular theory, as well as the connections between them.

Table I summarises the main features of the various theories under the following headings: objectives (i.e. behavioural assumptions), market assumptions, predictions, practical effects, and policy conclusions. This table is inevitably rather simplified and shorn of the complexities which we brought into the discussion of each theory in preceding chapters. To assist in rounding it out a little, we make the following observations:

(a) None of the theories assume or predict that peasant farmers are uniformly technically efficient, i.e. that they all operate on the same, 'best', production function. The simple conclusion to draw from this is that varying technical efficiency amongst peasant farms is always worth investigating irrespective of the microeconomic theory of the farm household.

(b) Two theories, the first and the fourth, predict that peasants are price efficient, and this means a positive output response to price changes, subject to technical constraints which may exist under (a) above.

(c) The same two theories depend on competitive markets. In the absence of competitive markets the predictions of these theories must be modified to take account of the nature and impact of market imperfections.

(d) Two theories, the second and fifth (tenant version), predict price inefficiency. This means underuse of variable inputs, and indicates policies to increase input use for output growth.

(e) Three theories – the second, third and fifth – are based on imperfect, incomplete, or non-existent markets. These are true peasant theories in the sense of our peasant definition.

(f) The entire range of agricultural policies is encompassed by one or other theory, with the table indicating in very general terms which policies are associated with which assumptions about household behaviour.

The goal of policy intervention in peasant agriculture, with the exception of pure welfare policies, is to increase productive efficiency, output growth, and peasant incomes. Implicit in this is to strip peasants of the attributes which make them peasants, whether these reside in household behaviour, in social norms, in technical constraints, or in market conditions.

From this viewpoint we can identify combinations between the theories which define 'the most desperate case' and 'the most hopeful case' respectively. The former award would surely go to a risk-averse, drudgery-averse, share tenant, peasant. The latter to a profit maximising farm household in competitive product and factor markets.

An effect of placing all these theories alongside each other is to emphasise the inseparability of household behaviour from the larger social system. Drudgery-aversion as a behavioural proposition cannot exist independently of certain factor market peculiarities. Likewise profit maximisation is nonsense without competitive markets. Economic agents behave according to the social relations of production of which they are a part; they do not, on their own, or through simple horizontal aggregation, make those social relations.

Table I. *A comparative summary of peasant theories*

Theory	Objectives	Market assumptions	Predictions	Practical effects	Policy conclusions
1. Profit max	Profit max. (trad. prod. constraints)	Competitive markets	Price efficient	+ ve supply response	New resources New technology Education Credit schemes
2. Risk-averse	Utility max. w.r.t. security	Natural hazards Social hazards Uncertain prices	Not efficient	Underuse variable inputs	Irrigation Price stab. Crop insurance Credit schemes
3. Drudgery-averse	Utility max. w.r.t. income/leisure	Competitive product market No labour market	Not efficient	Ambiguous – subjective responses	Cooperatives Education ('modernisation of the mind')
4. Farm household	Utility max. (general)	Competitive markets	Price efficient	+ ve supply response muted by gen. equil. effects	None *a priori*
5. Share cropping	Profit max.	Interlocked markets	Tenant – not 'efficient' Landowner – 'efficient'	Tenant – underuse variable inputs Landowner – interlocking for efficiency	Agrarian reform Tenant input subs. Tenant credit

Abbreviations: max. = maximisation, w.r.t. = with respect to, + ve = positive, stab. = stabilisation, subs. = subsidies, trad. prod. = traditional production, gen. equil. = general equilibrium.

Part III

Inside the peasant household

9

Women in the peasant household

The invisible peasant

Women are the invisible agricultural producers in peasant society. Across the agrarian communities of the world they contribute to the physical work of farm production as well as supporting the livelihood of the farm household in many other ways. It is only recently that the role of women has been placed on the agenda of analysis and research into peasant farm production. Most published data on rural economic activity – derived from censuses which tend to take male household heads as the primary data source – greatly underestimate the role of women in farm work, food processing, and many other productive activities.

Hitherto this book has taken the peasant farm household as the unit of economic analysis. The household has been a closed box; its internal working of little concern to theories which assume a single set of decisions across all household members. One purpose of this chapter is to open up this box and to subject its content to critical scrutiny. Another purpose is simply to make women more visible to peasant economic analysis. Some of the concerns which the chapter sets out to explore are:

(a) the division of labour between women and men in peasant societies;

(b) the impact of this division of labour on the time allocation of women and men in peasant households;

(c) the rigidities in this division of labour which inhibit the substitution of male and female labour across categories of economic activity;

(d) the control over resources which often resides in the male head of the household, and the effect this has on the economic independence, access to resources, and income share of women;

(e) the impact of these factors for relations of productivity, returns to labour, and income distribution within the farm household.

For reasons of scope and space this chapter restricts itself to issues surrounding the economic activity, and particularly the farm work, of women. Except in referring to the reproductive tasks of women, it does not deal with the role of children even though children contribute to farm production and to family incomes in most peasant societies. Nor does the chapter enter the large neoclassical economic literature on the determinants of fertility, family size, education, and nutrition in the farm household.

The chapter proceeds (a) to define certain concepts which are required for the analysis of women in the peasant farm household, (b) to summarise patterns, derived from fieldwork observations, of the economic situation of women in rural societies; (c) to reconsider the scope and limitations of the new home economics for analysing the economic role of farm women; (d) to examine how far non-market relationships within the household are susceptible to economic analysis; and, (e) to review briefly policy aspects of women in peasant agriculture.

Concepts for the analysis of women

The quest for a better integration of women into peasant economics begins with a set of concepts which are designed to place theoretical emphasis on differences in the economic situation of women and men. The meaning of these concepts varies in the literature, and their use here may not always accord with that found in other writing on this topic. The concepts are: gender division of labour, reproduction versus production, time allocation, non-wage labour, and the subordination of women.

Gender division of labour

In the present context this concept is used to describe the socially defined allocation of tasks between women and men in peasant households. The critical point of departure is that the division of labour between the sexes is not 'natural' in the sense of being ordained by the biological differences between them. Peasant households where women often do the most onerous physical tasks are living proof of this. Rather it reflects social customs, norms, and beliefs which govern and circumscribe individual behaviour.

For this reason it is misleading to refer to the division of labour between women and men as the 'sexual division of labour' with its overtones of causation by the biological differences between the sexes. An alternative is to refer to the 'gender division of labour' in which gender is used as a shorthand for the social meaning which is attached to the roles of women and men in different societies.

It follows from the idea that the division of labour between women and men is socially, not biologically, determined, that it is also susceptible to change. This susceptibility to change is at the centre of the feminist critique of social science analysis which takes the social roles of women and men as given and unchangeable.

Reproduction versus production

Closely related to the gender division of labour is the need to make distinctions about the role of women in reproduction and production. We have already discussed (Chapter 3) the concept of social reproduction, meaning the way the society as a whole (in both its social and economic aspects) is renewed over time. Within social reproduction an essential dimension is of course the reproduction of people, and this contains several different facets (Edholm, Harris & Young, 1977).

First, there is childbearing and the early nurturing of infants which may be defined as *biological reproduction*. Second, there is the care, upbringing, socialisation, and education of children, which – together with biological reproduction – is referred to as *generational reproduction*. Third, there are the recurrent tasks – cooking, collecting firewood and water, mending and washing clothes, cleaning the house etc. – concerned with the day-to-day material survival of the household, and this is referred to as *daily reproduction* or the *daily maintenance* of the household.

In most societies the tasks associated with these various categories of reproduction are predominantly assigned to women. However, only childbearing and the early nurturing of infants are of biological necessity restricted to women. All other tasks which fall within the categories of generational and daily reproduction can be (and sometimes are) undertaken by men as well as by women. The typical absence of men from such activities is a social rather than biological phenomenon.

Women in peasant societies also participate in productive activities. Here again some distinctions are usefully made. First, there is production for direct use in the household such as food processing, the weaving of mats, the making of pots and implements or clothes, the husking of grain, and so on. Second, there is non-farm income earning activity such as handicraft production for sale in the market. Third, there is work by women on the household farm, consisting of land preparation, weeding, fertilizing, harvesting, and so on. Fourth, there is off-farm wage labour which may consist of casual or intermittent work on neighbouring farms, domestic service for an adjacent landowner, or full-time wage labour in local mills, processing factories, and so on.

Time allocation

These reproduction and production activities can be summarised to provide a framework for the analysis of the use of time by women and men in the peasant household. Time allocation is an operational concept which provides the basis for practical investigation of the gender division of labour. It refers to the average number of hours spent by individual household members in different categories of activity.

The study of time allocation opens up differences between women and men in hours of work, productivity, and returns to labour. It is also a first step towards identifying areas of cooperation, conflict, independence, and obligation in the working patterns of women and men. The following categories are a simplified version of a time allocation framework set out in McSweeney (1979, 381):

A. *Reproductive activities*
    (a) Generational reproduction
          childbearing and infant care
          care and upbringing of children
    (b) Daily reproduction
          cooking
          cleaning
          washing
          mending clothes
          firewood collection
          water carrying
          house building and repair
B. *Productive activities*
    (a) Production for household use
          cultivation of food crops
          animal husbandry
          food processing
          tailoring
          craft work
    (b) Production for the market
          cultivation of cash crops
          food marketing
          wage work
          craft work for sale

C. *Leisure activities*
    meals
    personal hygiene
    social obligations
    many others

Of course not all activities can be unambiguously assigned under these labels. The farm work of women may be wholly or in part for direct use, rather than for the market, and other kinds of production for direct use may yield a surplus above household requirements which is then sold in the market. Moreover, an important feature of the work of women in farm households is that it often combines child care with the performance of other tasks.

Non-wage labour

A feature of most work undertaken by women in the farm household is that it is unpaid. This applies to the categories of reproductive activity we have identified, but also applies in varying degrees to productive activity, with the exception of wage work and independent involvement by women in agricultural marketing. Non-wage work arises in part because women's household activities are not confronted by market prices; it is production for use rather than for exchange. Where women are responsible for the food production needs of the farm family this also applies to their farm work.

However, the non-wage work of women has another important aspect. The product of this non-wage work is, almost by definition, available to meet the needs of the family as a whole. Indeed, for women to cook, wash clothes, carry water, collect firewood, husk grain, and so on solely on their own account would be so rare as to be safely discounted from analysis. The same is not necessarily true, however, of cash income generated from household activities which are mainly in the domain of men. Here the degree of sharing of the cash income component of the household product is a matter open to investigation, and one which has a direct impact on the material consumption of women compared to men.

The subordination of women

Related both to the gender division of labour and to non-wage work is the degree of control which men have over the way women conduct their lives, as well as over the intra-household allocation of tasks. The concept which describes the inferior social status of women in all its various manifestations is that of the subordination of women to men.

One particular manifestation of this concept which occurs in many peasant societies is *patriarchy*. This describes the power relationship of men over women when, socially, men control the property, resources, and income of the farm household. Other common features of patriarchy are control over the labour time of women, over their freedom of movement, and over their levels of consumption.

Time allocation and the economic role of peasant farm women

The purpose of this section is to review briefly certain economic aspects of women in the peasant farm household, with emphasis on patterns of time allocation. The section thus provides a link between the concepts set out above and the economic analysis of women in farm households which follows later. It should be noted that most information on women's activities in peasant farming comes from field studies of sample households in rural communities, not from national systems of economic statistics. This is because the latter do not typically collect any information on non-farm work in the household, and for farm production they understate the contribution of women because censuses and surveys are based on the household (or the farm) as a unit in which women tend to be assigned to the category of housewives (Beneria, 1981).

An earlier important work on the participation of women in peasant farm production was the book by Ester Boserup, *Woman's Role in Economic Development*, published in 1970. Boserup distinguished three main categories of peasant farming system according to the degree of women's engagement in farm work, the intensity of cultivation, and the availability to households of landless rural wage labour:

(a) The first category combined high female participation with extensive cultivation, low technology (the hoe), and the virtual absence of a labour market. This 'female farming system' was thought to apply mainly in African peasant farm communities south of the Sahara.

(b) The second category combined low or zero involvement of women in farm work with higher technology (the plough), more intensive cultivation, and availability of hired labour due to the presence of a rural class structure with landless labour. It was also associated with cultural values (e.g. in Islamic societies) which circumscribe the activities of women outside the home.

(c) The third category combined sharing of farm work between men and women with high population density, and even more intensive cultivation, in a situation of land scarcity and small farm size.

Though this simple threefold classification is no longer accepted as an accurate representation of the diversity of women's engagement in cultivation worldwide, Boserup's work nevertheless provided some useful insights into the economic conditions of women as peasants. She observed that changes in the division of labour between women and men often intensify the work of women while resulting in a loss of economic independence and social status; that changes in cropping patterns and farm technology often relegate women to the lowest productivity branches of production while increasing the productivity and income of men; and that these tendencies are reinforced by the bias towards men of state agricultural policies and projects.

A substantial amount of empirical work on women in peasant households has been undertaken since Boserup. Here we direct attention to the emerging picture of the time allocation of women and men in peasant societies.

The data cited in the following paragraphs are drawn from a number of different sources reporting the results of empirical research. Since these case studies vary considerably in their sample size, definitions, and time accounting units, certain liberties of interpretation were necessary in order to compile comparative tables. Rather than go into these in detail the reader is simply cautioned that the figures shown are for illustrative purposes only; they may not be strictly comparable according to the definitions used; they refer to sample households in villages or particular locations, not to nationwide averages; and the reader interested in their derivation should consult the sources cited:[1]

Hours of work

In many peasant societies women work longer hours than men. This can only be measured by the rigorous accounting of time for household members over the full length of the working day. Investigations which have done this substantiate the longer work hours of women in case studies scattered widely across rural areas of the developing countries. Some examples are given in Table 9.1.

Division of work

In all peasant societies, as elsewhere, there are rigidities in the division of tasks between women and men. The predominant pattern is for men to participate little in child care and the daily maintenance of the household, and to make much lower contributions than women to production for direct household use. If we term all non-market activity as 'household work', then the pattern in Table 9.2 is shown from various case studies.

Thus the contribution of men to household work varies from a mere fifteen minutes to one and a half hours, that of women from five to seven hours. The percentage time input of men varies from five per cent up to a maximum of about twenty per cent.

The converse of low male participation in household work is high male engagement in income earning activity. In those studies which examine the total number of hours spent in market-oriented work, we find the pattern shown in Table 9.3.

Table 9.1

Source	Location	Total hours work per day	
		Women	Men
McSweeney (1979)	Upper Volta	9.78	7.55
Evenson *et al.* (1979)	Philippines	9.51	7.90
Acharya & Bennett (1982)	Nepal	10.14	7.58

Table 9.2

Source	Location	Household work hours per day	
		Women	Men
Hanger (1973)	Uganda	6.15	0.43
McSweeney (1979)	Upper Volta	7.19	0.46
Evenson *et al.* (1979)	Philippines	6.33	1.70
Acharya & Bennett (1982)	Nepal	6.68	1.29
Cain *et al.* (1979)	Bangladesh	5.10	0.22
Hart (1980)	Java	5.65	1.35

Table 9.3

Source	Location	Income-earning hours per day	
		Women	Men
Evenson *et al.* (1979)	Philippines	2.33	7.44
Cain *et al.* (1979)	Bangladesh	1.61	7.04
Hart (1980)	Java	3.20	10.32

Farm work

The role of women in farm work varies considerably across different peasant societies. We have already noted the patterns identified by Boserup (1970). To these we can add the following points:

(a) that in the African context of high female participation there is often specialisation in which women work in food crops for domestic subsistence and men in cash crops for market sale;

(b) that throughout the developing countries the amount of farm work women do is inversely related to household income levels so that the poorer the household the higher the farm work hours of women;

(c) that women in poor farm households often work as casual wage labour on other farms, and this is especially prevalent where social differentiation is taking place (see Chapter 3) in labour intensive food production systems (e.g. in high yielding rice or wheat production in South and South East Asia).

Some examples of the farm work time of women and men are given in Table 9.4.

Summary

Several points of relevance for economic analysis can be derived from the above patterns.

First, the gender division of labour in most peasant societies strongly circumscribes the *substitutability* of female and male labour across the range of farm household activities. Economic theories of the farm household which treat men and women as perfect substitutes are therefore inaccurate about a critical aspect of labour use in farm production.

Table 9.4

			Crop production time	
Source	Location	Unit	Women	Men
McSweeney (1979)	Upper Volta	hours/day	2.97	3.10
Hanger (1973)	Uganda	hours/week	16.60	13.50
Barnum & Squire (1978)	Malaysia	hours/season	334	310
Cain et al. (1979)	Bangladesh	hours/day	0.28	2.26
Acharya & Bennett (1982)	Nepal	hours/day	2.26	2.65
Deere (1982)	Peru	per cent	25	75

Second, the long working hours of women, often unequal to those of men, stem from differences in the degree of this substitutability across different categories of activity. Substitution is typically lowest with respect to household chores, but it is sometimes higher in farm work and other market activity. Thus the varying engagement of women in farm work is superimposed on the rigidity of their time commitment to household work.

Third, the unequal distribution of time with respect to cash income earning activities is notable. The generalisation that, in effect, 'men control the purse strings' is widely applicable to peasant societies worldwide, with implications for the economic dependence of women and their share of the household total product.

Scope of the new home economics

The various theories of farm household decision-making which we have examined in preceding chapters of this book have as their point of departure the assumption of a single utility function for the farm family as a unit of analysis. In this and the next section we subject this assumption to scrutiny and consider both the scope and limitations of the new home economics for analysis of the division of labour between women and men in the farm household.

We begin with a brief summary of conceptual issues underlying the new home economics approach. The basic unit of neoclassical economics is usually the utility maximising individual rather than the entire household. This individual is deemed to hold a consistent preference ordering between various items of final consumption. Personal utility, or happiness, cannot be measured in this theory, and the amount of it derived by different people cannot be compared or added together. In pursuing their individual utility people confront each other as economic actors only through relative prices in the market.

The branch of neoclassical economics concerned with the interaction in the market between two or more utility maximising individuals is called welfare economics. One of its simplest results is that in a two-commodity, two-person world, the joint welfare of both people is maximised when each of them equates their marginal rates of substitution in consumption to the single market price ratio which they both confront. This means that in equilibrium the marginal rate of substitution of both individuals is the same, but this says nothing about the absolute amount of happiness each individual derives nor about the quantities of the two commodities they are able to purchase. The latter is determined by the initial income distribution between the two people, and income distribution falls outside the domain of joint welfare maximisation.

The closest neoclassical economics comes to defining an increase in social welfare is to state that this occurs when the welfare of one person is increased without reducing the welfare of any other person. This is called the Pareto criterion. Again it makes no allusion either to the comparative levels of welfare of the individuals before the change, nor to the initial income distribution between them.

Since the economic relationships between people within a household are not mediated by market prices, neoclassical economics prefers to treat the household as maximising a single utility function for purposes of the analysis of its decision-making behaviour. The strictness of the assumption underlying this single welfare function must be recognised. Since interpersonal comparisons of utility cannot be made, and personal utility functions cannot be added together, the single welfare function is not derived by summing the utility functions of the individual members of the household. Instead a strong assumption must be invoked, and this is that household members subordinate their individual inclinations to the pursuit of common household goals, a supposition which requires pure *altruism* as a behavioural trait within the home.

A dictionary definition of altruism is 'the principle of living and acting for the interest of others'.[2] In the present context it implies that utility is derived from the attainment of family rather than individual goals. Since various problems still remain concerning how joint family goals come to be formulated, and how to ensure that household members act in pursuit of these joint goals, it is easier to justify the single family welfare function by reference to an altruistic household head than by pretending it could be derived from the preferences of all family members. Altruism then collapses into the assumption that the household is ruled over by a benevolent dictator who sets the goals of the family in the interests of the family as a unit.

A paper by Nancy Folbre (1986) examines the paradoxes and limitations of the family utility function. Some of the points she makes are summarised as follows:

(a) The assumption of altruism in the home stands in sharp contrast to the presumed selfishness of individuals in the market upon which the edifice of neoclassical economics is built. If altruism works in the home then why not in society at large, in which case social organisation other than free markets could achieve maximum social welfare. And, vice versa, if the selfish pursuit of individual goals is the only basis of social welfare maximisation why should selfishness be left behind at the door of the home?

(b) The altruism assumption implies a degree of reciprocity in the home which outside the household would be regarded as a barrier to the efficient working of markets. We have here an interesting counterpoint between the *social* reciprocity and sharing which is held to distinguish, in part, peasant social relations from capitalist ones, and the *home* reciprocity which is seen as essential for the household to maximise its welfare in the context of a wider market economy.

(c) The single family utility function obscures and constitutes a barrier to the economic analysis of conflict and inequality in the home. In neoclassical economics conflict and exploitation cannot exist in the market because transactions do not occur unless both parties benefit from them. The altruism assumption ensures that they do not occur in the home either.

The assumption of altruism within the home underpins the new home economics theory which we introduced in Chapter 7. This theory appears at first sight to be a step forward in making household work visible to economic analysis. It recognises that work in the home has an opportunity cost in terms of the market wage; that it is productive work in that it contributes towards the material welfare of the household; and that the value of this work, costed at market wages, often exceeds the cash income obtained from work outside the home (e.g. King & Evenson, 1983).

In the new home economics the division of labour between women and men is explained by static comparative advantage in the maximisation of household welfare (Gronau, 1973). This means that individual household members specialise in those tasks at which they are relatively more efficient compared to other members. For example, if men and women are equally efficient at household chores, but men receive higher wages than women in the market, then men go out to work and women stay in the home.

It is recalled from Chapter 7 that Low (1986) uses this idea of comparative advantage to explain off-farm wage work by men and stagnation in farm output in Southern Africa. In this case the comparison was between different market wage rates for men and women and the same marginal product of labour for both sexes in farm production. Since men could obtain a market wage higher than the marginal product in farm work, they specialised in earning off-farm cash income. Likewise women faced a market wage lower than the farm marginal product and they stayed on the farm.

Static comparative advantage rules out social change which alters the status of women, unless it occurs through market forces. Thus a general rise in incomes might permit women to go out to work since it enables the purchase of labour-saving household technology. A rise in the market wage of women above that of men should in theory have the same effect.

The comparative advantage logic can be taken to somewhat bizarre lengths. For example, if the future wages of female children are predicted by the household to be lower than those of male children, then future-discounted welfare is maximised by depriving female children of current resources and putting these at the disposal of male children. This has been held to explain the high mortality rates of female children in some rural societies (Rosenzweig & Schultz, 1982).

This example gives some indication of the limitations of the comparative advantage principle. Its result is inconsistent with altruism. The direction of causation runs from the market to the utility function rather than the other way round, i.e. since the market is found to 'explain' female child neglect, it is inferred from this that the family utility function must contain a predisposition to treat female children unequally. The power relations of the household which permit this to occur are ignored. The failure of this logic to explain the more equal material treatment of children in other societies where boys and girls face unequal future earning potential is not explained.

Comparative advantage may go some way towards explaining the division of labour and resources in the home, but it does so in accordance with rules which ignore the social relations of the household:

(a) it relies on market prices as the sole explanatory force;
(b) it rules out all non-market reasons for the division of labour and resources in the home;
(c) it rules out men and women having unequal power in deciding household goals;
(d) it rules out men and women possessing areas of separate decision making in the home;
(e) in short, it captures only one facet – the opportunity cost of labour in the market – of the multi-faceted social concept of the gender division of labour.

Economics and intra-household relationships

There are many aspects of economic behaviour in the peasant farm household which cannot be explained by reference to a single utility function, comparative advantage, and market prices. A few commonplace examples are as follows:

(a) the much greater economic freedom often enjoyed by men

compared to women, including freedom in the disposal of cash income;

(b) the observed propensity of men to spend cash income on themselves, rather than, for example, on installing a water pipe which would save many hours of a woman's labour time;

(c) the social rigidity of task allocation, implying imperfect substitutability of male and female labour across different activities irrespective of relative market prices and returns to labour;

(d) the different access of women and men to productive resources, especially cultivable land, and their differing command over family labour time, and money for cash inputs;

(e) the preference of women for food crops over cash crops, perhaps in spite of lower returns for food crops measured in market prices;

(f) increasing work hours for women, and more leisure for men, following yield-increasing technical change in food production.

While instances like these are explained readily enough by reference to the social subordination of women, their impact on the material conditions of the household cannot be investigated if economic analysis stops at the door of the home. They include social constraints on the productivity and living standards of the household as a unit, in addition to the unequal status of women which they represent. On the other hand, since they involve non-market social relations of power, obligation, and custom between men and women, the economic method would seem to possess limited applicability to them.

One way forward is to recognise and build on the distinction between market and non-market areas of intra-household economic decisions. With respect to the latter Whitehead (1984: 93) uses the term *conjugal contract* to describe 'the terms on which husbands and wives exchange goods, incomes and services, including labour, within the household'. Women and men may also possess areas of independent economic action within which they are able to make decisions by reference to market criteria (e.g. women may be able to sell vegetables grown on their own plots). These areas are likely to be more constrained for women than for men, and this in itself is an important aspect of control over resource allocation and income distribution in the household.

The boundaries and content of the market/non-market distinction vary considerably between different peasant societies and, less so, across individual households within a given society. Nevertheless, it is possible to identify certain recurring patterns from the observation of women's role in different kinds of household farm system.

For example, a useful distinction has been made between the 'gender-specific' and the 'gender-sequential' farm work of women (Whitehead, 1984: 42–4). In the former, women work their own plots of land, separate from those of men, and carry out all the seasonal activities from sowing through to harvesting. In some cases, and most of the examples here come from Africa, women may also dominate in the marketing of the produce from their own farms which gives them a genuine degree of economic independence from men. This also means that the relationships of productivity and returns to women's work can be analysed, economically, separately from those of men.

In gender-sequential work, women and men work the same land, but there is a seasonal or task-specific division of labour in which, for example, men may do the ploughing, participate in the harvesting, and market the produce; women may do the weeding and spraying, participate in the harvesting, but have no hand in the marketing. In this case the work contribution of women is more likely to go unremunerated in terms of cash income; women lack economic independence; and they may work very long hours to improve the material welfare of the male head of the household rather than that of themselves or their children.

For some purposes it may be useful to consider the non-market area of household relationships as a *constraint* on farm output, in much the same way as fixed resources are constraints in linear programming (see Chapter 2). For example, the ability of women to allocate time to cultivation may be constrained in an absolute sense by prior obligations in the domains of reproduction and the daily maintenance of the household. Indeed this factor is pertinent in Low's (1986) explanation of farm stagnation in southern Africa, though the comparative advantage approach is not able to address the non-market character of this time allocation problem.

To construct a hypothetical example, consider a situation in which the woman of the farm household is wholly responsible for household chores, engages in the gender-specific production of the main food staple of the household, is responsible for feeding the entire household from this production, but receives none of the cash income from the sale of food which is surplus to household requirements. The situation of this woman can be illustrated by a production graph similar to those used throughout this book.

In Figure 9.1 the woman's total hours available are measured on the horizontal axis with farm work hours increasing from left to right, and household work hours from right to left. The production function of the food staple is measured in physical terms; it is a TPP curve. The graph shows two constraints: a minimum housework constraint, given as the vertical line T_2 which describes the irreducible number of hours which must be spent on household chores; and a minimum food consumption constraint, given as the horizontal line Q_1 which describes the subsistence needs of the household in terms of food.

It is clear that the only area of variation open to this woman peasant lies between A and B on the production function. It is also clear that this area of variation can readily be made to vanish either by raising the minimum consumption line or by moving the minimum household chores line towards the left. In other words the woman is in a straightjacket derived from the non-involvement of her man in household chores.

Assuming that an area of variation between A and B does exist, the question arises as to what determines the woman's labour input within this area. The neoclassical approach would be that this depends on her preference between extra income from the sale of food above household requirements and extra time which would permit her some 'leisure' in an otherwise toilsome day. In other words, it might occur at some point E, where her indifference curve trade off between income and time equals her

Figure 9.1. Time allocation of a farm woman.

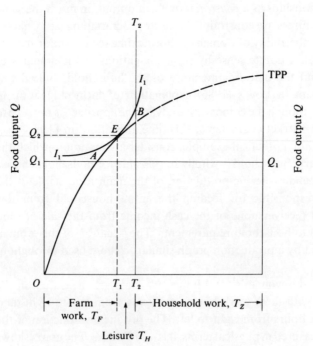

marginal value product in farm work, and this would permit her Q_2-Q_1 income and T_H hours of leisure.

This formulation raises some interesting issues. First, it dispenses with the family utility function and replaces it with a personal utility function for the woman. This may be considered dubious given the interdependence of household members, and it also places undue emphasis on the personal versus social determinants of this decision. Second, we have supposed that the male head of the household markets surplus food and pockets the cash. This means that on a personal utility basis extra income is zero, marginal utility of income is zero, and the indifference curve vanishes. Operation would then occur at point A, rather than E. Third, however, either altruism or the terms of the 'conjugal contract' may push the labour input to T_2 (point B on the production function) notwithstanding the absence of personal returns to extra labour time for this farm woman.

The outcome is inconclusive. To the extent that the female cultivator enjoys independence of action over this area of the production function then her operating position between A and B would depend both on her degree of altruism towards her husband and on her share of the surplus product. No altruism, no share, would dictate production at point A. However, rarely in peasant societies can individual women be thought to possess freedom of action in its neoclassical economic sense: social custom and obligation predominate over individual choice and decisions do not correspond to marginal utility criteria.

The main point made by Figure 9.1 is that the gender division of labour limits the scope for variation of personal labour time. This is emphasised further if we now assume that there exists a market for labour and a single wage which represents the opportunity cost of time for both men and women. This permits the economic optimum level of labour use in food production to be identified in the abstract from the social relations of the household. One possible such optimum position is shown in Figure 9.2 at point C, giving a total output of Q_3 and a labour input of T_3. At this point the marginal product of family labour would equal the market wage.

In this situation all points between A and B represent sub-optimal levels of labour use and output compared to the efficiency position. Thus a gender division of labour in which the man does not engage in food production results in lower output and incomes than would occur with more flexible labour use in the household. The optimum position at C could be reached either (a) by male involvement in household work, thereby releasing female labour time for food cultivation, or (b) by male involvement in food production to take the labour input from I_1 to I_3.

The impact of a rise in the price of the staple food which gives a new efficiency position at point D (the slope, w/p, of the wage cost line falls to zz') may also be considered. Whether this causes any increase in output depends on the critical factors already described, namely, first, the rigidity of the division of labour concerning household chores and, second, the extent to which men are prepared to engage in food production. In a situation which is negative on both these counts, it is possible that a zero or near zero response will prevail. Perhaps the woman would keep her labour input at point A throughout since she perceives no gain to be achieved by raising output above the minimum subsistence.

This model is purely illustrative. Its purpose is to suggest that certain analytical possibilities arise by disaggregating the farm household rather than treating it as an aggregate unit. The model is not, however, without some relevance to previous analysis in this book and to economic debates which have surrounded African peasant agriculture.

For example it gives a new dimension to the Chayanovian concept of family leisure preference since this is now seen to depend not just on household size and structure but also on the rigidities of time allocation between men and women in the household. In particular Chayanov ignored the importance of household chores for absorbing a large proportion of

Figure 9.2. Impact of a market wage.

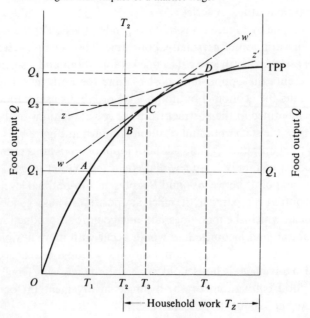

women's time, and this might result in low utility being attached to additional income by women where extra farm work extends the working day to absurd hours.

With respect to peasant agriculture in Africa, a number of writers have emphasised the division of both labour and cash income between men and women as important constraints on increased food production. These constraints become all the more severe where a division of labour develops (as it has done in some parts of Africa since colonial times) where men specialise in cash crop production, or wage labour off the farm, and food production is left in the hands of women who must also accomplish all the other household tasks.

The constraints are also tightened when seasonal factors are taken into account, since in African agriculture it is often the seasonal labour requirement (rather than land) which is the binding constraint on increased output. Hanger (1973) shows, using linear programming, how the joint output of several food and cash crops is significantly lower when a rigid gender division of labour between the crops is observed instead of flexible deployment of total family labour according to seasonal requirements. Moreover, the same constraints can wreck rural development projects based on wrong assumptions about male rights over land and male preparedness to deploy labour flexibly over both food and cash crop production.

In summary, this section is concerned with aspects of the economic organisation of the household which fall outside the scope of the family utility function and comparative advantage. It suggests that for practical purposes the non-market and market determinants of the division of labour and resources in the household must be distinguished. Non-market interactions may for certain purposes be identified as constraints on the flexible use of variable resources in farm production. This is because rigidities of time allocation, and unequal command over other resources, can result in the household being inflexible in its response to market forces. Where this is the case the subordination of women may sometimes be found to have a practical economic effect on the material conditions of survival of the household, quite apart from its meaning in terms of the inferior social status of farm women.

Policy aspects

The neglect of women in economic policies concerning peasant agriculture has tended to exacerbate the subordination of women and diminish the impact of policies designed to raise peasant output and incomes. The male bias of most agricultural development policy is well documented. It is invariably the male head of household who is approached to discuss new crops, new seeds, special credit facilities, improved input packages and so on. Extension workers are often male and relate exclusively to male peasants. Registration of private rights over traditional land is invariably made in male names even where the cultural tradition is for land to be passed down through the female line. Male peasants are encouraged to develop marketing skills and form farmer cooperatives even when women may have traditionally had an important role in such matters.

The impact of this male bias in agricultural policy is to diminish the status of women, isolate them increasingly in household work which may have previously been shared more equally by men, and reduce their economic independence while increasing that of men.

In order to reverse these trends, agricultural policy requires a conscious orientation towards women. Some main policy conclusions are as follows:

(a) National systems of data collection should attempt to obtain more accurate measurement of the productive contribution of women, the division of tasks within farm households, and the interaction between women and men in farm production.

(b) Women need to be taken into account much more than at present in the devising and implementation of agricultural projects, especially in regions where farm work and decision-making is largely in the domain of women. The same obviously holds true for farmer education and extension programmes.

(c) Many studies have concluded that the welfare of women can only effectively be improved by creating conditions in which they have sources of cash income independent of men. It is pointed out that helping women to become more productive is of little merit if the productivity gains accrue to men (Greeley, 1983). One proposal is the creation of marketing agencies, such as women-only cooperatives, which enable women to by-pass men altogether.

An evident problem with policy pleas for women is their implausibility in societies characterised by pervasive male dominance. The subordination of women never occurs in just some sectors or classes of society; it always permeates the social structure. Moreover, as is evidenced in certain industrial societies where feminist ideas have gained ground, the pace of change is very slow. For this reason small grassroots schemes for improving the situation of rural women may sometimes be more successful than projects which are more ambitious in their aims and scope, and which are thus more evidently threatening to the social status of men.

Summary

1 The purpose of this chapter is to explore the ways in which feminist issues can be drawn into the economic analysis of the peasant farm household.

2 The chapter begins by defining terms related to the role of women, and these include the concepts of the gender division of labour, of reproduction versus production, of non-wage work, and of subordination of women and patriarchy. These concepts place emphasis on the social, rather than biological or personal, determination of the division of labour and resources between women and men in the farm household.

3 Published evidence on patterns of time allocation in peasant households is summarised. It is observed that women often work much longer hours than men, that men participate little in household chores, that the farm labour input of women varies across different societies, that male and female labour is imperfectly substitutable across different activities, and that men predominate in activities which earn cash income.

4 The capacity of the new home economics to handle the gender division of labour is examined. This theory depends on a single family utility function and it thus rules out of its terms of reference social relations of power, obligation, conflict, or negotiation between men and women.

5 In the new home economics the division of labour between men and women is explained by static comparative advantage in the maximisation of family welfare. This comparative advantage can only be measured by reference to market prices, and thus non-market reasons for household economic behaviour cannot be captured or analysed.

6 In general the capacity of the economic method to deal with intra-household questions is limited by the non-market character of interpersonal relationships within the home. However, some scope for economic analysis exists by (a) distinguishing market from non-market areas of decision making, and (b) identifying areas of separate economic action open, unequally, to men and women.

7 An example is constructed to show how social rigidity in the allocation of tasks between men and women may lower farm output, and inhibit the capacity of the household to respond to

changes in market prices. Thus the social relations of the household do have implications for the efficiency of resource use in farm production, and these are to some degree susceptible to economic analysis.

8 On policy it is concluded that an active bias towards women is required in order to redress that typical male bias of agricultural development policies and projects. However it is also recognised that policies for rural women face formidable barriers in most societies.

9 In an important sense this chapter is a provisional attempt to identify the scope and limitations of economics for analysing interpersonal relationships within the farm household. A great deal more work needs to be done to define the limits of the economic method, to explore its relationship to social concepts, and to develop new concepts for analysing the division of labour between women and men in the household.

Notes

1 Some remarks are in order regarding data cited for Nepal and Java. The data for Nepal are simple averages calculated from figures covering eight separate rural samples (Acharya & Bennett, 1982:59). The data for Java are monthly hours divided by 30 and refer only to the 'Class I', peak month, sample (Hart, 1980: 204).

2 This is the definition given in *Chambers Twentieth Century Dictionary*, 1983 edition.

Further reading

A useful starting point for the economic study of women in peasant agriculture remains Boserup (1970). This needs to be supplemented in the first instance by advances in feminist theory which give greater precision to the social science analysis of women. Recommended here is the volume edited by Young *et al.* (1984), especially the papers by Mackintosh, Whitehead, and Harris. Also relevant are Beneria (1979), Beneria & Sen (1981), and Edholm, Harris & Young (1977). Secondly, an excellent review of the scope and limits of both neoclassical and Marxian theories of the household is given in Folbre (1986). The neoclassical theory of the family as a single welfare maximising unit is set out at length in Becker (1981), but summaries of this approach as given, for example, by Evenson (1976; 1981) and King & Evenson (1983), are more accessible and contain pertinent applications. There are several useful collections which contain papers on rural and farm women in developing countries and these are listed in the first section of the following reference list. Finally on time allocation and other economic aspects of women as peasants see, for *Africa*, McSweeney (1979), Nelson (1981), Hanger & Moris (1973); for *Asia*, Acharya & Bennett (1982), Cain, Khanam & Nahar (1979), King & Evenson (1983), IRRI (1985), Greeley (1983), Hart (1980); and for *Latin America*, Deere (1976; 1982) and Deere & Leon de Leal (1982).

Reading list

Useful collections

Afshar, H. (1985). *Women, Work, and Ideology in the Third World*. London: Tavistock.

Ahmed, I. (ed.) (1985). *Technology and Rural Women*. London: Allen & Unwin.

Beneria, L. (ed.) (1982). *Women and Development*. New York: Praeger.

Bunivic, M., Lycette, M.A. & McGreevey, W.P. (1983). *Women and Poverty in the Third World*. London: Johns Hopkins.

Hay, M.J. & Stichter, S. (eds.) (1984). *African Women South of the Sahara*. London: Longman.

International Rice Research Institute (IRRI) (1985). *Women in Rice Farming*. Aldershot: Gower.

Long, N. (ed.) (1984). *Family and Work in Rural Societies: Perspectives on Non-Wage Labour*. London: Tavistock.

Nelson, N. (ed.) (1981). *African Women in the Development Process*. London: Frank Cass.

Young, K. *et al.* (eds.) (1984). *Of Marriage and the Market*. 2nd edn. London: Routledge & Kegan Paul.

Time allocation studies

Acharya, M. & Bennett, L. (1982). *Women and the Subsistence Sector: Economic Participation and Household Decisionmaking in Nepal*. World Bank Staff Working Paper No. 526, Washington DC: World Bank.

Cain, M., Khanam, S.R. & Nahar, S. (1979). Class, patriarchy, and women's work in Bangladesh. *Population and Development Review*, Vol. 5, pp. 405–38.

Deere, C.D. (1982). The division of labour by sex in agriculture: a Peruvian case study. *Economic Development and Cultural Change*, Vol. 30, No. 4.

Hart, G. (1980). Patterns of household labour allocation in a Javanese village, Ch. 8 in Binswanger. H.P. *et al.* (eds.) *Rural Household Studies in Asia*, Singapore University Press.

King, E. & Evenson, R.E. (1983). Time allocation and home production in Philippine rural households. Ch. 3 in Buvinic *et al.* (eds.) (1983), pp. 35–61.

McSweeney, B.G. (1979). Collection and analysis of data on rural women's time use. *Studies in Family Planning*, Vol. 10, No. 11/12.

Other references

Becker, G.S. (1981). *A Treatise on the Family*. Cambridge, Mass.: Harvard University Press.

Beneria, L. (1979). Reproduction, production and the sexual division of labour. *Cambridge Journal of Economics*, No. 3.

Beneria, L. & Sen, G. (1981). Accumulation, reproduction, and women's role in economic development: Boserup revisited. *Signs*, Vol. 7, No. 2.

Boserup, E. (1970). *Woman's Role in Economic Development*, New York: Allen & Unwin.

Deere, C.D. (1976). Rural women's subsistence production in the capitalist periphery. *Review of Radical Political Economics*, Vol. 8, No. 1.

Deere, C.D. & Leon de Leal, M. (1982). Peasant production, proletarianization, and the sexual division of labor in the Andes. In Beneria, L. (ed.) *Women and Development*. New York: Praeger.

Edholm, F., Harris, O. & Young, K. (1977). Conceptualising women, *Critique of Anthropology*. Vol. 3, Nos. 9/10.

Evenson, R.E. (1976). On the new household economics. *Journal of Agricultural Economics and Development*, Vol. 6, pp. 87–103.

Evenson, R.E. (1981). Food policy and the new home economics. *Food Policy*, August.

Folbre, N. (1986). Hearts and spades: paradigms of household economics. *World Development*, Vol. 14, No. 2.

Hanger, E.J. & Moris, J. (1973). Women and the household economy. In Chambers, R. & Moris, J. (eds.) *MWEA: An Irrigated Rice Settlement in Kenya*, pp. 209–44. Munich: Weltforum Verlag.

Greeley, M. (1983). Patriarchy and poverty: a Bangladesh case study. *South Asian Research*, Vol. 3, No. 1.

Part IV

Farm size, technical change, overview

10

Farm size and factor productivity

Peasants and farm size

We turn in this chapter to a proposition which looms large in debates about strategies of agricultural development and the future of peasants. The proposition is that small farms make more efficient use of resources than large farms. The well-known policy implication of this proposition is that an agricultural development strategy based on the promotion of small rather than large farms can serve both growth and income distribution objectives. This simultaneous achievement of both efficiency and equity through small farm development deserves careful scrutiny. It implies compatibility between two aspects of economic life in a market economy which are more typically thought to work in opposition to each other.

The topic of farm size and relative productivity brings together a number of strands which have featured in previous chapters of this book. It links together issues of technical and price efficiency, land ownership structure, social differentiation, peculiarities of factor markets, and agrarian reform. It also involves the disentangling of various economic concepts related to farm size and scale of enterprise which can be, and are, sometimes muddled in comparisons of the economic attributes of different kinds of farms.

A few preliminary observations concerning the strategic significance of the farm size question help to place this topic in context. It has already been noted in earlier chapters that agrarian change under capitalism contains various opposing forces acting on the stability of peasant forms of farm production. Some of these forces – access to land, partial and varying engagement in the market, flexibility of resource use, social reciprocity – tend to conserve the peasant economy. Others – increased specialisation, higher dependence on market transactions, more competitive markets –

may tend to push peasants in the direction of family farm enterprises. Still others – distress land sales by poor peasants, concentration of land holdings, debt, monopoly power – tend to disintegrate the peasant economy and result in the emergence of capitalist farm enterprises hiring wage labour.

In the absence of state intervention the long run outcome of these forces is unpredictable and is likely to vary widely in different locations. Population pressure on land is obviously important, as also is the historical land ownership structure and the effects of changing technology. In many developing countries these factors appear to favour the growth of larger farms, while the small farm sector is increasingly marginalised.

A situation of zero state intervention is, however, rather hypothetical. Since in many countries land ownership and political power are closely related a built-in tendency to favour large landowners over small peasants often exists. Moreover, an earlier orthodoxy in development studies, which still has its adherents the world over, favoured a conscious bias by the state towards large commercial farms. The reason for this was the perceived need for agriculture to yield various surpluses, including a high marketed surplus of food, to assist the goal of rapid industrialisation. It was thought that the subsistence basis and other limitations of 'traditional' agriculture could not perform this role.

The advocacy of a small farm strategy clearly has much with which to contend. Not only does it oppose the weight of much received wisdom about modernisation and economic growth, but it also comes up against political and economic forces which tend to work in the opposite direction. The strategy is based on the capacity of the small farm sector to substitute for, and even possibly surpass, the marketed output performance of large farms, while at the same time fulfilling employment and equity goals which large farms do not meet. This does not, however, solve the problem of its political acceptance nor that of the pace and direction of agrarian change occurring outside the limits of state action.

The purpose of this chapter is to examine the logic of the case for a small farm bias in development strategy. At various points special attention is given to what is meant by small farms and large farms respectively. The arguments in favour of small farms tend to slide rather uneasily around distinctions purely in terms of *area* size, distinctions of economic *scale*, and distinctions of *kind* of farm enterprise (family versus capitalist). This confuses the logic of the case and results in areas of ambiguity which require clarification.

The chapter proceeds as follows. The next section examines the economic concepts of scale and farm size which need to be kept in mind throughout the chapter. The third section considers the central argument that farm efficiency is inversely related to farm size. The nature of the evidence, its proximate causes, and its possible defects are examined. The fourth section deals with the major economic explanation of the inverse relationship located in different relative factor prices confronting different kinds of farms. The section is thus concerned with the distinction between social and private efficiency in farm production. The fifth section summarises the strands of the argument and looks again at the strategic and policy issues to which they give rise.

Economic concepts of scale and farm size

Debates about the appropriate size of farms and the existence or not of economies of farm size are often confusing due to the mixing of concepts with different meanings. A common problem is the confusion of the area size of farms with their economic size as units of production. The former treats farm size as described solely by the physical quantity of the single resource, land, available for production. The latter treats farm size as a description of the total economy of the farm as an enterprise, and this might be measured by the joint volume of resources used in production, by gross farm output, or by the quantity of capital (both fixed and working) tied up in farm production.

For reasons of directness and simplicity we use the term 'farm size' in this chapter to refer only to the area size of farms. This is the perception of the term which springs most immediately to the mind of most people, and it avoids confusion in subsequent discussion. The term 'scale of farm enterprise' or simply 'farm scale' is used to describe differences in the overall economic size of farms.

The concept of scale has a pure definition in economics which is more of theoretical than practical intent. It is recalled from Chapter 2 that in microeconomics changes of scale refer very precisely to the simultaneous increase of *all* productive resources in the same proportion. If this simultaneous and identical increase in all resources results in the same percentage increase in output, it is referred to as *constant returns to scale*; if it results in a smaller percentage increase in output it is *diminishing returns to scale*; and if it results in a larger percentage increase in output it is *increasing returns to scale*.

The reason for specifying a pure concept of scale in this way is to make clear the analytical distinction between the effect of increasing scale, on the one hand, and the effect of varying the level of some resources while holding others fixed, on the other. The received wisdom on returns to scale in agriculture is that they tend to be constant. In other words if 100 days of labor, one bullock pair, and one hectare of land produce 3 metric tons of paddy, then 200 days of labour, two bullock pairs, and two hectares of land would produce 6 metric tons of paddy.

In practice equal across-the-board changes in resource use are rarely, if ever, observed. While a farm family might be able to double the use of variable inputs like labour and fertilizer, and may even sometimes be able to double the land under cultivation, it would be rare for all items of fixed capital (buildings, machinery etc.) to be doubled, and impossible for the farm family to duplicate itself. For this reason the term 'scale' is often used in an impure way, to refer to a large change in the volume of resources committed to production (e.g. the purchase of a tractor) without adhering to the equal percentage change in all inputs. Such changes perforce involve some element of varying factor proportions as well as pure scale effects because the equal increase in *all* resources no longer holds.

An example of a large shift in farm resource use which is sometimes confused with the pure concept of scale is farm mechanisation. Machines are *indivisible* resources the services of which are not typically available in continuous small increments (unless a competitive market exists for the hire of machine services, which is rare). The purchase of a machine, such as a tractor of given size, thus involves variations in production costs according to the quantities of other resources combined with this fixed resource. Indivisible resources, like tractors, result in cost economies related to their optimum level of use. These cost economies are sometimes rather inaccurately referred to as 'economies of scale'.

Even though conceptually distinct, resource indivisibility and farm scale are related when it comes to defining optimum scale in farming. This is because the cost economies associated with indivisible resources have a direct impact on the volume of output – the scale – which minimises unit production costs in the short and long run.

The standard textbook treatment of cost economies is the U-shaped average cost curve in the theory of the firm (Figure 10.1). Average fixed costs (the AFC curve) decline steeply as the utilisation of a fixed resource, like a tractor, increases until the resource is used to its physical capacity. When combined with average variable costs (the AVC curve) which rise with diminishing returns to variable factors, we get an average total cost (ATC) curve which is U-shaped, and which defines a minimum total cost for the prevailing level of farm technology.

The theory of the firm predicts that competition will force all farms towards operation at the minimum point on the ATC curve (point *E* in Figure 10.1). This minimum point then defines the *optimum scale of enterprise* for a given technology of farm production. This optimum scale of enterprise has, as one of its aspects, an area size required to operate at minimum unit cost, and it is in this sense that optimum farm size is defined.

More generally the optimum scale of enterprise in farming may be defined as the scale which minimises average unit production costs in the long run, and this scale will change with advances in farm technology. At a particular moment in time the optimum scale results from opposing cost economies and diseconomies for a given technology.

Cost economies are thought to result from:

(a) the indivisibility of fixed capital (declining unit costs as capacity utilisation increases);
(b) specialisation of tasks and division of labour on the farm;
(c) market economies in the bulk purchase of variable inputs or bulk sales of output (in the tropics likely to apply only to plantation enterprises).

Cost diseconomies are associated with:

(a) limits to effective management and supervision of labour as scale increases;

Figure 10.1. Cost curves and optimum scale.

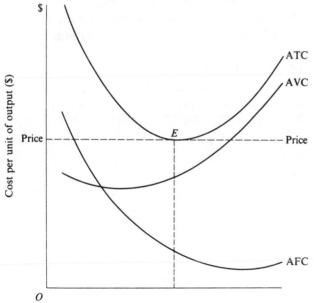

(b) limits to the detailed grasp of agronomic factors over larger land areas;

(c) the changing nature of risk as the scale of farm enterprise increases.

Amongst these, indivisible resources are by far the most common reason for notions of economies of farm size in agriculture. Indivisible machines often require a larger area size of farm in order to achieve minimum average costs, and changes in this kind of mechanical technology are thus held to be the principal cause of increases in average farm size in the industrial countries. However, the decision to purchase such machines in the first instance depends on the relative cost of capital against labour, and it is around this that much of the debate about farm size in the developing countries revolves. Management limitations are often cited as the main diseconomies which ultimately limit the area size of farms.

Two further terms require clarification in the context of farm size and scale. These are *intensive* and *extensive* cultivation. The most common use of these terms is to refer to the quantity of other resources which combine with a given amount of land. Thus a small area size of farm combined with large quantities of other resources is referred to as *intensive cultivation*, while a large area size of farm combined with small quantities of other resources is *extensive cultivation*. This is the sense in which the terms are used here. However the reader should note that some economists refer to 'land intensive cultivation' meaning exactly the opposite – a large quantity of land compared to other resources. Note also that in our sense of the terms, more intensive cultivation implies increased scale of enterprise for a given land area.

In summary, farm size and farm scale are distinct concepts with different meanings. The former refers only to the area size of farms, the latter to their total economic size in terms of all resources used in production. The concept of optimum farm size refers to the area size of farm which minimises the long run average unit cost of production for the given technology confronting all farmers. Optimum farm size will obviously vary for different crops, different crop-specific technologies, relative factor prices, and the balance between size-related cost economies and diseconomies. Finally intensive cultivation refers to small farm size with relatively large inputs of other resources, while extensive cultivation refers to large farm size with low inputs of other resources.

Inverse relationship of farm size and productivity

It is convenient to examine the relationship of farm size and productivity in two separate steps. The first step focuses on the physical productivity of farms of different sizes. It is thus concerned with relative technical efficiency. The second step focuses on factor market imperfections which result in different outcomes for small and large farms of correct private allocative behaviour by both of them. The two steps are linked because it is the differences in the factor prices they confront which result in large farms adopting technologies which are socially less efficient than those of small farms.

To anticipate the results of later discussion, it is the way factor markets work, and especially rural labour markets, which is the decisive factor in the logic of the inverse relationship. First, however, we consider technical aspects of this proposition.

The point of departure for comparisons of physical productivity is the output of farms per unit area of land. Here a volume of evidence across different countries seems to reveal an inverse relationship between farm size and yields per unit area. A fair proportion of this evidence is collected and analysed in Berry & Cline (1979). For illustrative purposes we reproduce parts of two tables from that book here. The first of these refers to a farm survey undertaken in northeast Brazil in the early 1970s, and we cite the figures for Zone A of that survey in Table 10.1.

This example has its own peculiarities. The range of farm sizes is large, and the gross outputs per unit area indicate an agriculture of low productivity throughout. But the example serves to reveal in an extreme form the strength of the inverse relationship which has excited attention in the literature. The second example refers to a survey undertaken across India, again in the early 1970s, and extracts from the relevant table are given in Table 10.2.

Again a continuous decline in the area productivity of farms appears to occur as farm size increases, such that the productivity of the largest size category of farms is less than half that of the smallest category. More

Table 10.1

Size group (ha)	Average farm size (ha)	Gross output per hectare ($US)
0–9.9	3.7	85.92
10–49.9	25.5	30.73
50–99.9	71.9	16.19
100–199.9	138.9	8.80
200–499.9	313.2	5.00
500 and over	1178.0	2.20

Source: Berry & Cline (1979: Table 4–1, p. 46)

research has been undertaken on this inverse relationship in India than elsewhere, and its validity is one of the most debated issues in Indian agricultural economics. We return to some of the conceptual and statistical problems below, but in the meantime we consider the proximate technical reasons for the inverse relationship which are noted in various studies.

(a) *Land use intensity.* Average figures for land productivity such as those cited in the Tables 10.1 and 10.2 are obtained by dividing total farm output (or value added, or net farm income) by the total area of farms. In many cases the inverse relationship of farm size and yield is explained by a parallel inverse relationship between farm size and the proportion of farm area in productive use. In other words declining land productivity as farm size increases results from underutilisation of the total land area available.

(b) *Output composition.* The output composition of larger farms may be oriented more towards land extensive enterprises (like livestock pasturing) or lower value crops than smaller farms.

(c) *Multiple cropping.* Smaller farms have been found to do more multiple cropping than larger farms, for the same crop (such as paddy) in the same locations. The effect of multiple cropping is, of course, to raise the total output value for a given area of land. In this context a distinction is sometimes made between *net sown area*, which counts a given amount of land only once in yield calculations, and *gross sown area* which counts land twice when it is used for two successive crops.

(d) *Soil fertility.* Large farms may have on average less fertile soils than small farms, and various explanations have been given for this. One is that high population density and fragmentation of holdings tend to occur in locations of high natural soil fertility. Another is that large farms only 'improve' the best land within their total farm area and ignore the productive potential of less favourable land. However, the relationship of fertility and farm size is unproven as a general hypothesis, even though it may occur in some locations.

Table 10.2

Size group (acres)	Average farm size (acres)	Income per acre (Rupees)
0–5	2.95	737
5–15	9.3	607
15–25	19.5	482
Over 25	42.6	346

Source: Bhalla (1979) in Berry & Cline, Table A–1, p. 149

(e) *Irrigation.* Some studies reveal an inverse relationship between farm size and the proportion of the total farm area under irrigation. Where this occurs it evidently gives one technical reason for the inverse yield relationship.

(f) *Labour intensity.* Allied to the inverse yield relationship is an inverse relationship between farm size and the quantity of labour used per unit area. Smaller farms use more labour per unit area than large farms (see Berry & Cline (1979) for evidence on this). Higher labour intensity helps to explain other factors like the higher amount of double cropping on small farms.

The pattern of ideas which emerge from these points may now be drawn out. First, the proposed superior efficiency of smaller farms rests largely on the intensity of utilisation of land as a resource, *not* in differences of yields per hectare on a strictly comparable basis. Thus the logic is not that the yield of a single crop of maize or rice under the same conditions is higher on small farms than that on large farms. Rather it is that larger farms *underutilise the total land area at their disposal* in comparison to smaller farms. And this relative underutilisation of land may occur due to a lower proportion of land being used for production, lower value of outputs, less double cropping, less irrigation, or generally less commitment of other resources which combine with land to produce output.

The explanation of lower land utilisation by larger farmers must be sought outside the technical conditions of production. Specifically it is thought to reside in the much lower implicit price of land for larger than for smaller farms, and this is part of the factor market aspect to which we turn in the next section.

An alternative explanation is that large landowners sometimes hold or purchase land for reasons other than its use as a productive resource. One reason thought to be relevant in countries with unstable economies and periodic high inflation is the holding of land as a portfolio investment. Another is for reasons of social prestige and the political influence this prestige confers. In both these cases landowners are likely to derive their income from non-farm economic activity (they are absentee landowners), and their possession of land represents either a hedge against inflation or a form of consumption as distinct from productive investment.

Second, lower intensity of land use as farm size increases means lower use of other inputs per unit area of land. The existence of lower labour use with increasing farm size is well documented, and like the use of land its explanation is sought in peculiarities of the way labour markets work for small and large farms respectively. Lower use of other inputs is not so well documented. There are evident problems of comparability where labour is substituted by machines and farms of different sizes operate with different technologies.

Third, the scale of farm enterprise has not so far entered the argument. Declining yields with larger farm size could be consistent with decreasing returns to scale, but because land is not the only factor of production the two are not necessarily linked. If decreasing returns to scale were found to be important then this would suggest that it was the kind of farm (family versus wage labour) rather than the size of farm which was the operative factor at work. This is because diseconomies of both scale and size seem to be related to the management function rather than to other economic considerations.

Various objections have been made to the inverse physical relationship, both with respect to its statistical validity in certain cases (particularly in the Indian context) and to its economic limitations. Here we note briefly the nature of some of these objections before turning to the factor price question.

(a) Size class averages can obviously obscure a great deal, and may lead to the spurious finding of a continuously inverse correlation where none exists in the underlying data. Many of the major studies of inverse relationship publish their findings without any indication of the standard deviation of yields around the mean levels in each class. These standard deviations could be large for all size classes, implying that yields in reality vary randomly over the entire range of farm sizes (Barbier, 1984).

(b) The area ranges of the size classes can be manipulated to show declining yields, when alternative ranges on the same data would show constant or increasing yields. An interesting example of the effect of changing the area ranges which define class sizes is given in Barbier (1984). It shows for an Indian case study how the finding of lower cropping intensity as farm size increases disappears when the size classes are changed.

(c) Scale may be much more important than is suggested by the area based studies (Patnaik, 1972). The finding that yields decline with farm size does not imply that they decline with farm scale, and, indeed, Patnaik finds the opposite: yields increase with true scale. Since size and scale need not be closely related, especially in the Indian context where the difference between a large and small farm is often taken to be greater than or less than 10 acres, the undue fascination with farm size results in an inaccurate perception of variations in farm efficiency. We shall return to this point later.

(d) Partial productivity measures, like yields or labour product, inevitably result in ambiguity about the relative efficiency of farms of different sizes. Land productivity is low when labour productivity is high (e.g. on mechanised farms) and vice versa. Farm efficiency comparisons should be based on the productivity of all factors of production, not the land area alone. This is notoriously difficult to measure because resources can only be aggregated in value terms, and many problems attend on the prices used and on the measurement of fixed capital between farms. One approach is to value resources at prices which are thought to reflect social, rather than private, scarcity values (see below). Berry & Cline (1979) contains examples of total factor productivity analysis, and the results seem to confirm the inverse relationship for overall farm efficiency.

Imperfect factor markets and social efficiency

So far we have observed (a) that yields seem to decline with farm size, (b) that this decline reflects variations in the intensity of land utilisation between small and large farms, (c) that the labour intensity of production likewise declines with farm size, and (d) that aside from partial explanations such as prestige land holding these variations require an economic explanation outside the technical conditions of farm production. Such an economic explanation exists, and it is at the core of the emphasis on small farm development in a number of major works on rural development (Griffin, 1979; Johnston & Kilby, 1975; Lipton, 1977).

The explanation is that small farmers confront different factor prices to large farmers due to imperfections in factor markets. Specifically, small farmers confront a low price for labour combined with high prices for land and for capital; while large farmers confront a higher price for labour combined with low prices for land and for capital. These differences in relative factor prices result in:

(a) small farmers committing more labour to production than large farmers;

(b) large farmers treating land as a relatively abundant resource even in a land scarce economy;

(c) large farmers substituting machines for labour even in the capital scarce, labour abundant, economy;

(d) large farmers being overall less *socially efficient* agricultural producers than small farmers.

The concept of *social prices* is critical to this explanation, since it provides both an implicit benchmark against which actual prices are compared and the basis of the inferred social inefficiency of large farms. Social prices refer to the opportunity cost of resources for the economy at large. Thus in a labour abundant, land and capital scarce, economy the social price of labour is low and the social prices of both land and capital are high. It is argued that if competitive conditions were to prevail in such an economy all farms would use labour intensive techniques in preference to land extensive or capital intensive alternatives.

By reference to these social prices small farmers confront an implicit labour cost which is lower than the social wage, and land and capital prices which are higher than their social value. Large farmers, by contrast, face labour costs which are above the social wage, and land and capital prices which are below their social levels. This induces large farmers to substitute capital for labour and hence to adopt socially inefficient techniques of production.

These points may be illustrated by reference to an isoquant diagram as in Figure 10.2. In this diagram all farmers face the same technical substitution possibilities between labour (L) and inputs of working and fixed capital (K), as indicated by the single isoquant, Q. Big farmers confront relative factor prices (isocost line bb') such that labour is expensive and capital inputs are cheap. Optimum resource allocation for them occurs at point F. Small farmers confront relative factor prices (isocost line ss') such that labour is inexpensive and capital inputs are dear. Their optimum resource allocation occurs at point D, implying higher labour use and less capital input for a given output than big farmers.

Figure 10.2. Optimal factor proportions for big and small farmers.

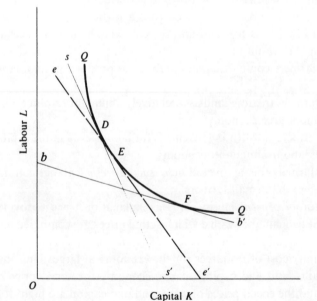

Social efficiency prices occur somewhere between the price ratios experienced by big and small farmers. Relative resource availabilities in most developing countries would suggest that social efficiency prices are closer to the prices confronted by small farmers than large farmers, as indicated by the broken isocost line ee' and equilibrium point E in Figure 10.2. This means that the factor proportions of big farmers tend to depart more from the socially optimal resource combinations than do those of small farmers.

Small and big farmers confront different factor prices due to imperfections in factor markets. The nature of these factor market imperfections are considered here, taking each major resource in turn.

Land

There are various reasons why land as a resource may appear cheap to the large landowner and expensive to the small peasant. In most countries the land ownership structure is a legacy of lengthy phases of past history. It changes relatively little in a lifetime, let alone in the short or medium term. Large landowners inherit their landholdings from their forebears, they themselves may have little connection with the land, and they may undervalue its merits as a productive resource. Further, large farmers are able to finance land purchases with loans from formal credit institutions at comparatively low rates of interest (see also capital below). Moreover, land tends to become concentrated into larger holdings when small farmers are forced into sale by accumulated debt or imminent starvation (distress sales), at which point the land is at its lowest price within a general context of land scarcity.

For small farmers none of these conditions prevail. They may also acquire land by inheritance, but often in inadequate amounts (due to fragmentation) for optimum farm operation. They have no financial capacity to finance land purchases and can only borrow money at exorbitant rates of interest. Many small farmers rent land either as cash tenants or sharecroppers, and in both cases their payment for the use of land is above the market clearing price which would prevail in a more competitive land market (see chapter 8).

Capital

The nature of imperfections in rural capital markets was noted earlier in this book in the context of sharecropping and interlocked factor markets. For various reasons – size of money income, risk of default, lack of collateral – small farmers rarely have access to formal channels of credit at competitive interest rates. Instead they tend to depend on local moneylenders, traders, or landowners as the source of credit at interest rates which reflect the peculiarities of each transaction rather than a market clearing condition.

Large farmers, by contrast, tend to have access to formal financial institutions, and they are better placed to take advantage of subsidised credit schemes when these are on offer. There are other reasons too why capital may be cheap to those farmers in a position to purchase capital goods. For example, overvalued exchange rates, common in many developing countries, artificially reduce the price of imported capital goods.

Labour

We have left labour until last here because the arguments about the relative price of labour for small and large farms are more subtle and complex than those for the other factor markets. Moreover, many writers consider that the way labour markets work is the critical feature of the farm size question.

Most explanations of the different labour costs confronting small and large farms are based on some version of *labour market dualism*. Dualism decidedly shifts the emphasis of the argument from the area size of farms to their type of production, and specifically to the way labour enters production in family labour versus hired labour (capitalist) farms.

For the family labour farm the marginal product of labour (MVP_L) is not determined by equalisation to the market wage, but by subjective criteria internal to the family (Chapter 6). It is thought that in locations of high population density, scarce land, and small farm size, the marginal product of labour on family farms is pushed beyond the point of equality to the market wage. Thus the marginal product of labour is below the market wage and may even tend towards zero (Sen, 1962; 1964). The internal family 'wage' is the share of each working member in the total value product of the farm, i.e. it is the *average* product of labour which is higher than the marginal product of labour. A floor to the market wage is set by the average product of labour on family farms, since households do not hire out labour at a wage below their average product.

Even if the farm family were willing to hire out labour on a marginal product equivalent basis, it would discount market wages by the risk attached to job search, and this would place the market wage, w, well above the MVP of labour in the family farm sector. Thus if the probability of finding a job were only p ($p < 1$), then the market wage, w, would need to be at least high enough to make $p \cdot W$ equal to the MVP of labour in order to attract any labour. Or, to give an example, if the probability of finding a job is 50 per cent and the MVP of labour on the family farm is $1.00 per day, then the market wage would need to be at least $2.00 per day for family labour to offer itself in the labour market. In this example the market wage would need to be twice the marginal product of labour in family farms.

From the labour hiring side, there are also downward rigidities in the formation of wages. One explanation of this is the so-called 'efficiency wage hypothesis' which applies more to the employment of landless labour with no other source of income than to peasant households. In this the wage needs to be at least high enough to ensure the bodily strength of the worker, for at lower wages the worker would not be able to purchase enough to eat and work performance would decline. Another explanation is seasonality, timeliness, and dependability of labour supply since the correct quantity of labour in peak periods is essential.

These labour market imperfections provide the most convincing explanation of the various physical productivity relationships which have been observed. Family farms make intensive use of labour at low marginal productivity and thus obtain the highest possible yields per unit area of land. They are also better placed to even out seasonal variability in the labour requirements of farming, and one of the ways they do this is by double cropping.

Large farms employ labour at the market wage, w, which is above the marginal product of labour in the farm sector at large. By operating with a labour use which equates their internal marginal product of labour to this wage, they employ too little labour and are *socially inefficient*. Moreover, where large farms find themselves in a monopoly position in local labour markets, they may restrict labour use even further in order to avoid driving up the market wage against themselves. Finally, large farms may find that it is uneconomic from a private perspective to keep hiring and firing labour over successive peaks of labour demand, and may therefore restrict themselves to one annual crop even when two successive crops are possible.

Taken together these factor market imperfections provide an array of reasons for promoting small, or family, farm development rather than emphasising large farms. From this strategic perspective, other reasons are added to those already discussed. An extension of the dual factor markets proposition is that small farms could be even more productive if they were able to acquire land or credit at nearer the social efficiency prices of those resources. This is due to the *complementarity* of abundant labour with variable inputs, like new seeds or fertilizer, which require high labour time in soil preparation or application. Small farms are thus thought to require relatively small quantities of additional non-labour resources to result in large gains in additional output. Large farms, in contrast, require large quantities of capital to achieve the same yield increases using mechanised technology. Since capital is a scarce resource this is a socially inefficient alternative for achieving output growth in agriculture.

Further considerations

We are now in a position to draw together the threads of the argument about farm size and to review its strengths and its weaknesses. The main *empirical* basis of the argument is the observation of lower physical productivity per unit of area as farm size increases, and this seems to turn mainly on lower intensity of land use by larger farms compared to smaller ones. Its main *economic* basis is that large farms confront different relative factor prices from small farms which lead them either (a) to treat land as a relatively abundant resource using extensive methods of production, or (b) to substitute capital for labour through farm mechanisation. In both cases these economic decisions reflect the departure of private prices from social opportunity costs, and they result in a socially inefficient allocation of resources.

The outcome is that the pursuit of a small farm, rather than large farm, strategy of agricultural development simultaneously achieves greater social efficiency of resource use in agriculture and greater social equity via the employment creation and more equal income distribution attributes of small farms. One way this strategy has been posed is as a *unimodal* farm size strategy, in contrast to the *bimodal* strategy which results from the neglect of the small farm sector and the promotion of large commercial farms (Johnston & Kilby, 1975).

In some countries a prior condition for the pursuit of such a strategy is a massive change in the ownership structure of land. This is because the private ownership of land is so heavily skewed towards large holdings that no amount of tinkering with relative prices or taxes could produce the desired shift in land allocation. Thus *agrarian reform* is often a prerequisite of a small farm strategy. Generally the policy conclusions of the farm size argument are:

(a) that development resources should be committed to the small rather than the large farm sector;

(b) that where there are investment choices (say, in new crop production schemes) they should take the form of small rather than large farm projects;

(c) that factor price distortions which favour mechanisation and expansion of farm size should be removed.

The farm size argument contains certain ambiguities which need to be considered. Three linked aspects which we consider briefly here are (a) the neglect of scale, (b) the dividing line between large and small, and (c) the small versus family farm distinction.

First, the relative neglect of scale in making comparisons between farms may result in an inaccurate perception of the kind and size of farm which it is desirable to promote for strategic reasons. Area size and scale are not continuously related in the way the inverse hypothesis suggests, and, indeed, ranking by scale may display an opposite trend of area productivity to ranking by size (Patnaik, 1972). The optimum farm size for strategic purposes requires some combination of scale and area size considerations. If only the area size is taken, then the logic of the argument suggests that land should be divided into the smallest possible parcels on which families could survive. However, while this might maximise employment and equalise incomes at a minimum survival level, it would cause the marketed surplus to disappear and prohibit output growth. Some farm size above this minimum level is needed to permit a positive impact on output and marketed supply from increases in the intensity of resource use.

Second, the dividing line between small and large is often arbitrary and not dictated by economic logic. For example, in the Indian literature 10 acres is often taken as the dividing line in statistical studies, but there are infinite gradations of types of farm (family with no hiring, family with hiring, pure hiring, sharecropping), resource intensity, and cropping intensities in a wide range around this figure. Again the singular fascination with area size obscures many other factors which require definition for strategic purposes.

Third, we have noted several components of the farm size argument in which it is the family farm, not the farm size *per se*, which seems to be the decisive factor. This applies especially to labour market dualism, but it also lurks in the background of the entire bundle of propositions about efficiency. Family farmers are said to have more direct motivation, more intrinsic grasp of the agronomic attributes of their land, more flexibility in seasonal labour deployment, and so on. Capitalist farms, by contrast, have supervision and motivation problems with labour, rigidities of seasonal employment, and less detailed knowledge of the land and its capabilities.

These three points are linked by the *type of farm* which should form the basis of agricultural development. Advocates of the small farm strategy clearly have a preference for family farms over capitalist farms, but this is not always made explicit. Making it explicit provides a sharper basis for resolving the ambiguities of appropriate farm size, since the upper limits would be determined by the size which can be managed by family members with minimum recourse to hired labour.

Summary

1 This chapter examines the proposition that the productivity of resource use in agriculture is inversely related to the area size of farms.

2 This proposition is based in part on the observation of physical productivity differences between farms of different sizes, and in part on departures of factor prices from the social opportunity cost of resources.

3 The physical productivity aspect rests mainly on declining yields as farm size increases, reflecting less intensive land use with increasing farm size.

4 The factor price aspect explains the lower intensity of land use by reference to different factor prices confronting large and small farmers.

5 These price differences occur due to imperfections in land, capital, and labour markets which result in prices which differ from their social efficiency values.

6 A decisive aspect is the working of rural labour markets which, due to dualism and efficiency wage effects, result in the market wage being above the social opportunity cost of labour. This encourages the inefficient substitution of labour by capital in the labour-abundant economy.

7 Certain ambiguities of the argument are drawn out. It is often unclear where the cut off point between small and large farms lies; the argument is somewhat ambiguous as to whether it is the smallness of size or the family basis of small farms which is the decisive attribute; and neglect of relationships of scale which may differ from those of area size is a significant omission.

8 In brief conclusion an array of economic reasons can be deduced for promoting small, family, farms in labour-abundant agrarian economies. In the terms of this book, this implies emphasis on the transition of peasants into competitive family farmers rather than capitalist farmers, as well as the creation of new family farms from larger land holdings. The political problems of the latter should not be minimised. While small farm bias may be well founded in pure economic logic, it is perhaps rather naive in its sense of political processes and the rhythm of capitalist development.

Further reading

Perhaps the best textbook introduction to economic concepts of farm scale and size remains that given in Heady (1952, Ch. 12). It may seem strange to refer to a textbook published so long ago, but most recent agricultural economics texts (such as those cited at the end of Chapter 2) tend to give scale and size only passing mention. The logic and evidence of the inverse relationship of farm size and productivity are treated at length in Berry & Cline (1979). Factor market imperfections and social efficiency are given most explicit treatment in Griffin (1979, Ch. 2), but they are also crucial throughout Lipton (1977). A useful summary of the meaning of relative economic efficiency is contained in the first few pages of Barnum & Squire (1978). Lastly the Indian debate on this question provides a wealth of interesting material amongst which the following are recommended in date order: Sen (1962), Khusro (1964), Patnaik (1972), Bardhan (1973), Chattopadyhay & Rudra (1976), Carter (1984), and Barbier (1984).

Reading list

Barbier, P. (1984). Inverse relationship between farm size and land productivity: a product of science or imagination? *Economic and Political Weekly*, Vol. XIX, Nos. 52 & 53.

Bardhan, P.K. (1973). Size, productivity and returns to scale: an analysis of farm level data in Indian agriculture. *Journal of Political Economy*, Vol. 18, pp. 1370–86.

Barnum, H.N. & Squire, L. (1978). Technology and relative economic efficiency. *Oxford Economic Papers*, Vol. 30.

Berry, R.A. & Cline, W.R. (1979). *Agrarian Structure and Productivity in Developing Countries*. Baltimore: Johns Hopkins.

Carter, M.R. (1984). Identification of the inverse relationship between farm size and productivity: an empirical analysis of peasant agricultural production. *Oxford Economic Papers*, Vol. 36, pp. 131–45.

Chattopadhyay, M. & Rudra, A. (1976). Size-productivity revisited. *Economic and Political Weekly*, Review of Agriculture. Sept.

Griffin, K. (1979). *The Political Economy of Agrarian Change: An Essay on the Green Revolution*. 2nd edn. London: Macmillan.

Heady, E.O. (1952). *Economics of Agricultural Production and Resource Use*. Englewood Cliffs, New Jersey: Prentice-Hall.

Khusro, A.M. (1964). Returns to scale in Indian Agriculture. *Indian Journal of Agricultural Economics*, Vol. 19, No. 1.

Lipton, M. (1977). *Why Poor People Stay Poor*. London: Temple Smith.

Patnaik, U. (1972). Economics of farm size and farm scale: some assumptions re-examined. *Economic and Political Weekly*, Special Number, August.

Sen, A.K. (1962). An aspect of Indian agriculture. *The Economic Weekly*, Annual Number, February.

11

Technical change

Peasants and technical change

The final topic of this book is technical change. Peasant households carry out their productive activities in a world economy in which every aspect of economic life is in a state of flux and change. The terms of survival of the farm household, as well as of entire farming communities, alter continuously as prices of inputs and outputs change, new production methods are devised, new crops or new varieties of existing crops appear, and new pressures are exerted by the larger economic system. While some households and communities may experience varying degrees of insulation from these changes, none escape them entirely, and it is only a matter of time before adaptation to them must take place.

The topic of technical change is concerned with this adaptation of production to the changing circumstances, pressures, and opportunities which farm households confront. Adaptation in this context means the adoption of new or different methods of production. For various reasons this may, and often does, occur differentially between farm households, or between farm communities in different locations, and this in turn may intensify the pressure for change on other farmers or may irrevocably undermine their basis for survival as agricultural producers.

Thus technical change is never just about the advent of new, more productive, methods of production taken in the abstract from the social conditions of survival of farm families. It is always also about those survival conditions themselves. And it involves far reaching strategic questions about the nature of new technology, its diffusion and adoption between different kinds of farm enterprise, and its social effects as well as its economic attributes.

Technical change is a large topic and many entire books have been written about it in the context of agrarian change in developing countries. This chapter is therefore selective in its coverage. Its main emphasis is on clarifying the economic tools which are used to conceptualise technical change, since these are often given only brief mention in agricultural economics textbooks.

The structure of the chapter is as follows. The next section is concerned with the economic analysis of technical change, and is divided into three components. The first is concerned with defining terms, the second with the distinction between neutral and biased technical change, and the third with a theory of technical change in agriculture known as induced innovation. The subsequent two sections are concerned with the application of these concepts, respectively, to labour-saving technical change (farm mechanisation) and land-saving technical change (new seeds). A final section considers the wider implications of technical change for the future of peasant household forms of production.

Economic analysis of technical change
Defining terms

A first task is to define economic terms and distinguish technology from technique, change in technology from technical change, factor substitution from technical change, embodied technical change from disembodied technical change, process innovation from product innovation.

Technology is defined by some economists as all those methods of production which have been developed or could be developed with the existing state of scientific knowledge. If this is accepted then *technological change* would refer only to advances in scientific knowledge from which new production methods can be derived. Other economists, however, prefer to restrict technology to mean only the techniques already developed and available at a given moment in time from which a choice can be made. This is a sub-set of those techniques which could be developed from existing scientific knowledge.

A *technique* is any single production method, i.e. it is a precise combination of inputs used to produce a given output. A technique may be represented by any single point on an isoquant or iso-product curve, such as point A in Figure 11.1.

Two different types of change in technique are shown in Figure 11.1. The first is a change in input proportions along an existing isoquant illustrated by the move from point A to point B. The second involves an inward shift in the entire isoquant as occurs in the move from point A to point C.

Neoclassical economics refers to the former of these two alternatives as *factor substitution*, and the latter as *technical change*. This distinction is crucial for the way neoclassical economics conceptualises technical change, and it is also found to be a useful one for assessing the nature of observed changes in farm production methods.

Factor substitution means a change in the combination of inputs used to produce the same level of output. Under the usual assumption of profit maximising behaviour, the main features of factor substitution are as follows:

(a) A change in relative prices (e.g. a fall in the price of labour) changes the slope of the isocost lines, as illustrated by the change from P_1 to P_2 in Figure 11.1;

(b) This change has both an output and a substitution effect, and these are analogous to the income and substitution effects in consumption theory;

(c) The output effect means that a higher level of output can be obtained for the same total cost after the input price fall, and this is represented in Figure 11.1 by operation at point D on isoquant I_2;

(d) The substitution effect is the movement from A to B in Figure 11.1,

Figure 11.1. Factor substitution versus technical change.

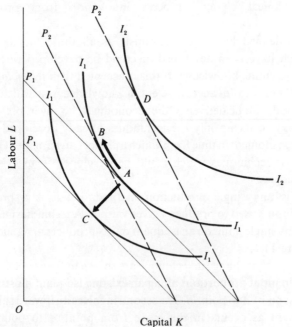

i.e. it is the operating position on the old isoquant at the new factor price ratio, after the increase in output has been taken away;

(e) Factor substitution is this pure substitution effect of a change in relative factor prices, holding technology constant (i.e. the substitution occurs within the existing set of available techniques, represented by isoquant I_1).

Technical change, in contrast, means a reduction in the quantity of resources required to produce a given output; or, alternatively, more output for the same level of resources. On an isoquant diagram like Figure 11.1 it is shown by the movement of the equilibrium position from A to C, corresponding to the technological change which moves the same isoquant, I_1, inwards towards the origin. The main features of technical change are as follows:

(a) There is a reduction of the quantity of one or more inputs required to produce a given output, *irrespective* of what happens to relative factor prices;

(b) This means that the efficiency or productivity of one or more resources has increased;

(c) Technical change implies a reduction in total production cost for given factor prices as indicated by the parallel inward shift of the iso-cost line, P_1.

The foregoing suggest two alternative ways in which technical change might be measured. The first is to measure the increase in output obtained from the same level of inputs. The second is to measure the decrease in total costs for the same level of output at constant input prices. The former has the disadvantage that the old combination of inputs may not be suitable for the new technology. For example new seed varieties typically require better soil preparation, more regular water supply, and higher fertilizer use in order to achieve their yield potential. For this reason the latter approach is often preferred to the former, and for practical purposes 'technical change is usually defined as the proportional decrease in costs of production achievable by the innovation when both the old and the new techniques operate at their optimal input combination and when factor prices are held constant' (Binswanger, 1978: 20).

The relevance of the distinction between factor substitution and technical change for the analysis of alternative production methods should now be becoming clear. If we take an example like the purchase of a tractor on a farm which has previously used manual labour, it makes a considerable difference to the assessment of the impact of this change in method whether it involves (a) the same level of output for a different combination of inputs and different factor prices (factor substitution), or (b) higher output for the same production cost at constant factor prices (technical change).

The standard neoclassical approach to technical change treats it as *exogenous* to the economic system. The move from A to C in Figure 11.1, unlike the move from A to B, is not explained by any economic forces visible to the production decision.

Technical change is termed *disembodied* when the reasons for the increased productivity cannot be identified. This is not very helpful for the analysis of technical change in agriculture where identification of the cause of an increase in productive efficiency is usually the main object of interest. In practice, technical change is always *embodied* in the particular resource which results in greater efficiency. For example if higher yields per unit area result from using new seeds, then technical change is *embodied* in the new seeds.

Note that identification of the resources which embody higher productivity does not, by itself, make technical change *endogenous*. Endogenous change requires technical change to be a response to visible economic forces, i.e. to changing relative prices (see below).

Innovation is virtually synonymous with technical change – it refers to the first practical use of a new, more productive, technique. A *process innovation* is one which changes the amount, combination, quality, or type of inputs required to produce the same kind of output. Most innovations in agriculture are process innovations in which the output produced (wheat, rice, potatoes etc.) remains unchanged. A *product innovation* is one in which the nature of the output changes, and it is usually considered more prevalent in industry than in agriculture.

The manufacturing sector often undertakes product innovation in the production of agricultural inputs (new machines, chemicals etc.) which then become process innovations in agricultural production. This distinction tends to become blurred in the case of new seeds, which although mainly regarded as a process innovation may give an output which is sufficiently different in appearance, taste etc. to be a product innovation as well.

Neutral and biased technical change

The technical change shown in Figure 11.1 is called 'neutral' technical change. It is a parallel movement of the isoquant inwards towards the origin, implying that *at given factor prices* the ratio of the inputs (L/K) is the same after the change as before the change. Neoclassical economists often like to think of technical change as being 'neutral' because this means that technical change itself cannot be blamed for altering the combination of labour and capital used in production (which can only be altered if their relative prices change).

If technical change is 'biased' in favour of using more of one resource than another, then different social as well as economic implications follow from technical change. Figure 11.2 shows a technical change which is biased in favour of capital and against labour. Instead of moving in parallel inwards towards the origin, the isoquant representing a given level of output is skewed inwards making it much steeper. This change of slope means that more labour (dL) is displaced for a given increase in capital (dK) than on the previous isoquant. Or, more formally, the marginal rate of substitution of capital for labour ($MRS_{K,L}$) increases between the two technologies.

In Figure 11.2, point A is the initial equilibrium representing efficiency of resource use for a given inverse factor–price ratio, r/w, which underlies the slope of the iso-cost line, P_1. At point A labour use is L_1 and capital use is K_1. The biased technical change results in a new equilibrium at point B for the same factor price ratio, entailing a greater decline in labour use (L_1 to L_2) than increase in capital use (K_1 to K_2). It is *labour-saving* technical change. The factor ratio, L/K, falls, and at given factor prices so too does the share of labour, wL, in the total value of output.

Figure 11.2. Bias in technical change.

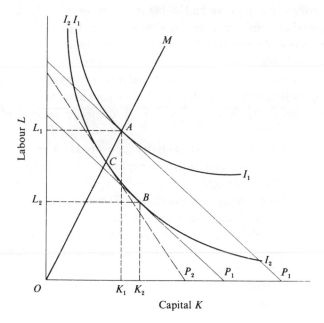

Capital K

An alternative expression of the bias of technical change is to consider the direction of change in relative factor prices which would be required in order to maintain the same factor proportions, L/K, as before. Constant factor proportions are shown by the ray, OM, passing from the origin through A, which joins together all points with the same L/K ratio on the graph. In order to keep the same factor proportions with the new technology at point C, the price of labour, w, must fall relative to the price of capital, r, yielding a new iso-cost line, P_2. This fall in the price of labour relative to capital reduces the share of labour, wL, in the total value of output for a given L/K ratio.

Technical change bias can thus be identified according to whether the income share of a factor, like labour, rises, stays the same, or decreases, for constant factor proportions. If the income share of labour, wL, rises relative to that of capital, rK, then we have labour-biased or *capital-saving* technical change; if the income shares of factors stay the same, we have *neutral* technical change; and if the share of labour, wL, falls we have capital-biased or *labour-saving* technical change. These alternatives are defined with respect to a definition of neutrality – the constant L/K ratio – which is known as Hicks-neutrality after the economist, J.R. Hicks, who posed the analysis of technical change in this way.

These conceptual distinctions are more than abstract niceties. Labour-saving technical change implies a lower share of total income accruing to labour in the production process and a higher share of total income accruing to non-labour resources. In farm production it means lower employment and gross earnings to direct farm labour, and higher payments to purchased variable inputs or fixed capital which accrue to owners of resources outside the farm sector. When purchased inputs and fixed capital goods are imported this means, in addition, higher payments to foreign factors of production and lower payments to domestic factors of production.

Amongst the main kinds of technical advance experienced in developing country agriculture, new seeds are considered to represent a land-saving (or land-augmenting) technical change, while some kinds of mechanisation are considered to be labour-saving technical change. These concepts should not be confused with those of scale discussed in Chapter 10, even though they are related. New seeds are land-augmenting because they increase yields per unit area. They are also thought to be *scale neutral*, because both the seeds themselves and the resources like fertilizer and water required to complement them are infinitely divisible across all ranges of output. Tractors, on the other hand, may be biased with respect to both technical change and scale. They have a labour-saving bias in technical change (assuming that they result in lower production costs per unit of output), and they have a *scale bias* towards larger farm size due to resource indivisibility.

Induced innovation

The distinction between factor substitution and technical change in neoclassical economics poses some difficulty for the analysis of the *causes* of change and their *direction* in terms of factor proportions. Firms may be presumed to innovate due to competitive pressures which force them continuously to seek cheaper ways of producing the same output or to develop new outputs for which a market potential exists. But the absence of relative input prices from this explanation means that technical change remains a *deus ex machina*; it simply occurs in response to competition with no explanation as to why it should take one path rather than another.

In order to explain the direction of technical change relative factor prices must be brought into the picture. One approach is to propose that changes in relative factor prices *induce* firms to search for production methods which use less of the resource which has become more expensive. This is the basis of a theory of technical change known as *induced innovation* which seeks to explain paths of technological development in agriculture in terms of changing relative factor scarcities over time (Hayami & Ruttan, 1985). This theory merits examination, not only with respect to the way it gets round the distinction between technical change and factor substitution, but also because it purports to provide a general theory of the causes, direction, and agencies of agricultural innovation. Its elements are first set out descriptively as follows:

(a) As agriculture develops over time particular resources become scarce and their costs rise relative to other resources.

(b) The resources which become scarce vary between regions according to land availability, population density and growth, and the nature of economic growth in the larger economy. Thus in North America or Australia labour tended to become the scarce resource; in Japan and in many of today's developing countries land emerges as the scarce resource while labour is plentiful.

(c) While these two examples by no means exhaust patterns of emerging resource scarcity, they serve to define two major paths of technological development in agriculture.

(d) In the labour scarce, land plentiful, economy farmers seek innovations to increase output while saving labour. The potential demand for such innovations *induces* manufacturing industry to devise and produce labour-saving machines.

(e) In the labour abundant, land scarce, economy farmers seek innovations to raise the productivity of land. This *induces* a search for yield-increasing technologies by both private and public agencies.

(f) More generally emerging relative resource scarcities manifest themselves in changing relative factor price levels of which all agencies, both private and public, are conscious. Thus relative prices *induce* both public and private research into innovations which save on the most expensive resource.

(g) This process is assisted by institutional arrangements which enable farmers to influence the ordering of research priorities. Thus decentralised public research in a context of representation by farmer groups on the boards of research bodies, and a pluralistic and participatory democracy, help to guide innovation along its appropriate path in terms of factor scarcities.

We defer a consideration of the problems of this theory to the end of this section. First we examine its economic logic as a theory of *endogenous* technical change, to be contrasted with the exogenous technical change of standard neoclassical theory. Technical change is endogenous in this theory because it is induced by relative factor prices.

Figure 11.3 illustrates the induced innovation model for the case of labour-saving technical change or *farm mechanisation*. The farm sector initially operates on a short term isoquant, I_1, with limited substitution possibilities between labour and land. Equilibrium is at A. This short term function is one of a whole family of such functions which could exist along an innovation possibility curve (IPC_1). The IPC describes the whole range of production techniques which could be developed with existing scientific knowledge. However, at prevailing factor prices only those techniques consistent with I_1 are available.

Labour now becomes scarce, pushing up the wage, and causing a shift in the factor price ratio from P_1 to P_2. The initial short term reaction is to attempt to move to B on I_1 (factor substitution), but this is only the start of a dynamic process of adjustment to the change in relative prices. First, the production method at B is not the most efficient technique which could be developed with existing knowledge along IPC_1. Second, the change in factor prices *induces* research and development into labour-saving new technology. The outcome of this R & D is an inward shift of the IPC to IPC_2, representing a neutral technological change (IPC_2 is parallel to IPC_1). A new equilibrium is reached on a new short term production function, I_2, at C. The path of technological change is given by the ray

(A,M) which shows the combination of machines and land which result from the increasing adoption of labour-saving technology. This model has some interesting features:

(a) It brings into play both definitions of technology we gave earlier.

(b) The factor price comparison is not directly between labour and capital, hence knotty problems about the measurement of capital and its price are avoided. Instead mechanical innovation enters the model as the indirect means by which farmers can cultivate more land with less labour.

(c) Point B on the original short term production function is illusory. The change of method is directly from point A to point C, *induced* by the efforts of farmers to try to get to point B.

(d) A corollary is that factor substitution disappears. In the induced innovation model all changes of production method are technical change.

Figure 11.3. Induced mechanical technical change (adapted from Hayami & Ruttan, 1985:91).

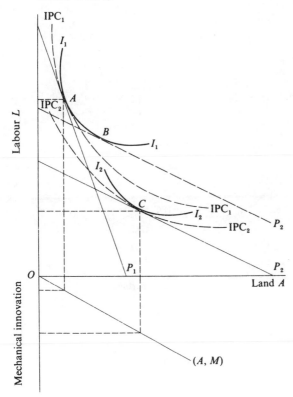

(e) The move from A to C is a capital-biased technical change, but this has been induced by the change in relative factor prices, it does not result from inherent bias in research (hence the neutrality of the shift from IPC_1 to IPC_2).

Biological innovation (new seeds, fertilizer etc.) is handled by the induced innovation theory in the same way (Figure 11.4). Here the cause of induced innovation is a rise in the price of land relative to variable inputs like fertilizer. The relative shortage of land *induces* a search for new crop varieties which can be combined with cheap variable inputs to produce more output per unit of scarce land. Here the ray (F,A) describes a path of technological change in which fertilizer is combined with new seeds, better cultivation, water management and so on to produce higher yields. Strangely enough labour does not enter this model directly, but it must be presumed that the authors of the theory implicitly include abundant labour in the resource requirements of land-augmenting technical progress.

Figure 11.4. Induced biological technical change (adapted from Hayami & Ruttan, 1985:91).

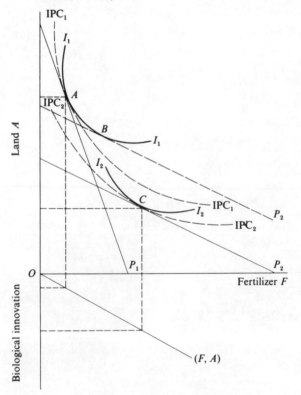

With its emphasis on market prices as the arbiter of the pace and direction of technical and institutional change, induced innovation needs to be considered with some reservation. Objections to the theory hinge on its reliance on assumptions of competitive markets and pluralistic participation by farmers in institutional decisions:

(a) In a dualistic agriculture small and large farmers confront different factor scarcities and different relative factor prices (Grabowski, 1979). This means that large farmers press for access to technologies, like mechanisation, which are inappropriate for the social efficiency of resource use.

(b) It is naive to project onto developing countries the avenues of access to public sector agencies which farmers purportedly possess in North America. Again, the largest landowners and farmers may well have access to, and influence upon, public sector agencies, but such access is non-existent for most peasants in developing countries.

(c) The theory neglects the issue of transfer of technology between the industrialised and developing countries, and the associated impact of market power and penetration by global corporations.

The response to these objections is that the appropriate path of technological progress in agriculture is induced in the manner predicted by the model *provided* that relative factor prices properly reflect underlying factor scarcities. The policy implication is that factor market distortions should be removed, and more 'democratic' avenues of farmer participation instituted where these do not at present exist.

This policy implication probably underestimates the degrees of unequal resource ownership and unequal access to political and economic power which prevail in many contemporary developing countries. Induced innovation may be retrospectively insightful about the paths of technical change in agriculture which occurred in some now industrialised countries, but this does not mean that it provides a ready blueprint for countries with entirely different patterns of social development. Since the roots of political and economic power in the material base of the productive economy are exogenous to the theory, they fall outside its capacity to handle or predict.

Farm mechanisation

The induced innovation theory discussed in the preceding section distinguishes two broad paths of technological development in agriculture corresponding to labour-saving and land-augmenting technical change respectively. This distinction is a common one in the literature because it seems to correspond reasonably closely to the different character of farm mechanisation from biological innovation. It also yields broad perceptions about the appropriate path of innovation in peasant agriculture, which it is thought should be oriented more closely to biological than to mechanical innovation.

Of course the technical options in peasant agriculture are a great deal more complex than this. Not all mechanisation is of necessity labour-saving, and not all biological innovation is of necessity labour-using. For example mechanisation in the shape of irrigation pumps, very important in wet rice cultivation, is complementary with more labour use since it permits more intensive cultivation and the potential for double cropping. Likewise biological innovation in the form of weedicides is labour-saving.

In this section we consider briefly some of the main issues surrounding farm mechanisation in developing countries, with emphasis on tractors and big machines since these are the form of mechanisation which excite the most controversy, and which seem to depart most from considerations of social efficiency, employment creation, and more equal income distribution. The following points may first be made with respect to mechanisation in general:

(a) Machines come in all different shapes, sizes, and functions. There are small water pumps and large water pumps, tools for oxen and buffaloes as well as for tractors, two-wheel tractors, four-wheel tractors of various sizes, and combine harvesters.

(b) It is facile to generalise about mechanisation *per se*. Rather each separate item of mechanical equipment must be assessed on its merits, taking into account whether it substitutes or complements labour, its farm size requirements for optimal operation, and the basis of its claims to raise farm output.

(c) For most developing countries the pace and direction of mechanical innovation in agriculture is well within the capacity of the state to regulate, via import and sales taxes which determine the relative cost of different machines for farmers. A corollary is that inappropriate mechanisation takes place by conscious state decision or collusion, reflecting the political basis of governments in power.

Most of the debates surrounding mechanisation in countries with large peasant populations concern the impact of *tractors* on farm size, productivity, and employment. Two lines of argument may be identified and these have been referred to as the *substitution view* and the *net contribution view* respectively (Binswanger, 1978: 3–6). These of course correspond to the concepts of factor substitution and technical change in economic analysis; and they emphasise, on the one hand, tractorisation as pure substitution for animal power and labour, and, on the other hand, the *net* increases in productivity achieved by tractors.

The substitution view is straightforward. It argues that the net effect of tractorisation is more or less pure substitution for animal draft power and human labour. There is little or no reduction in the overall cost of producing a given output, and no net efficiency gains in terms of higher output. Higher yields, if observed, are offset by higher production costs, especially if resources are valued at social, rather than private, efficiency prices.

The net contribution view is built up on a series of reasons to expect a net increase in output from using tractors. These are listed briefly as follows:

(a) Tractors allow previously unutilised land to be brought into production. This may be due to the superior capacity of the tractor to plough heavy soils, to work difficult and uneven terrain, to drain swampy ground, and so on; or it may simply be due to the larger area which can be cultivated where land is not the binding constraint (e.g. parts of Africa).

(b) Tractors permit seasonal shortages of labour to be overcome and/ or they release labour in critical periods for other productive tasks. If seasonal labour availability is the binding constraint on area cultivated this reason collapses into the previous one. If tractors release labour for the production of other crops they should result in higher total farm output.

(c) Tractors result in higher yields per unit area due to more timely ploughing, better seed bed preparation, more accurate delivery of variable inputs, and so on.

(d) Tractors may be essential for high rates of double cropping, due to the need for rapid land preparation between sequential crops.

(e) The tractor is a many-splendoured thing. It is not only used for cultivation, but can also be used for improving the farm infrastructure (drainage, irrigation, field size etc.), for driving pumps and mills, for carrying to and from market, and so on. Tractors also reduce the drudgery of farm work for the farm family, and can be used to take the family to town or to the cinema. These latter are, however, uses of tractors for consumption rather than production.

A great many case studies have been undertaken in an effort to reach firmer conclusions about the impact of tractors. Some of these are listed in the reference section to this chapter. While the balance of results inevitably remains to some degree contentious, the weight of evidence seems to indicate that the net productivity contribution of tractors is low or non-existent in most developing countries. The substitution view thus seems to approximate more closely the nature and impact of tractors than the net contribution view. Some points which emerge from the literature are as follows:

(a) Cultivation of previously unutilised land is the only net contribution which obtains substantive support across an array of empirical evidence.

(b) Farm size increases with tractorisation, and in Asia this mainly occurs through non-renewal of leases to cash or share tenants, and through the purchase of adjacent small farms.

(c) Yield increases are often falsely attributed to tractors when they stem in fact from the simultaneous introduction of new seeds and variable inputs.

(d) The capital cost of tractors is high and only farms of the largest sizes fully utilize them at efficient unit costs.

(e) In the absence of tractor hire services, the use of tractors by most farmers in developing countries cannot be justified on grounds of economic efficiency.

(f) Farmers that do purchase tractors make considerable use of them for consumption purposes, such as all-purpose transport.

(g) Tractors have been encouraged in many countries by direct subsidies, tax concessions, and overvalued exchange rates which have accelerated tractorisation compared to the pace which would have occurred in the absence of such distortions.

(h) Tractors typically possess a high foreign exchange cost, whether manufactured domestically or not, for capital and component imports, spares and services, fuel and running costs.

We conclude this section with a simple model designed to illustrate the larger economic impact of the adoption by a peasant farm household of a big mechanical innovation. The example is consciously made outrageous in order to emphasise its results. We suppose that a combine harvester for rice is introduced into a peasant farm system, and we initially assume that the individual household can make use of this innovation on a competitive hire basis. The model is set out in Figure 11.5.

The production function for the farm household shifts from I_1 to I_2, representing a labour-saving bias in technical change. It pays the household to use this innovation since a reduction in cost for a given output is involved. Equilibrium moves from point A to point B at prevailing factor prices. This causes a substantial reduction in labour use from L_1 to L_2, and a moderate increase in capital from K_1 to K_2 representing the hire of the harvester.

However, at point B, the farm household is characterised by substantial unemployment of labour. The diagram then shows how much output would need to increase at the new technology for this labour to be re-absorbed. For full employment of family labour to occur output would need to expand outwards to I_3 giving an equilibrium at C with labour use $L_3 = L_1$. This requires a vast increase in the *scale* of output as manifested by the increase of capital to K_3, and a vast increase in farm size in order to achieve optimal economies of scale with the innovation. The shift is equivalent to a change from a peasant farm to a North American family grain farm.

If we drop the assumption of harvester hire the initial movement from point A to point B disappears. Peasants do not normally have access to mechanised technology on a competitive hire basis, and the size and shape of their farms is not typically suitable for large machine operation. Thus the more likely impact of this innovation is a movement directly from point A to point C. The peasant household disappears, and a large-scale farm enterprise takes its place. The simultaneous disappearance of several peasant households, necessitated in order to achieve the optimum farm size for the harvester, swells the ranks of landless labour and the rural unemployed: a quantum leap from peasant to proletarian has taken place.

Figure 11.5. Farm-level impact of labour-saving technical change (adapted from Donaldson & McInerny, 1973:836).

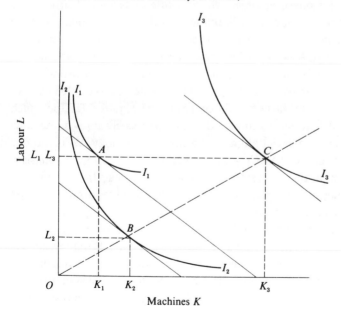

The graph in Figure 11.5 illustrates a general point about innovation at the farm level. Technical change does not only mean that existing output can be produced more efficiently. It also means that resources, in this case labour, are released. For big mechanical technology this release of labour has wide ranging social and economic effects for the size structure of farms, for type of farms, for unemployment, and for the living standards of the mass of the rural population.

Modern varieties

In this section we provide a brief summary of issues surrounding the adoption of new crop varieties in peasant farm sectors. In common with recent usage we refer to innovation associated with new crop varieties as the study of *modern varieties* and their impact. This kind of technical change is also referred to in the literature variously as the Green Revolution, high yielding varieties (HYVs), biological innovation, or plant technology.

The term Green Revolution has tended to fall into disuse because modern varieties have certainly not miraculously transformed the economic situation and prospects of developing countries, even though they may have prevented famine in some of them. The term high yielding varieties places rather too much stress on just one attribute – their potential to achieve greater output per unit area of land – at the expense of other attributes like disease or pest resistance, drought tolerance, and shorter growing seasons.

A feature of modern varieties which is often overlooked, leading to spurious arguments about their limitations, is that they change over time through the activities of a worldwide network of International Agricultural Research Centres (IARCs) and local research agencies. This means that the observation of a defect in, say, a particular strain of rice grown in one region over a couple of crop seasons – perhaps it was acutely susceptible to a pest, had low tolerance to variations in moisture, or required far too much fertilizer for most farmers to afford – does not necessarily apply to the same region a few years later, let alone to the entire technology. While no one would pretend that the IARCs work perfectly – much current emphasis is placed on making their research more relevant to small farmer growing conditions – they are continuously redefining the attributes of crop varieties and severe defects have tended to be rectified fairly rapidly.

Modern varieties are developed with a great number of factors in view. High yield responsiveness to plant nutrients is one. Wind resistance, drought resistance, pest resistance, toleration to variations in soil and water, shorter growing seasons, and acceptability in consumption are others. The technology has also extended over a great many more crops –

sorghum, millets, root crops, pulses – than was the case earlier in its application.

The arguments concerning the social and economic attributes of modern varieties differ from those associated with tractors. Few people doubt the output increasing capability of modern varieties. Their net impact is technical change rather than factor substitution. However, controversy has existed concerning their differing rates of adoption by different kinds of farmers, their reliance on high levels of complementary purchased inputs, regional disparities in their uptake, and their overall impact on income distribution. For the purposes of disentangling the arguments it is useful to separate their technical–economic attributes from the nature of the societies into which they are inserted. Confusion between these two dimensions, as well as neglect of continuous change in the varieties themselves, leads to incorrect perceptions about their disadvantages.

Bearing these considerations in mind, we present here a summary of points concerning the nature of new seed technology, its effects in countries where its adoption has been widespread (mainly South and South East Asia, but also Latin America), its advantages and its disadvantages:

(a) Modern varieties have resulted in substantial output increases, and have averted almost certain famine, in those countries where their adoption is widespread.

(b) The main basis of these output increases is higher yields per unit area, though some proportion is attributable to more double cropping and some to bringing new land into cultivation.

(c) Many, but not all, modern varieties require complementary inputs in the form of artificial fertilizer and water control (irrigation) in order to attain their potential yields. However, it is not true, as a blanket generalisation, that in the absence of such inputs they invariably do less well than traditional varieties. Drought resistance and higher response to organic inputs are also appearing in newer strains of modern varieties.

(d) Peasant farmers are observed to be as capable of the adoption and yield increases of modern varieties as large commercial farmers, though often there is a lag in rates of adoption between the two types of farm enterprise.

(e) The greater reliance on purchased inputs locks peasant farmers more firmly into the market, and may therefore make them more prey to the unequal exercise of market power in imperfect markets. The interpretation placed on this is perforce ambiguous since higher cash incomes are traded against the loss of security in subsistence.

(f) Some modern varieties are more susceptible to yield variability than traditional varieties. They thus involve an increase in production risk, though this must be traded against their higher yields.

(g) Modern varieties are technically *scale neutral*. Both the seeds themselves and the complementary inputs are infinitely divisible, and the smallest farms are able to attain the same yield levels as large farms. Scale biases, where observed, reside not in the varieties themselves but in the way the larger economic system favours some producers over other producers.

(h) In the absence of tractorisation, modern varieties are labour-using. More labour is required for cultivation, weeding, input application, water control, double cropping, and harvesting. Modern varieties have increased rural employment, though due to population growth and increasing landlessness in some countries this has not necessarily caused an increase in real wages.

(i) The higher incomes from modern varieties have resulted in less farm work by women members of peasant households. At the same time they have greatly increased the casual wage employment of women from landless or very poor rural families.

(j) Higher output has meant lower food prices, and this has benefited both urban consumers and the landless rural poor.

(k) Nutritional effects are mixed. Lower grain prices mean more staple food for poor people. On the other hand, locally, the tendency to monocrop modern varieties in preference to the diverse production of traditional foods may lower the nutritional status of farm families.

(l) Large regional disparities in the adoption and benefits of modern varieties have been observed, corresponding especially to natural endowments of water and the location of irrigation facilities. Farm families in locations which cannot adopt modern varieties due to these constraints lose from the lower prices of grains. However, the potential genesis of varieties suitable to such locations should not be neglected.

These points demonstrate the inadequacy of generalisations about modern varieties based on partial aspects observed in a few locations over a few crop seasons. The pessimism about their impact prevalent in the 1970s derived in part from (a) premature conclusions drawn at an early stage of diffusion; (b) confusion of the intrinsic technical features of the varieties with their insertion into societies already rife with unequal land ownership, unequal economic power, and imperfect factor markets; (c) confusion of the impact of new varieties with the conceptually separate impact of tractorisation; and (d) wrongly attributing to new varieties the effects of political decisions favouring irrigation in some areas rather than others, subsidised tractor purchase by large farmers, and so on.

Modern varieties are not a panacea for inequality and poverty in the developing countries, but then no purely technical solution to such problems will ever occur. But, more so than other innovations, their potential benefits are about as neutral between rich and poor, large farmer and small farmer, as one is ever likely to get. Moreover perceived defects of modern varieties – whether on agronomic, ecological, economic, or social grounds – remain more susceptible to corrective action than is true of other technologies.

Peasants again

In terms of our definition of peasants (Chapter 1) most technical change, whether machines or modern varieties, lock peasants increasingly into the market economy and hasten their demise as peasants. In some countries new technology, combined with population growth and land scarcity, has accelerated the polarisation of peasant society into landless rural labour and family or capitalist farmers. In others, where population density and land scarcity are less pressing, its social impact is less pronounced.

Technology on its own does not make the difference between peasant and other forms of farm production. Even where technical change has been most rapid, there are formidable barriers to the complete transition from peasants to commercial family farmers or capitalist farm enterprises. This resides partly in the continued semi-subsistence basis of a great proportion of farm families, and partly in the continued high degree of market imperfection in most agrarian economies. These two aspects are linked because market imperfections, in the shape of inequalities of power and access, continue to make complete specialisation unacceptably risky for many farm families.

Summary

1 This chapter is concerned with technical change and its impact on peasant farm households. The first half of the chapter covers the approach to technical change in economic analysis, including the meaning of various concepts, the notion of bias in technical change, and the theory of induced innovation.

2 The distinction between factor substitution and technical change is emphasised since this is relevant for assessing whether a change in production method merely substitutes one input for another or makes a positive net contribution to productivity and output.

3 The application of these concepts to mechanisation, and to

tractors in particular, is considered. It is observed that machines come in all shapes and sizes, and that it is not useful to generalise the economic impact of mechanisation *per se*.

4 However, four-wheel tractors and larger machines possess biases both to large farm size, due to their indivisibility, and to labour-saving. At prevailing social prices, reflecting factor availabilities in most developing countries, the impact of tractors is almost pure substitution with negligible gains in social efficiency. The private purchase of tractors often contains a strong consumption component in addition to its productive uses.

5 By contrast modern varieties involve net technical change. They increase yields more than in proportion to the additional inputs required in their production. Modern varieties are variable input intensive, labour-using, and technically neutral to scale.

6 Earlier criticism of the social effects of modern varieties resulted from confusing their technical attributes with the nature of the society and politics of countries where they were introduced; confusing their impact with that of the simultaneous permissive growth of tractors; and underestimating the evolution of them over time.

7 It is observed that modern varieties are bred for certain attributes. Should these attributes prove undesirable for technical, economic, ecological, or social reasons, they are susceptible to change. While it is legitimate to argue for desirable properties of these varieties, it is incorrect to attribute to them all the social and economic ills of the societies in which their adoption has been widespread.

8 Where peasants are concerned, a broad effect of technical change is to integrate them more closely into the market economy, and thus to hasten the demise of their peasant status. Whether this also means polarisation into distinct rural social classes depends on a great many other factors than technology alone.

Further reading

A useful introduction to many of the concerns of this chapter is given in Ruthenberg & Jahnke (1985, Chs. 3–4). The theory of induced innovation is set out in various different ways in Hayami & Ruttan (1985, Ch. 4), Binswanger & Ruttan (1978, Ch. 2), and Hayami & Ruttan (1984). For related discussion of bias in technical change see Thirtle & Ruttan (1987, Ch. 2) and Kislev & Peterson (1981). A critique is contained in Grabowski (1979). Farm mechanisation is examined in Binswanger (1978,

1984), Clayton (1983, Ch. 8), Donaldson & McInerney (1973), and Agarwal (1981). Collections containing case studies are ILO (1973) and IRRI (1983). Other case studies of mechanisation are Disney & Elbashir (1984), Gill (1983), Lingard (1984), Lingard & Sri Bagyo (1983), and Roy & Blase (1978). The classic critical tract on the Green Revolution is Griffin (1979), and also see Byres & Crow (1983). For a recent assessment Lipton & Longhurst (1986) is much recommended. Other items on this topic are Blyn (1983), Bowonder (1981), Lipton (1978), Pinstrup-Andersen & Hazell (1985), and Prahladachar (1983). The reference list which follows is divided into three sections, corresponding to general analysis, mechanisation, and modern varieties respectively.

Reading list

Analysis of technical change

Binswanger, H.P. & Ruttan, V.W., (eds.) (1978). *Induced Innovation: Technology, Institutions, and Development*. Baltimore: Johns Hopkins.

Grabowski, R. (1979). The implications of an induced innovation model. *Economic Development and Cultural Change*. Vol. 27, No. 4.

Hayami, Y. & Ruttan, V.W. (1985). *Agricultural Development: an International Perspective*. 2nd edn. Baltimore: Johns Hopkins.

Hayami, Y. & Ruttan, V.W. (1984). The green revolution: inducement and distribution. *The Pakistan Development Review*. Vol. XXIII, No. 1.

Kislev, Y. & Peterson, W. (1981). Induced innovations and farm mechanisation. *American Journal of Agricultural Economics*. Vol. 63, No. 3.

Ruthenberg, H. & Jahnke, H.E. (1985). *Innovation Policy for Small Farmers in the Tropics*. Oxford: Clarendon Press.

Thirtle C.G. & Ruttan, V.W. (1987). The role of demand and supply in the generation and diffusion of technical change. *Fundamentals of Pure and Applied Economics*, Vol. 21, London: Harwood Academic Press.

Farm mechanisation

Agarwal, B. (1981). Agricultural mechanisation and labour use: a disaggregated approach. *International Labour Review*, Vol. 120, No. 1.

Binswanger, H.P. (1978). *The Economics of Tractors in South Asia*. New York: Agricultural Development Council.

Binswanger, H.P. (1984). *Agricultural Mechanisation: A Comparative Historical Perspective*. World Bank Staff Working Papers, No. 673, Washington D.C.: World Bank.

Clayton, E.S. (1983). *Agriculture, Poverty and Freedom in Developing Countries*. Ch. 8. London: Macmillan, 1983.

Disney, R. & Elbashir, A.A. (1984). Mechanisation, employment and productivity in Sudanese agriculture. *Journal of Development Economics*, Vol. 16.

Donaldson, G.F. & McInerney, J.P. (1973). Changing machinery, technology and agricultural adjustment. *American Journal of Agricultural Economics*, Vol. 55, No. 5.

Gill, G.J. (1983). Mechanised land preparation, productivity and employment in Bangladesh. *Journal of Development Studies*, Vol. 19, No. 3.

Lingard, J. (1984). Mechanisation of small rice farms in the Philippines: some income distribution aspects. *Journal of Agricultural Economics*, Vol. XXXV, No. 3.

Lingard, J. & Sri Bagyo, A. (1983). The impact of agricultural mechanisation on production and employment in rice areas of West Java. *Bulletin of Indonesian Economic Studies*, Vol. XIX, No. 1.

Roy, S. & Blase, M.G. (1978). Farm tractorisation, productivity and labour employment: a case study of the Indian Punjab. *Journal of Development Studies*, Vol. 14, No. 2.

Modern varieties

Blyn, G. (1983). The green revolution revisited. *Economic Development & Cultural Change*. Vol. 31, No. 4.

Bowonder, B. (1981). The myth and reality of high yielding varieties in Indian agriculture. *Development and Change*, Vol. 12, No. 2.

Byres, T.J. & Crow, B. (1983). *The Green Revolution in India*. Open University, Third World Studies Course U204, Case Study 5, Milton Keynes: Open University Press.

Griffin, K. (1979). *The Political Economy of Agrarian Change: An Essay on the Green Revolution*. 2nd edn. London: Macmillan.

Lipton, M. (1978). Inter-farm, inter-regional and farm-non-farm income distribution: the impact of the new cereal varieties. *World Development*, Vol. 6, No. 3.

Lipton, M. & Longhurst, R. (1986). *Modern Varieties, International Agricultural Research, and the Poor*. Consultative Group on International Agricultural Research (CGIAR), Study Paper No. 2, Washington D.C.: World Bank.

Pinstrup-Andersen, P. & Hazell, B.R. (1985). The impact of the green revolution and prospects for the future. *Food Reviews International*, Vol. 1, No. 1.

Prahladachar, M. (1983). Income distribution effects of the green revolution in India: a review of empirical evidence. *World Development*, Vol. 11, No. 11.

12

Peasant economics in perspective

This book is a theoretical textbook. It is not a manual of methods for practical problem-solving, even though it makes reference to some of the practical circumstances confronting peasants. The role of theory is to provide a coherent structure of ideas within which to undertake practical work. Some of these ideas may have only broad contextual relevance to a given situation, for example the debate about the persistence of peasant household production in a capitalist world economy. Others have more immediate technical application by indicating a chain of logic which follows from a set of initial conditions, for example the farm household theories. Still others provide a social dimension within which to interpret economic analysis, for example the class structure of rural societies where share tenancy is prevalent, or the impact of the social subordination of women on the division of labour in the peasant household.

In what follows the main themes and components of the book are restated in a form designed to bring out the relationships between them. This summary is not a substitute for the content of previous chapters. It involves condensation of preceding material, as well as selective emphasis. The five main elements identified are:

- Definition of peasants
- Farm household economic theories
- Political economy
- Intrahousehold relations
- Social and economic change

Definition of peasants

The book begins with a definition of peasants for the purposes of economic analysis. Peasants are household agricultural producers characterised by partial engagement in incomplete markets. This definition serves a number of purposes throughout the book:

(a) it recognises that peasants are part of a larger economic system, and therefore that their economic behaviour as agricultural producers depends on how the larger system works for them;

(b) it allows peasants some limited capacity for survival independent of the larger system, and this may sometimes be important for explaining peasant economic behaviour;

(c) it emphasises that peasant production takes place in a context of factor and product markets which are not fully formed, and depending on which markets are incomplete (e.g. the land market, the labour market, the credit market) this has an important impact both on their relative autonomy as agricultural producers and on the kind of economic decisions they make;

(d) it serves to distinguish peasants both from capitalist farm enterprises (hiring wage labour) and from commercial family farmers operating in the context of fully formed factor and output markets;

(e) it lends a strategic perspective to agricultural policies which are often concerned with accelerating the transition of peasants into commercial family farmers by improving the working of markets, increasing the use of purchased inputs, and removing the social and economic constraints which distinguish peasants from other economic actors in the market economy.

Farm household economic theories

The book contains a set of farm household microeconomic theories. These seek to explain peasant economic behaviour by making logical deductions from a set of prior assumptions about household goals, and about the nature of markets within which households make their decisions. These theories are not mutually exclusive. They have much in common – in starting point, approach, logical method, and sharing of certain key assumptions – which means that they are variations on a single theme:

(a) the farm household is taken as a single decision-making unit for purposes of economic analysis;

(b) the household maximises a single utility function, representing the joint welfare of its members;

(c) where income is the only variable in the utility function, then profit maximisation and utility maximisation coincide;

(d) where all input and output markets are fully formed and competitive then profit maximisation is always a component of utility maximisation, even though there may be several other variables in the utility function (e.g. food security, 'leisure' time);

(e) differences in the logic and predictions of different theories arise from different assumptions about the working of factor and product markets rather than from different assumptions about household goals;

(f) varying assumptions about labour markets and the allocation of household labour time are often the critical feature which distinguishes one theory from another;

(g) in short, household economic behaviour depends on social relations which make markets work in certain ways for some peasants and in different ways for other peasants.

Thus the different farm household theories examined in the book spring from the same theoretical apparatus, with certain components being altered while others are held constant. A brief summary of the theories described in Part II of the book makes this clear:

Profit maximisation

This theory treats the household as a farm firm, operating in fully formed and competitive input and output markets. Utility is solely a function of income, and utility maximisation coincides with profit maximisation. The theory predicts a positive response by the household to market price changes, i.e. an increase in the real price of output results in higher input use, higher output, and higher net income.

By our definition of peasants – partial engagement in incomplete markets – profit maximisation would seem an inadequate portrayal of their economic behaviour. It permits no conflicts or trade-offs between higher income and other household goals, and these arise due to the absence of markets in some commodities and services. However, the degree of market integration of most contemporary peasants means that some elements of the economic calculus characterised by profit maximisation are almost always present in peasant economic behaviour.

Risk aversion

This theory recognises uncertainty as an important factor in household decision making. Uncertainty enters the utility function of the household as a preference for security in the face of subjective risk. Utility maximisation involves a trade-off between higher income and greater security, as two separate household goals. This may mean lower input use than is suggested by profit maximisation (avoidance of the loss which could be incurred by a high outlay on inputs), and cropping patterns which do not correspond to the highest net return.

Risk aversion is evidently a modification of the profit maximisation model, not a different theory. The pursuit of security as a goal occurs because risk avoidance cannot be purchased in the market. Unstable input and output markets are part of the problem, and no market in crop insurance exists.

In many countries the state steps in to provide the security which private markets cannot deliver. Here there is a big contrast between farmers in the temperate industrialised countries and peasants in developing countries. The former not only experience less environmental variation than the latter, they also operate in protected markets where output prices are stabilised within narrow limits by state action.

Drudgery aversion

This theory assumes that no labour market exists, and that the farm household is entirely reliant on family labour. The lack of a labour market causes time not working on the farm to enter the utility function as a goal separate from income. Utility maximisation involves a trade-off between higher income and more time to spend on activities other than farm work (avoidance of the drudgery of farm work). Labour use and output are not determined by the factor/product price ratio – which no longer exists – but rather by family size and structure which varies across households.

Again this theory only modifies the logic of the profit maximising model, and is not an entirely different approach. Time for non-farm activity is pursued by the household as a separate goal because labour time cannot be purchased or valued in the absence of a labour market.

Farm household theories

These can vary considerably in their specification, but they have in common the idea derived from the new home economics of household utility maximisation subject to production and time constraints. Farm profit maximisation is here one aspect of a larger picture of the household in which (a) the farm may not be the only income source, (b) a labour market exists so that hiring in and hiring out of labour is possible, (c) different household members may confront different market wages, (d) the farm-gate and retail prices of farm output may differ, meaning that sale and purchase of food have different relative price implications for household decisions.

In farm household theories, utility maximisation is synonymous with full income maximisation, within which farm net income is not necessarily the only component. Trade-offs between alternative household goals (e.g. family versus hired labour; own consumption versus sale of a food crop) affect the distribution of full income, but they do not affect its size at given market prices. Nor do they affect optimum resource use in farm production which follows standard profit maximising criteria.

Share tenancy

Economic theories of share tenancy, whether tenant or landlord oriented, are based on the profit maximising model. This time it is the non-market nature of access to land as a productive resource which results in modifications to the standard theory. From the tenant perspective, given otherwise working markets, share tenancy would seem to imply lower inputs and outputs than under cash tenancy. From the landlord perspective, share tenancy cannot be explained by a competitive model, and recourse must be had to various market flaws to explain this form of land tenure.

The related phenomenon of interlocked factor markets also occurs due to flaws in the working of markets. Again it is the absence of fully formed markets in farm inputs – land, labour, credit, and so on – which results in modifications to the profit maximising logic, not changes in the rationale of household decision making which remains the same.

Political economy

The comparison between microeconomic theories makes clear that it is departures of varying kinds from fully working markets which result in different explanations of farm household behaviour. This links to the peasant definition which emphasises incomplete markets as a central feature of peasant production. Incomplete markets in turn reflect the prevailing social relations of production of which peasant households are a part.

The political economy dimension of the book is designed to bring out the inseparability of short run household decisions from the wider social relations of production. As the discussion above shows, it is misleading to treat microeconomic theories as if they have universal validity independent of particular social relations. Incomplete markets reflect the uneven transition from pre-capitalist to capitalist social relations of production in different settings. The following points summarise some of the insights obtained into the situation of peasants from Marxian political economy:

(a) most peasants are located within the capitalist mode of production, characterised by the separation of direct labour from the means of production, production for exchange rather than direct use, competition, and the prevalence of market relations;

(b) the more peasants become locked into market exchanges, the more they must compete on the terms dictated by the larger economic system, and the less is their capacity to disengage from that system;

(c) this process of integration into market relations occurs unevenly so that full commitment to a particular market (e.g. the market for a commodity output) does not mean either that all markets work or that households rely on market exchanges for all inputs and outputs;

(d) the efficiency of peasant households as farm production units cannot be divorced from the degree to which they are subject to the pressures and discipline of market relations, and thus efficiency is a relative term which has no meaning independent of the social relations of production;

(e) in the long term the spread of capitalist social relations means the disappearance of peasants, but not necessarily the end of household types of farm production;

(f) the orthodox prediction that peasant society polarises into capitalist farmers and landless labour may prove correct under certain conditions but not others;

(g) household production in agriculture remains important throughout the advanced capitalist countries, and this suggests that an alternative transition can occur, from peasants to family farm enterprises fully integrated into working markets.

Intrahousehold relations

A significant limitation of the household as a unit of economic analysis is that it tends to ignore the impact of intrahousehold relations on economic behaviour. Purely economic arguments fail to address the social nature of the relationships between people within the household:

(a) the economic situation of individuals within households is not freely determined by each household taken in isolation, it corresponds to social norms of behaviour to which most farm households in a given society comply;

(b) the division of property, labour and income within the household is socially – not biologically – determined, and particular economic roles are socially assigned to men, women, and children;

(c) the term gender division of labour is used to focus especially on the social demarcation of tasks between men and women, and the time allocation of men and women tends to follow this social demarcation closely;

(d) household microeconomic theories tend to assume that male and female labour is substitutable across the range of household economic activities: this is rarely, if ever, the case;

(e) in practice rigidities of time allocation may inhibit the capacity of the household to respond to market signals;

(f) for example a gender division of labour which allocates all childcare, household chores, and water carrying to women constrains the capacity of women to participate in farm production irrespective of opportunities indicated by the market;

(g) likewise the same gender division of labour may result in a fall in output if men become engaged in off-farm wage work leaving women to try to combine farm work with their other chores;

(h) more generally the gender division of labour needs to be given more consideration in microeconomic analysis: it may have a major impact on total farm output, the pattern of farm output, constraints on seasonal labour inputs, and responsiveness to price changes;

(i) the gender division of labour is one aspect of the social subordination of women prevalent in most peasant societies, and this is crucial for considering the impact of social and economic change on the material well-being of women compared to men;

(j) most agricultural policies and projects ignore the role of women in farm production, both as cultivators and as decision makers, and this male bias reduces the effectiveness of policy and diminishes the social status of women.

Social and economic change

A final component of the book is concerned with social and economic change. Social change is implicit in the definition of peasants and in the approach of peasant political economy. However the penultimate two chapters of the book are concerned with the technology of production as a central feature of social change.

Changes in technology alter the combinations of inputs used to produce farm outputs, introduce new inputs, and affect the viability of different types of farm enterprise in different ways:

(a) the large versus small farm debate is about strategic choices concerning production technology;

(b) the arguments in favour of small farms centre on the farm input combinations which should occur given social resource availabilities, given that in many developing countries land and capital are in short supply and labour is in abundant supply;

(c) departures of actual prices from their social efficiency levels occur due to market imperfections, and these may encourage large farms and capital intensive production;

(d) market imperfections in this context cover a multitude of sins, and include social features such as highly skewed land ownership structures or political processes which systematically favour access to resources by some social groups or classes while excluding access by others;

(e) farm size also enters the discussion of labour-saving versus land-augmenting technical change in agriculture, a distinction which permeates the economic analysis of technology and the adoption of innovations;

(f) the evidence on labour-saving technology, or farm mechanisation, suggests that the substitution of labour by machines can rarely be justified on social efficiency grounds;

(g) land-augmenting, or biological, technology is neutral with respect to size and scale, and thus offers family farmers scope for increasing real incomes without increasing farm size;

(h) many modern varieties require high levels of complementary purchased inputs in order to achieve their yield potential, and for this reason their adoption by peasants locks them ever more firmly into wider market relations.

Conclusion: Variation versus uniformity

The study of peasant farm households and their problems is a complex matter, with many different points of entry and levels of engagement. This book has focused on production rather than distribution, on economics rather than social analysis or politics, on theory rather than practice.

It is appropriate to end the book where it began, which is with the use of the term 'peasant' and its relevance for thinking about the problems of farm families in developing countries. Agricultural economics as a discipline usually makes no distinctions with respect to the social organisation of farm production. A single economic rationale is put forward as having universal applicability to all farm production in space and time. In this perspective the social and historical dimensions of farm production are not considered relevant and they disappear.

This book has taken a different position. The term peasant was adopted precisely in order to emphasise that short term economic decisions are inseparable from the larger social relations within which production takes place. For economic analysis these social relations are manifested by departures of varying degrees from the pure market relations on which the main body of microeconomic theory is predicated. Peasants differ from capitalist farm enterprises and from other family farmers because non-market interactions still figure in their access to resources, in the farming systems they adopt, and in the social principles to which they conform.

The failure of agricultural policy to take into account local variation in these social relations frequently results in a waste of resources and unintended side effects. For example a fertilizer subsidy aimed at improving the income of share tenants is doubly misapplied if it first increases landowner income via interlocked markets, and then results in land concentration and the eviction of the same tenants. There is no 'quick technical fix' to the problems of poor peasants independent of the social conditions of their livelihood.

The approach of this book emphasises variation rather than uniformity. The transition towards fully developed market relations occurs unevenly in different societies. This means that there is great variation in the way resource and output markets work in different places. The book will have achieved some of its purpose if it results in the avoidance of superficial generalisation about peasant economic decisions and the social contexts within which they are made.

References

Acharya, M. & Bennett, L. (1982). *Women and the Subsistence Sector: Economic Participation and Household Decisionmaking in Nepal*. World Bank Staff Working Paper No. 526, Washington DC: World Bank.

Adams, J. (1986). Peasant rationality: individuals, groups, cultures. *World Development*, Vol. 14, No. 2.

Afshar, H. (1985). *Women, Work, and Ideology in the Third World*. London: Tavistock.

Agarwal, B. (1981). Agricultural mechanisation and labour use: a disaggregated approach. *International Labour Review*. Vol. 120, No. 1.

Ahmed, I. (ed.) (1985). *Technology and Rural Women*. London: Allen & Unwin.

Ahn, C.Y., Singh, I. & Squire, L. (1981). A model of an agricultural household in a multi-crop economy: the case of Korea. *The Review of Economics and Statistics*, Vol. LXIII, No. 4.

Anderson, J.R., Dillon, J.L. & Hardaker, J.B. (1977). *Agricultural Decision Analysis*. Ames: Iowa State University Press.

Barbier, P. (1984). Inverse relationship between farm size and land productivity: a product of science or imagination? *Economic and Political Weekly*, Vol. XIX, Nos. 52 & 53.

Bardhan, P.K. (1973). Size, productivity and returns to scale: an analysis of farm level data in Indian agriculture. *Journal of Political Economy*, Vol. 18, pp. 1370–86.

Bardhan, P.K. (1980). Interlocking factor markets and agrarian development: a review of issues. *Oxford Economic Papers*, Vol. 32, No. 1.

Barker, R., Herdt, R.W. & Rose, B. (1985). *The Rice Economy of Asia*. Washington DC: Resources for the Future.

Barnum, H.N. & Squire, L. (1978). Technology and relative economic efficiency. *Oxford Economic Papers*, Vol. 30.

Barnum, H.N. & Squire, L. (1979). *A Model of an Agricultural Household: Theory and Evidence*. Occasional Paper No. 27. Washington DC: World Bank.

Basu, K. (1984). *The Less Developed Economy: A Critique of Contemporary Theory*. Oxford: Basil Blackwell.

Bates, R.H. (1981). *Markets and States in Tropical Africa*. Berkeley: University of California Press.

Beattie, B.R. & Taylor, C.R. (1985). *The Economics of Production*. New York: Wiley.

Becker, G.S. (1965). A theory of the allocation of time. *Economic Journal*. Vol. 75.

Becker, G.S. (1981). *A Treatise on the Family*. Cambridge, Mass.: Harvard University Press.

Beneke, R.R. & Winterboer, R. (1973). *Linear Programming Applications to Agriculture*. Ames: Iowa State University Press.

References 243

Beneria, L. (1979). Reproduction, production and the sexual division of labour. *Cambridge Journal of Economics*, No. 3.

Beneria, L. (1981). Conceptualizing the labor force: the underestimation of women's economic activities. *Journal of Development Studies*, Special Issue on African Women in the Development Process, Vol. 17, No. 3.

Beneria, L. (ed.) (1982). *Women and Development*. New York: Praeger.

Beneria, L. & Sen, G. (1981). Accumulation, reproduction, and women's role in economic development: Boserup revisited. *Signs*, Vol. 7, No. 2.

Bernstein, H. (1979). African peasantries: a theoretical framework. *Journal of Peasant Studies*, Vol. 6, No. 4.

Berry, R.A. & Cline, W.R. (1979). *Agrarian Structure and Productivity in Developing Countries*. Baltimore: Johns Hopkins.

Bhaduri, A. (1973). A study in agricultural backwardness in semi-feudalism. *Economic Journal*, Vol. 83.

Bhaduri, A. (1983). *The Economic Structure of Backward Agriculture*. London: Academic Press.

Bhaduri, A. (1986). Forced commerce and agrarian growth. *World Development*, Vol. 14, No. 2.

Bhalla, S.S. (1979). Farm size, productivity, and technical change in Indian agriculture. Appendix A in Berry, R.A. & Cline, W.R. (1979), pp. 141–93.

Binswanger, H.P. (1978). *The Economics of Tractors in South Asia*. New York: Agricultural Development Council.

Binswanger, H.P. (1980). Attitudes toward risk: experimental measurement in rural India. *American Journal of Agricultural Economics*, Vol. 62, No. 3.

Binswanger, H.P. (1984). *Agricultural Mechanisation: A Comparative Historical Perspective*. World Bank Staff Working Papers, No. 673, Washington DC: World Bank.

Binswanger, H.P. & Rosenzweig, M.R. (1986). Behavioural and material determinants of production relations in agriculture. *Journal of Development Studies*, Vol. 22, No. 3.

Binswanger, H.P. & Ruttan, V.W. (eds.) (1978). *Induced Innovation: Technology, Institutions, and Development*. Baltimore: Johns Hopkins.

Binswanger, H.P. & Sillers, D.A. (1983). Risk aversion and credit constraints in farmers' decision-making: a reinterpretation. *Journal of Development Studies*, Vol. 20, No. 1.

Bliss, C.J. & Stern, N.H. (1982). *Palanpur: The Economy of an Indian Village*. Oxford: Clarendon Press.

Blyn, G. (1983). The green revolution revisited. *Economic Development & Cultural Change*, Vol. 31, No. 4.

Boserup, E. (1970). *Woman's Role in Economic Development*. New York: Allen & Unwin.

Bowonder, B. (1981). The myth and reality of high yielding varieties in Indian agriculture. *Development and Change*, Vol. 12, No. 2.

Braverman, A. & Srinivasan, T.N. (1981). Credit and sharecropping in agrarian societies. *Journal of Development Economics*, Vol. 9.

Braverman, A. & Stiglitz, J.E. (1982). Sharecropping and interlinking of agrarian markets. *American Economic Review*, Vol. 72.

Bunivic, M., Lycette, M.A. & McGreevey, W.P. (1983). *Women and Poverty in the Third World*. London: Johns Hopkins.

Byres, T.J. (ed.) (1983). *Sharecropping and Sharecroppers*. London: Frank Cass.

Byres, T.J. & Crow, B. (1983). *The Green Revolution in India*. Open University, Third World Studies Course U204, Case Study 5. Milton Keynes: Open University Press.

Cain, M., Khanam, S.R. & Nahar, S. (1979). Class, patriarchy, and women's work in Bangladesh. *Population and Development Review*, Vol. 5, pp. 405–38.

Carter, M.R. (1984). Identification of the inverse relationship between farm size and productivity: an empirical analysis of peasant agricultural production. *Oxford Economic Papers*, Vol. 36, pp. 131–45.

Chattopadhyay, M. & Rudra, A. (1976). Size-productivity revisited. *Economic and Political Weekly*, Review of Agriculture.

Chennareddy, V. (1976). Production efficiency in South Indian agriculture. *Journal of Farm Economics*, Vol. 49.

Cheung, S. (1968). Private property rights and sharecropping. *Journal of Political Economy*, Vol. 76.

Cheung, S. (1969). *The Theory of Share Tenancy*. University of Chicago.

Clayton, E.S. (1983). *Agriculture, Poverty and Freedom in Developing Countries*. Ch. 8. London: Macmillan.

Deere, C.D. (1976). Rural women's subsistence production in the capitalist periphery. *Review of Radical Political Economics*, Vol. 8, No. 1.

Deere, C.D. (1982). The division of labour by sex in agriculture: a Peruvian case study. *Economic Development and Cultural Change*, Vol. 30, No. 4.

Deere, C.D. & de Janvry, A. (1979). A conceptual framework for the empirical analysis of peasants. *American Journal of Agricultural Economics*, Vol. 61, No. 4.

Deere, C.D. & Leon de Leal, M. (1982). Peasant production, proletarianization, and the sexual division of labor in the Andes. In Beneria, L. (ed.) *Women and Development*, New York: Praeger.

Dillon, J.L. & Hardaker, J.B. (1980). *Farm Management Research for Small Farmer Development*. FAO Agricultural Services Bulletin 41. Rome: FAO.

Dillon. J.L. & Scandizzo, P.L. (1978). Risk attitudes of subsistence farmers in northeast Brazil: a sampling approach. *American Journal of Agricultural Economics*, Vol. 60.

Disney, R. & Elbashir, A.A. (1984). Mechanisation, employment and productivity in Sudanese agriculture. *Journal of Development Economics*, Vol. 16.

Doll, J.P. & Orazem, F. (1984). *Production Economics: Theory with Applications*. 2nd edn. New York: Wiley.

Donaldson, G.F. & McInerney, J.P. (1973). Changing machinery, technology and agricultural adjustment. *American Journal of Agricultural Economics*, Vol. 55, No. 5.

Durrenberger, E.P. (ed.) (1984). *Chayanov, Peasants, and Economic Anthropology*. New York: Academic Press.

Edholm, F., Harris, O. & Young, K. (1977). Conceptualising women. *Critique of Anthropology*, Vol. 3, Nos. 9/10.

Ellis, F. (1983). Agricultural marketing and peasant-state transfers in Tanzania. *Journal of Peasant Studies*, Vol. 10. No. 4.

Evenson, R.E. (1976). On the new household economics. *Journal of Agricultural Economics and Development*, Vol. 6, pp. 87–103.

Evenson, R.E. (1981). Food policy and the new home economics. *Food Policy*, August.

Evenson, R.E., Popkin, B. & King-Quizon, E. (1979). Nutrition, work, and demographic behaviour in rural Philippine households. *Economic Growth Centre Discussion Paper*, No. 308, Yale University.

Folbre, N. (1986). Hearts and spades: paradigms of household economics. *World Development*, Vol. 14, No. 2.

Friedmann, H. (1980). Household production and the national economy: concepts for the analysis of agrarian formations. *Journal of Peasant Studies*, Vol. 7, No. 2.

Gill, G.J. (1983). Mechanised land preparation, productivity and employment in Bangladesh. *Journal of Development Studies*, Vol. 19, No. 3.

Grabowski, R. (1979). The implications of an induced innovation model. *Economic Development and Cultural Change*, Vol. 27, No. 4.

Greeley, M. (1983). Patriarchy and poverty: a Bangladesh case study. *South Asian Research*, Vol. 3, No. 1.

Griffin, K. (1979). *The Political Economy of Agrarian Change: An Essay on the Green Revolution.* 2nd edn. London: Macmillan.

Gronau, R. (1973). The intrafamily allocation of time: the value of housewives' time. *American Economic Review*, Vol. LXIII, No. 4.

Hamal, K.B. & Anderson, J.R. (1982). A note on decreasing absolute risk aversion among farmers in Nepal. *Australian Journal of Agricultural Economics*, Vol. 26, No. 3. pp. 220–5.

Hanger, E.J. (1973). Social and Economic Aspects of the Contribution of Women to the Farm Household Economy: Two East African Case Studies. Unpublished MSc. Thesis, University of East Africa.

Hanger, E.J. & Moris, J. (1973). Women and the household economy. In Chambers, R. & Moris, J. (eds.) *MWEA: An Irrigated Rice Settlement in Kenya*, pp. 209–44. Munich: Weltforum Verlag.

Hardaker, J.B., MacAulay, T.G., Soedijono, M. & Darkey, C.K.G. (1985). A model of a padi farming household in central Java. *Bulletin of Indonesian Economic Studies*, Vol. XXI, No. 3.

Harris, O. (1984). Households as natural units. Ch. 7 in Young, K. *et al.* (eds.) (1984), pp. 136–56.

Harrison, M. (1975). Chayanov and the economics of the Russian peasantry. *Journal of Peasant Studies*, Vol. 2, No. 2.

Harrison, M. (1977). The peasant mode of production in the work of A.V. Chayanov. *Journal of Peasant Studies*, Vol. 41, No. 4.

Harriss, J. (ed.) (1982). *Rural Development: Theories of Peasant Economy and Agrarian Change.* London: Hutchinson.

Hart, G. (1980). Patterns of household labour allocation in a Javanese village. Ch. 8 in Binswanger, H.P., Evenson, R.E., Florencio, C.A. & White, B.N.F. (eds.) *Rural Household Studies in Asia*. Singapore University Press.

Hay, M.J. & Stichter S. (eds.) (1984). *African Women South of the Sahara.* London: Longman.

Hayami, Y. & Ruttan, V.W. (1984). The green revolution; inducement and distribution. *The Pakistan Development Review*. Vol. XXIII, No. 1.

Hayami, Y. & Ruttan, V.W. (1985). *Agricultural Development: an International Perspective.* 2nd edn. Baltimore: Johns Hopkins.

Hazell, P., Pomareda, C. & Valdes, A. (eds.) (1986). *Crop Insurance for Agricultural Development,* Baltimore: Johns Hopkins.

Heady, E.O. (1952). *Economics of Agricultural Production and Resource Use.* Englewood Cliffs, New Jersey: Prentice-Hall.

Herdt, R.W. & Mandac, A.M. (1981). Modern technology and economic efficiency of Philippine rice farmers. *Economic Development and Cultural Change*, Vol. 29, No. 2.

Hiebert, L.D. (1974). Risk, learning, and the adoption of fertilizer responsive seed varieties. *American Journal of Agricultural Economics*, Vol. 56, No. 4.

Hopper, W.D. (1965). Allocation efficiency in a traditional Indian agriculture. *Journal of Farm Economics*, Vol. 47, No. 4.

Hsiao, J.C. (1975). The theory of share tenancy revisited. *Journal of Political Economy*, Vol. 83.

Hunt. D. (1979). Chayanov's model of peasant household resource allocation and its relevance to Mbere division, Eastern Kenya. *Journal of Development Studies*, Vol. 15.

Hyden, G. (1980). *Beyond Ujamaa in Tanzania: Underdevelopment and an Uncaptured Peasantry.* London: Heinemann.

Hymer, S. & Resnick, S. (1969). A model of an agrarian economy with nonagricultural activities. *American Economic Review*, Vol. 59, No. 4.

International Labour Organisation (ILO) (1973). *Mechanisation and Employment in Agriculture*. Geneva: ILO.

International Rice Research Institute (IRRI) (1978). *Economic Consequences of the New Rice Technology*. Los Banos, Philippines: IRRI.

International Rice Research Institute (IRRI) (1983). *Consequences of Small-Farm Mechanisation*. Los Banos, Philippines: IRRI.

International Rice Research Institute (IRRI) (1985). *Women in Rice Farming*. Aldershot: Gower.

de Janvry, A. (1972). Optimal levels of fertilization under risk: the potential for corn and wheat fertilization under alternative price policies in Argentina. *American Journal of Agricultural Economics*, Vol. 54, No. 1.

de Janvry, A. (1981). *The Agrarian Question and Reformism in Latin America*. London: Johns Hopkins.

Jaynes, G.D. (1982). Production and distribution in agrarian economies. *Oxford Economic Papers*, Vol. 34, No. 2.

Johnston, B.F. & Kilby, P. (1975). *Agriculture and Structural Transformation*. New York: Oxford University Press.

Khusro, A.M. (1964). Returns to scale in Indian agriculture. *Indian Journal of Agricultural Economics*, Vol. 19, No. 1.

King, E. & Evenson, R.E. (1983). Time allocation and home production in Philippine rural households. Ch. 3 in Buvinic M. *et al.* (eds.), (1983). pp. 35–61.

Kislev, Y. & Peterson, W. (1981). Induced innovations and farm mechanisation. *American Journal of Agricultural Economics*, Vol. 63, No. 3.

Kitching, G. (1982). *Development and Underdevelopment in Historical Perspective*. London: Methuen.

Kroeber, A.L. (1948). *Anthropology*. New York: Harcourt, Brace & Co.

Lee, E. (1979). Egalitarian peasant farming and rural development: the case of South Korea, Ch. 2 in Ghai, D. *et al.* (eds.), *Agrarian Systems and Rural Development*. pp. 24–71. London: Macmillan.

Lenin, V.I. (1967), *The Development of Capitalism in Russia*. (first published 1899). Moscow: Progress Publishers.

Levi, J. & Havinden, M. (1982). *Economics of African Agriculture*. Ch. 4. London: Longman.

Lingard, J. (1984). Mechanisation of small rice farms in the Philippines: some income distribution aspects. *Journal of Agricultural Economics*, Vol. XXXV, No. 3.

Lingard, J., Castillo, L. & Jayasuriya, S. (1983). Comparative efficiency of rice farms in central Luzon, the Philippines. *Journal of Agricultural Economics*, Vol. XXXIV, No. 2.

Lingard, J. & Sri Bagyo, A. (1983). The impact of agricultural mechanisation on production and employment in rice areas of West Java. *Bulletin of Indonesian Economic Studies*, Vol. XIX, No. 1.

Lipton, M. (1968). The theory of the optimising peasant. *Journal of Development Studies*, Vol. 4, No. 3, pp. 327–51.

Lipton, M. (1977). *Why Poor People Stay Poor*. London: Temple Smith.

Lipton, M. (1978). Inter-farm, inter-regional and farm-non-farm income distribution: the impact of the new cereal varieties. *World Development*, Vol. 6, No. 3.

Lipton, M. (1979). Agricultural risk, rural credit, and the inefficiency of inequality. Ch. 8 in Roumasset, J.A. *et al.* (1979).

Lipton, M. (1984). Family, fungibility and formality: rural advantages of informal non-farm enterprise versus the urban-formal state. In Amin, S. (ed.) *Human Resources, Employment and Development Vol. 5: Developing Countries*. London: Macmillan.

Lipton, M. & Longhurst, R. (1986). *Modern Varieties, International Agricultural Research, and the Poor*. Consultative Group on International Agricultural Research (CGIAR), Study Paper No. 2, Washington DC: World Bank.

Littlejohn, G. (1977). Peasant economy and society, in Hindess, B. (ed.), *Sociological Theories of the Economy*. London: Macmillan.

Long, N. (ed.) (1984). *Family and Work in Rural Societies: Perspectives on Non-Wage Labour*. London: Tavistock.

Low, A. (1986). *Agricultural Development in Southern Africa: Farm Household Theory & the Food Crisis*. London: James Currey.

Mackintosh, M. (1984). Gender and economics: the sexual division of labour and the subordination of women. Ch. 1 in Young, K. *et al*. (eds.) (1984), pp. 3–17.

Mann, S.A. & Dickinson, J.M. (1978). Obstacles to the development of a capitalist agriculture. *Journal of Peasant Studies*, Vol. 5, No. 4.

Marshall, A. (1956). *Principles of Economics*. 8th edn. London: Macmillan.

McInerney, J.P. & Donaldson, G.F. (1975). *The Consequences of Farm Tractors in Pakistan*. World Bank Staff Working Paper, No. 210, Washington DC: World Bank.

McSweeney, B.G. (1979). Collection and analysis of data on rural women's time use. *Studies in Family Planning*, Vol. 10, No. 11/12.

Mellor, J.W. (1963). The use and productivity of farm family labor in the early stages of agricultural development. *Journal of Farm Economics*, Vol. XLVIII.

Mellor, J.W. (1966). *The Economics of Agricultural Development*. Ch. 9. New York: Cornell University Press.

Michael, R.T. & Becker, G.S. (1973). The new theory of consumer behaviour. *Swedish Journal of Economics*. Vol. 75, No. 4.

Mintz, S.W. (1974). A note on the definition of peasantries. *Journal of Peasant Studies*, Vol. 1, No. 3.

Nakajima, C. (1970). Subsistence and commercial family farms: some theoretical models of subjective equilibrium. In Wharton, C.R. (ed.), *Subsistence Agriculture and Economic Development*. London: Frank Cass.

Nakajima, C. (1986). *Subjective Equilibrium Theory of the Farm Household*. Amsterdam: Elsevier.

Nelson, N. (ed.) (1981). *African Women in the Development Process*. London: Frank Cass.

Newbery, D.M.G. & Stiglitz, J.E. (1979). Sharecropping, risk sharing and the importance of imperfect information. Ch. 17 in Roumasset, J.A. *et al*. (eds.), *Risk, Uncertainty and Agricultural Development*. New York: Agricultural Development Council.

Norman, D.W. (1974). Rationalising mixed cropping under indigenous conditions: the example of northern Nigeria. *Journal of Development Studies*, Vol. 11.

Norman, D.W. (1977). Economic rationality of traditional Hausa dryland farmers in the north of Nigeria. In Stevens, R.D. (ed.) *Tradition and Dynamics in Small-Farm Agriculture*. Ames: Iowa State University Press.

Patnaik, U. (1972). Economics of farm size and farm scale: some assumptions re-examined. *Economic and Political Weekly*, Special Number, August.

Patnaik, U. (1979). Neo-populism and Marxism: the Chayanovian view of the agrarian question and its fundamental fallacy. *Journal of Peasant Studies*, Vol. 6, No. 4.

Pinstrup-Andersen, P. & Hazell, B.R. (1985). The impact of the green revolution and prospects for the future. *Food Reviews International*, Vol. 1, No. 1.

Prahladachar, M. (1983). Income distribution effects of the green revolution in India: a review of empirical evidence. *World Development*, Vol. 11, No. 11.

Quibria, M.G. & Rashid, S. (1984). The puzzle of sharecropping: a survey of theories. *World Development*, Vol. 12, No. 2.

Ray, S.C. (1985). Measurement and test of efficiency of farms in linear programming models: a study of West Bengal farms. *Oxford Bulletin of Economics and Statistics*, Vol. 47, No. 4.

Ritson, C. (1977). *Agricultural Economics: Principles and Policy*. London: Crosby Lockwood Staples.

Rosenzweig, M.R. & Schultz, T.P. (1982). Market opportunities, genetic endowments, and intrafamily resource distribution: child survival in rural India. *American Economic Review*, Vol. 71, No. 4.

Roumasset, J.A. (1976). *Rice and Risk: Decision-Making Among Low-Income Farmers*. Amsterdam: North Holland.

Roumasset, J.A., Boussard, J.M. & Singh, I. (ed.) (1979). *Risk, Uncertainty and Agricultural Development*. New York: Agricultural Development Council.

Roy, S., and Blase, M.G. (1978). Farm tractorisation, productivity and labour employment: a case study of the Indian Punjab. *Journal of Development Studies*. Vol. 14, No. 2.

Rudra, A. (1973). 'Allocative efficiency' of Indian farmers: some methodological doubts. *Economic and Political Weekly*, Vol. 8, January.

Rudra, A. (1982). Myth of allocative efficiency, Ch. 1 in his *Indian Agricultural Economics: Myths and Realities*. New Delhi: Allied Publishers.

Ruthenberg, H. & Jahnke, H.E. (1985). *Innovation Policy for Small Farmers in the Tropics*. Oxford: Clarendon Press.

Sahlins, M. (1974). *Stone Age Economics*. London: Tavistock.

Sahota, G.S. (1968). Efficiency of resource allocation in Indian agriculture. *American Journal of Agricultural Economics*, Vol. 50.

Saini, G.R. (1968). Resource use efficiency in agriculture. *Indian Journal of Agricultural Economics*, Vol. 24.

Saith, A. & Tankha, A. (1972). Economic decision-making of the poor peasant household. *Economic and Political Weekly*, February.

Schluter, M.G.G. & Mount, T.D. (1976). Some management objectives of the peasant farmer: an analysis of risk aversion in the choice of cropping pattern, Surat district, India. *Journal of Development Studies*, Vol. 12, No. 3, pp. 246–61.

Schultz, T.W. (1964). *Transforming Traditional Agriculture*. New Haven: Yale University Press.

Scott, J.C. (1976). *The Moral Economy of the Peasant*. New Haven: Yale University Press.

Sen, A.K. (1962). An aspect of Indian agriculture. *The Economic Weekly*, Annual Number.

Sen, A.K. (1964). Size of holdings and productivity. *The Economic Weekly*, Annual Number.

Sen, A.K. (1966). Peasants and dualism with or without surplus labour. *Journal of Political Economy*, No. 74.

Shanin, T. (1971a). Introduction. In his (ed.) *Peasants and Peasant Societies*, Harmondsworth: Penguin.

Shanin, T. (1971b). Peasantry: delineation of a sociological concept and a field of study. *European Journal of Sociology*, Vol. 12.

Shapiro, K.H. (1983). Efficiency differentials in peasant agriculture and their implications for development policies. *Journal of Development Studies*, Vol. 19, No. 2, pp. 179–90.

Singh, I., Squire, L. & Strauss, J. (eds.) (1986a). *Agricultural Household Models*. Baltimore: Johns Hopkins.

Singh, I., Squire, L. & Strauss, J. (1986b). A survey of agricultural household models: recent findings and policy implications. *World Bank Economic Review*, Vol. 1, No. 1.

Stern, N. (1986). Book Review in *Economic Development and Cultural Change*, pp. 257–8.

Stiglitz, J.E. (1986). The new development economics. *World Development*, Vol. 14, No. 2.

Thirtle, C.G. & Ruttan, V.W. (1987). The role of demand and supply in the generation and diffusion of technical change. *Fundamentals of Pure and Applied Economics*. Vol. 21, London: Harwood Academic Press.

Thorner, D., Kerblay, B. & Smith, R.E.F. (1966). *Chayanov on the Theory of Peasant Economy*. Homewood, Illinois: Richard D. Irwin.

Upton, M. (1973). *Farm Management in Africa: The Principles of Production and Planning*. London: Oxford University Press.

Upton, M. (1976). *Agricultural Production Economics and Resource-Use*. Oxford University Press.

Walker, T.S. & Jodha, N.S. (1986). How small farm households adapt to risk. In Hazell, P., Pomareda, C. & Valdes, A. (eds.) *Crop Insurance for Agricultural Development*. pp. 17–34. Baltimore: Johns Hopkins.

Whitehead, A. (1984). I'm hungry mum: the politics of domestic budgeting. Ch. 5 in Young, K. *et al*. (eds.). (1984), pp. 93–116.

Whitehead, A. (1985). Effects of technological change on rural women: a review of analysis and concepts. Ch. 3 in Ahmed, I. (ed.) (1985). pp. 27–64.

Williams, G. (1976). Taking the part of peasants. In Gutkind, P. & Wallerstein, I. (eds.) *The Political Economy of Contemporary Africa*. London: Sage Publications.

Wolf, E.R. (1955). Types of Latin American peasantry: a preliminary discussion. *American Anthropologist*, Vol. 57. No. 3.

Wolf, E.R. (1966). *Peasants*. Englewood Cliffs, New Jersey: Prentice-Hall.

Wolf, E.R. (1982). *Europe and the People without History*. Berkeley: University of California Press.

Wolgin, J.M. (1975). Resource allocation and risk: a case study of smallholder agriculture in Kenya. *American Journal of Agricultural Economics*, Vol. 57, No. 5.

Yotopoulos, P.A. (1968). On the efficiency of resource utilization in subsistence agriculture. *Food Research Institute Studies*, Vol. 8, No. 2.

Yotopoulos, P.A. & Nugent, J.B. (1976). *Economics of Development: Empirical Investigations*. New York: Harper & Row.

Young, K. *et al*. (eds.) (1984). *Of Marriage and the Market*. 2nd edn. London: Routledge & Kegan Paul.

Author index

Subject index